THE WEALTH
OF COMMUNITIES

'I commend this charming book to those who already believe – as well as to those who still doubt – that deep within our human spirit there is an innate ability to live sustainably with nature.'
From the Foreword by HRH The Prince of Wales

So much written about the environment conveys unremitting doom and the sense that time is running out. The problems are, indeed, serious, yet there are grounds for optimism, and communities all over the world are making intelligent use of the resources on which they depend.

This book tells the stories of 10 such communities, from the Philippines to Poland, from Los Angeles to Zimbabwe. Whether reviving depleted fisheries, finding novel ways of waste disposal, controlling industrial pollution or replanting forests, they are shaping their own destinies and meeting their own needs while at the same time protecting the environment – often in the face of hardship and opposition.

The Wealth of Communities is a book about hope and ingenuity, written in a vivid and memorable style to which the accompanying photographs lend immediacy and depth. These ten tales will help pave the way for the success of future ventures: they are a tonic for hard times.

Charlie Pye-Smith is author of numerous books including *Crisis and Conservation* (1984), *Travels in Nepal* (1989) and *In Search of Wild India* (1992). Grazia Borrini Feyerabend heads the Social Policy Service at The World Conservation Union (IUCN). Richard Sandbrook is Executive Director of the International Institute for Environment and Development (IIED).

'... small is not necessarily beautiful. It can be ugly and evil. It can be depressing, destructive and burdensome. It can be monotonous and boring. In fact, smallness can contain any and every natural and human quality – good or bad. It has, however, one overwhelming advantage over giantism. Whatever is contained in smallness is within the human scale. It is in this respect that smallness, for better or worse, makes humans more human. This is the essence of its beauty.'

Manfred Max Neef

THE WEALTH OF COMMUNITIES

STORIES OF SUCCES IN LOCAL ENVIRONMENTAL MANAGEMENT

CHARLIE PYE-SMITH AND GRAZIA BORRINI FEYERABEND
WITH RICHARD SANDBOOK

WITH A FOREWORD BY
HRH THE PRINCE OF WALES

KUMARIAN PRESS

Published in the United States of America by Kumarian Press Inc
630 Oakwood Avenue, Suite 119, West Hartford, Connecticut
06110-1529 USA
ISBN 1-56549-038-X

Published in the United Kingdom by Earthscan Publications Ltd
120 Pentonville Road, London N1 9JN, United Kingdom
ISBN 1 85383 175 1

Printed and bound in Great Britain by Clays Ltd, St Ives plc
Typeset by Saxon Graphics Ltd, Derby
Cover design by Zoë Davenport

Library of Congress Catalog Card Number 94 75606

98 97 96 95 94   5 4 3 2 1
First printing 1994

CONTENTS

"The Wealth of Communities" tells the stories of ten communities which are making intelligent and sustainable use of the world around them. It is about people seeking sustainable livelihoods, often in very difficult circumstances. The stories are heart-warming, full of hope and enthusiasm. They are a marvellous palliative to the daily diet of gloom and doom served up by so much of the mass media.

There are, it is true, many problems afflicting the world: war, floods, famine, suffering, and so much more that involves tyranny, corruption, greed and deceit. The list of problems and disasters seems endless, and yet there are still plenty of reasons for optimism. As this remarkable book shows, people in communities, in many different circumstances and with few incentives, are the stewards of the planet, and can achieve remarkable results with the barest of resources. Whether they are reviving depleted fisheries in the Philippines, conserving water and sparse pastures in the deserts of Mauritania, or transforming Calcutta's sewage into fish and vegetables, each of the communities featured in "The Wealth of Communities" is shaping its own destiny <u>and</u> protecting and enhancing the environment.

These stories from around the world confirm many of the things revealed to me in the United Kingdom and by the work of the various Trusts in which I am involved. For example, in the inner cities we see what can be achieved by different groups working together; how a little help to the local entrepreneur can transform the quality of life in a depressed area; how a supporting framework of law and local government can liberate people so that they are able to find their own solutions to their difficulties. In the rural areas it is the same, but local custom plays an important part as well. Local practice and culture is, after all, often the result of finding the best way to survive in a particular circumstance.

I commend this charming book to those who already believe - as well as to those who still doubt - that deep within our human spirit there is an innate ability to live sustainably with nature.

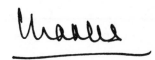

ACKNOWLEDGEMENTS

We are very grateful to the Ford Foundation for providing us with the funds to research and write *The Wealth of Communities*. Without the Foundation's help, and the support and guidance of the International Institute for Environment and Development, this book would never have seen the light of day. We were honoured and delighted that HRH The Prince of Wales was happy to write the foreword to *The Wealth of Communities*.

During the course of a year we visited ten countries around the world and received the help and advice of hundreds of people. Wherever we went we met with generosity and kindness, and along the way we made several friends. Our very special thanks go to the following:

Calcutta Astam Kumar Bag, Gouranga Biswas, Mukut Roy Choudhury, Dhrubajyoti Ghosh, Bonnari Kakkar, Niranta Makal, Shambhu Mondal, Ashok Patra.

Nepal Filip Debruyne, Bhakti Kumari Gurung, Chandra Prasad Gurung, Chij Kumari Gurung, Dibya Gurung, Jagan Gurung, Lal Gurung, Min Bahadur Gurung, Prem Chandra Gurung, Tek Bahadur Gurung, Anil Manandhar, Anil Ranjit, Dharani Sharma, Mani Ratna Sharma, Hari Gopal Shrestha.

Zimbabwe Elliot Chauke, Phineas Chauke, David Cumming, Kias Farmada, Charles Gore, Roy Martin, Simon Metcalf, Robert Monro, Sam Moyo, Marshall Murphree, Achim Steiner, Clive Stockil, Julian Sturgeon.

Uganda John Arube-Wani, Tom Barton, John Okodoi, Stanley Okurut and *all* the PACODET committee.

Mauritania Mohamed Abu, Eli Ould Ahmedou, Mohamed Ould Ahmedou, Ahmadou Ould Aly, Mohamed Lemin Ould Azize, Habib Ould el Bekay, Mohamed Mahmod Ould Beya, Cheik Ould Dih, Baby Abdoul Kader, Brahim Vall Ould Mohamed Lemine, Mohamed Lemme, Mohamed Ould Moktar, Zeinabou Mint Salem, Sow Souleimane.

Krakow Aleksandra Chodasewicz, Ton van Eck, Pawel Gluszynski, Marek Goczal, Janusz Kala, Grzegorz Pesko, Darek Szwed.

Los Angeles Lisa Duran, Juliana Gutierrez, Lisa Hoyos-Tweten, Eric Mann, Chris Mathis, Carlos Molina, Kikanza Ramsey, Geoffrey Ray.

Costa Rica Melvin Baker, Teodoro Lopez, Diego Lynch, Elena Murillo, Noël Paine, Luis Rodriguez, Juana Sanchez, Armando Vasquez, Felix Vasquez, José Luis Zuniga.

Ecuador Thomas Alcedo, Gauke Andrikseen, Rosario Auraucela, Rutged Boelens, Father Juan Bottasso, Bayron Casignia, Marco Guillelmo Flores, Carlos Herz, Victor Janchaliquin, Johanna Jansen, Jolanda Kakabadse, Pablo Morales, Juan Piana, Father Antonio Polo, Francisco Roman, Ligla Samoniego, José Sanchez Parga, Guillelmo Teran, Jorge Utrillas, Pepe Sola Villena, Gabriel Zurita.

Philippines Ilyo Aala, Estelito Alday, Beloy Alicaya, Silving Alicaya, Dominga Alicaya, Boyd Alexander, Roman Botones, Kiko Caisip, Balbina Destreza, Lyn Lacsamana, Mayette Rodriguez, Peter de la Salis, Julio Tan, Paul Valentin.

And elsewhere Patricia Barnett, Fiorella Bomé, Patricia Bond, Maria Teresa Cobelli, Broughton Coburn, Marta Guidi, Mark Halle, Françoise Lieberherr, Hemanta Mishra, Richard Moorehead, Jules Pretty, David Satterthwaite, Thomas Schwedersky, Dudley Spain, Tricia Spanner, Louise Sperling, Mario Tapia, Camilla Toulmin, Doreen Ward, Ann Waters-Bayer.

1

CALCUTTA

The Mudialy Fishermen's Cooperative Society

'Nature has given us the means of purifying water'

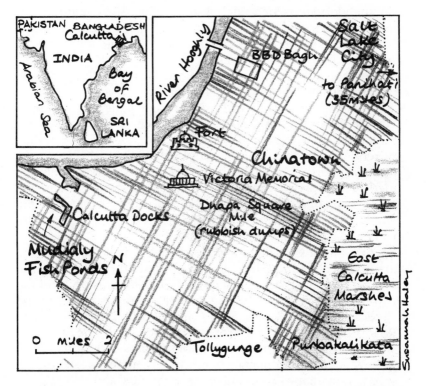

'**B**efore I joined the fishermen's cooperative', explained Niranta Makal, 'I was a robber, a bag-snatcher. I used to hang around with a gang – there were about seven or eight of us – and we'd rob people in the docks and break into factories.' Niranta was a thin, swarthy character with a broad smile; he was somewhat abashed about his nefarious youth and giggled nervously when invited to discuss past misdemeanours.

We were sitting with Shambhu Mondal, the chairman of the Mudialy Fishermen's Cooperative Society, on the third floor of their new office block in a suburb some ten miles south of central Calcutta. An orange sun was sinking fast, throwing the feathery fronds of scattered palms into sharp relief. From the dusty streets below rose the excited babble of an Indian dusk. A dozen children were playing cricket in a narrow alley with a table-tennis ball and a bat which had seen better days; three teenagers stood among them, oblivious to the noise, fluttering their distant kites across the pale blue sky. Women lounged on the doorsteps of their pantiled shacks, or attended to goats, babies and the washing; a group of men sat cross-legged outside the office, chatting quietly while they smoked *beedis* and repaired fishing nets.

'Before Niranta joined us', explained Shambhu, 'his gang was causing all sorts of problems. Then one day he and some of his accomplices came to us and asked if they could join the society. We took them on probation and I went to see the police. I told them that the gang was going to reform. The police weren't very happy about it. They said: "OK, but if there's any more robberies, you'll be responsible".' The society always tried to help people in trouble, explained Shambhu; and in any case, turning crooks into fishermen was in the interests of the whole community. Of the society's 430-odd workers, Shambhu reckoned about 50 were reformed criminals.[1]

Early the next morning, an hour before dawn, we clattered along Calcutta's pot-holed streets towards the small wetland managed by the Mudialy fishermen. The city's history, and the nature of the port, seemed to be written in the names of the streets: Karl Marx Sarani, King George's Dock, Oil Installation Road; there was even a Proposed Road. At the heart of this shabby landscape with its miserable *bustees* and monumental godowns, its vast container parks and fly-tipped wasteground, was a remarkably beautiful oasis of ponds and greenery. It was still dark when we arrived but a score of fishermen had already begun work in one of the larger ponds. Some held one end of a long net close to the shore while others waded out, a hundred yards or more, unravelling it as they went. Once the net had been stretched to its full length the distant fishermen curved back towards the shore, drawing the net into a circle and splashing the water to drive the fish into its clutches. It took them a quarter of an hour to draw in the net, by which time dawn had broken in a blaze of gold and red over the cranes and gantries on the far side of the pond, and we could make out the glint of fish leaping high above the heads of the fishermen as they tried to escape. Most didn't, and were transferred to aluminium urns and floated back to the shore. The process was repeated three more times and by 8 o'clock the day's fishing was complete. A group of merchants had gathered beneath the trees near the main entrance to the wetland and it took an hour to auction off the catch.

When Shambhu Mondal's father arrived here in the 1930s with five other families – all poor fishing people who had left their homes in Howrah District when the Damoda River had dried up – they found a large area of soggy marshland with scattered ponds and a floating population of criminals. Over the years the owners, the Calcutta Port Trust, nibbled away at the marshes, converting some areas into industrial sites and using other parts for the dumping of waste. Between 1960 and 1980 the wetlands shrank from 250 hectares to 80 hectares. By 1980 the Mudialy Fishermen's Cooperative Society was well established – it had begun life in 1961 – but the fish catch was relatively low compared to the present. In 1980/1, the society harvested 65 tonnes of fish; ten years later the annual yield had risen to 288 tonnes. Over the same period earnings had risen from 800,000 rupees ($42,000) to 5 million rupees ($263,000), and today the only criminals you'll see at the Mudialy wetlands are reformed ones like Niranta Makal.

Niranta had abandoned the life of crime and turned to fishing for two good reasons. First, he was afraid of the police: 'They shot at me once', he recalled, 'and even though they missed, I decided it was time to become an honest man.' More importantly, Niranta saw that the Mudialy fishermen had steady work and a regular income which far exceeded his own.

Few places in the world have been so persistently reviled as Calcutta, Kipling's 'City of Dreadful Night', whose very name conjures up images of poverty, overcrowding and death. Founded just over three centuries ago on the marshy banks of the River Hooghly by an English merchant called Job Charnock, Calcutta's past has been both glorious and gruesome. With its marvellous collection of neo-classical palaces, its fine churches and splendid government buildings, Calcutta's architecture is a match for any city in the world. And there is much else to recommend it too. Its people, for example: the native Bengalis possess a wit and intelligence which makes India's more prosperous cities – one thinks, for example, of Delhi or Madras – seem parochial. Nevertheless, the misery of the millions who live on the streets and in the overcrowded slums is as palpable as the pollution which at times renders the air almost unbreathable. A city built for a million people is now home to over ten times that many; starved of funds, and crippled by apathy and overmanning, the municipal authorities struggle to keep Calcutta working. The public services – whether of transport, telecommunications or power supply – are a shambles, although the situation is by no means unremittingly bleak. Kipling described Calcutta as the city 'where the cholera, the cyclone, and the crow come and go, by the sewerage rendered foetid, by the sewer made impure'. Perhaps; yet over the last hundred years Calcutta has developed a system of sewage and waste disposal which is among the most enlightened in the world.

The architects of this system – which transforms sewage and organic waste into fish and vegetables – are the fishermen and farmers of places like Mudialy and the East Calcutta Marshes. Every day the Mudialy Cooperative takes in 25 million litres of polluted water – an oxygenless cocktail of sewage and industrial effluent – and every day it harvests over 1 tonne of fish and expels some 23 million litres of reasonably clean water. Meanwhile, on the other side of the city, in the East Calcutta Marshes, 20,000 people daily transform over a third of the city's sewage and almost all its domestic waste into 150 tonnes of vegetables and 20 tonnes of fish. This is not only one of the most efficient and productive systems of sewage treatment in existence, it is very probably the cheapest. In India's expanding cities, the links between people and nature become ever more tenuous: the Mudialy wetlands and the East Calcutta Marshes provide a marvellous exception, with the fishermen and vegetable farmers doing the people of the city, and the municipal authorities, an immense favour.[2]

Shambhu Mondal's father and the small group of associates who came to the Mudialy wetlands over half a century ago were not concerned with looking after the environment; they simply wished to scratch a living at the one occupation they knew, which was fishing. Life was very difficult for them at first. The wetlands were covered with garbage and the scattering of shallow ponds provided just enough fish to sustain the newcomers. 'In 1950', explained Shambhu as we wandered around the tree-fringed ponds one afternoon, 'my father and five others decided to organize a *samity*, a society, and they approached the Calcutta Port Trust and asked for a lease on the wetland.' In 1952 they were given a three-year lease for a fee of 16,000 rupees. They shifted some of the waste, enlarged the ponds and began to prosper in a modest way. 'Then in 1957', recalled Shambhu, 'a rich *zamindar*, a landlord from another district, bought the lease off CPT and my father and his friends were forced to become his labourers. They became poorer and poorer.' The following year they decided that each member of the *samity* should make a daily contribution of 25 paisa – a quarter of a rupee – to a collective fund. After a year they had raised 4,500 rupees; a further 12,000 rupees were collected from other sources and in 1960 they bought back the lease. In 1961, at the insistence of the CPT, they formed the Mudialy Fishermen's Cooperative Society with 53 members. The next 20 years witnessed steady growth in the society's membership; sales from fish provided each family with a respectable living, in addition to which the society was able to pay some of the members' education and health costs. However, in 1986 the society's activities – and the wetlands themselves – were transformed following the arrival of Mukut Roy Choudhury, a mild, self-effacing ecologist from the West Bengal Fisheries Department. 'We call him remote control,' said Shambhu affectionately.

'When I arrived the fishermen resented my presence,' said Mukut as he drove us out to Mudialy one morning. Shambhu agreed: 'Yes, we were angry at first. Mukut said we should change the shape of the ponds and plant trees. We said: "No, why should we? We're *bona fide* fishermen. We don't know anything about trees".' It took a while for Mukut to convince the fishermen that great improvements could be made to the fisheries. 'I spent months talking to them,' he recalled. 'I lived with them, I got to know their problems and gradually they saw that I had their best interests at heart. In those days there were still many rowdies hanging about here. I often met them at night, and they threatened to kill me if I tried to evict them.' The rowdies gradually drifted away as Mukut's plan to improve the wetlands took shape.

Since 1986 the society has planted almost 100,000 trees, two-thirds of which have survived, and the whole system of water use has been refined. Previously, the polluted water which seeped in at one end of the wetland was subject to a fairly anarchic process of filtration by wetland plants. Now this water is passed through a series of six square tanks and connecting canals. 'In this one', explained Shambhu as we peered into the first of these, 'there's no oxygen at all and the BOD, the biological oxygen demand, is sometimes as high as 250.' BOD, he explained, was a good index of water quality; the higher the figure, the worse the pollution. 'By the time we discharge water back into the Hooghly', he continued, 'the BOD is down to around 15, the water is thoroughly oxygenated and it's almost drinkable.' Indeed, by the time the polluted water reaches the third tank – just a couple of hundred feet away from the point of entry – it has been purified enough for several hardy species of fish to survive; further along the line, in the main stocking tanks, it is clean enough to support over 40 species, 14 of which are commercially important. 'We don't use any chemicals except lime, which kills anaerobic bacteria,' explained Shambhu. 'Nature has given us the means to purify water, and that's what we do here.' Dense beds of water hyacinth (*Eichhornia crasspies*) and reed (*Phragmites* species) leach heavy metals like lead and mercury out of the water, and *Leptocloa chinensis* (Shambhu's love of Latin suggests a classicist manqué) absorbs the oil and grease. The water which reaches the stocking tanks is a sewagy soup devoid of nasty chemicals but rich in nutrients. This is the food of the algae and animal plankton, which in turn are devoured by the fish.[3]

Attention to detail is not confined to life in the water, and many of the 70-odd species of tree planted along the embankments are here for a good reason. The leathery-leaved fig trees along the boundary of the park help to absorb the dust which comes swirling in from the industrial estates nearby; species like *neem* absorb a variety of gaseous pollutants; and beside the water's edge leguminous trees provide extra fodder for the fish. The trees have already begun to generate an income. 'Last year', explained Mukut, 'the society sold 40 tonnes of timber. This year we're hoping to double that.' When Mukut arrived in 1985/6 the yield of fish per hectare was 1.9 tonnes and total earnings for the year were 1,300,000 rupees (or $68,000). By 1987/8, the yield had risen to 3.75 tonnes per hectare and earnings had almost trebled. Two years later, in 1989/90, the yield had risen to 5.6 tonnes and earnings were past the 5 million rupee mark. The fishermen are ambitious: they see no reason why they shouldn't get 600 tonnes of fish a year, double the present figure, by 1995.

The society's book-keeping is exemplary, and the members know exactly how much money is earned and how it is used. Approximately half of all earnings goes on salaries and daily running costs, and half is ploughed back into developing the fisheries and the society. The most experienced members of the cooperative – and the six members of the board of directors (all of whom are elected) – receive 51 rupees a day, or 1,500 rupees a month. To put this in perspective, it amounts to double the wage a manual labourer would receive for industrial work, or four times that of an agricultural day-labourer. Those beginning work for the society – they will generally be unmarried teenagers – start at the bottom of the scale, with around 20 rupees a day. Gradually, their salaries rise towards the higher level. Each member of the cooperative also receives an annual bonus of between 4,500 rupees ($180) and 10,000 rupees ($400), which most invest in government bonds.

About a tenth of the society's earnings goes on educational costs, medical care, funeral expenses, building loans and charitable donations. An indication of the society's rising prosperity can be gauged from the amount of money spent on festivals: in 1982/3 it was 10,000 rupees; by 1989/90 it had risen to 30,000 rupees. Talk to any of the fishing families in Mudialy and they will tell you how their lives have improved over the past ten years. Take Astam Kumar Bag, for example, now the society's accountant. 'When I joined the society in 1961', he said, 'our living conditions were dreadful. I lived in a one-room mud hut and couldn't afford to eat much. Since 1986, our standard of living has risen dramatically.' We asked him whether he considered himself wealthy now. He laughed: 'Yes, more or less, I suppose!' Like most members of the society, he lives a couple of miles away from the wetland in the suburb of Mudialy. He has a three-room home beside a large tank, or pond, with a pleasant garden and plenty of space. His young daughter and son eat three decent meals a day, with fish every lunch; it is a far cry from the penury of his youth. He is especially proud of the community's educational

7

achievements. In 1980 barely a fifth of the members' children attended school; most were sent out to work from an early age. Now that the society pays educational costs from its profits from fishing, all the members' children go to school.

The most tangible sign of prosperity is in the building boom at Mudialy. After we left Astam Kumar Bag we went to inspect a half-built house a stone's throw from the society's office. A young man with the looks of a film star and the build of an athlete proudly showed us round the ground floor, then took us on to the roof, where his family were drinking up the dying rays of the setting sun. In another couple of months, he explained, their house would be complete. He and his brother had saved 60,000 rupees ($2,400) from their salaries and taken an interest-free loan of 70,000 rupees ($2,800) from the Mudialy Fishermen's Cooperative Society. They would pay the loan back within ten years: 'No problem,' he said. 'We're making enough money from fishing; we'll find it easy to pay off our debts.' He said they were going to paint the whole house bright green. It should clash nicely with the lurid orange building – also constructed with loans from the society – next door. On our way back to the fishermen's office – a chasmy, concrete job four inelegant storeys high and constructed with the society's profits – he showed us the home which he and his family of eight would soon be leaving: with its russet pantiled roof and mottled walls, it was certainly picturesque, but it was cramped, dingy and less than half the size of their new house.

In the early weeks of 1992 the magazine *India Today* ran a short piece under the title 'Sewage Nightmare – Calcutta in eco-peril'. The article suggested that if the East Calcutta Marshes were developed for building – or parts were turned into a trade-fair park and zoo, as the state government evidently wished – the city would soon smother in its own sewage. At last, it seemed, Calcutta would really deserve the opprobrium heaped upon it a century before by Kipling. In February an organization called PUBLIC – People United for Better Living in Calcutta – filed a writ in the high court to halt any further development of the wetlands; the judge passed an interim order prohibiting any changes in land use while the court duly considered the issues in detail. Nine months later the order was made permanent. (Pradeep and Bonnari Kakkar, two prominent members of PUBLIC, were in Delhi when the final judgement was made. The hotel receptionist handed them the following message from their lawyer, who had telephoned the news from Calcutta: 'We have one hand towel. I will be in Delhi tomorrow.' What he had actually said was: 'We have won hands down. I will be ...')

The person who has done most to establish the significance of the East Calcutta Marshes is Dr Dhrubajyoti Ghosh, a sanitary engineer by training and now the executive engineer for the Calcutta Metropolitan Water and Sanitation Authority. We met late one morning in his office in BBD Bagh, the square named after three revolutionaries – Binoy, Badal and Dinesh – hanged by the British for conspiring to kill Lord Dalhousie, the first governor of Bengal. We were soon reminded of Calcutta's revolutionary element when a Marxist demonstration within the decrepit and dusty building made conversation all but impossible. However, we struggled on during the occasional gaps in the chanting and clapping.

The East Calcutta Marshes, explained Dr Ghosh, constituted the largest and finest traditional sewage and waste-disposal system in the world. He estimated that somewhere in the region of a third of the city's sewage ended up in the marshes, to be processed in the most ingenious ways. A little under 7,500 acres is taken up by sewage-fed fishponds or *bheris*. Each year these fisheries produce 7,500 tonnes of fish. While some of the sewage goes straight to the *bheris*, some is detained for use by the 'garbage farms'. Much of Calcutta's domestic refuse is dumped on the fringes of the marshes and picked over by several thousand people; while some collect plastic, others gather tin, copper wire, paper, rubber, whatever. By the time they have done their work, all that remains is a vast pile of organic matter which, when dispersed and irrigated with sewage water, becomes a fertile substrate for vegetable production; every day Calcutta gets 150 tonnes of vegetables from these garbage farms. The effluent from the fishponds is also used, mostly in the rice paddies which are dotted around the outer reaches of the marshes. 'It is a system of genius', explained Dr Ghosh, 'and it's perfectly suited to countries in the developing world: the two basic requirements seem to be poverty and sunshine, and we have plenty of both.'

A journey from central Calcutta into the heart of the marshes takes no more than an hour. The approach is distinctly unpromising; before you leave Calcutta you cross a long humped bridge, on either side of which live thousands of Bangladeshi refugees in conditions of appalling squalor. A little later, the cabbagy smells of defecation and decay – the odours of the slums – are replaced by the more acrid fumes of Chinatown's tanneries. On the opposite side of the road from Chinatown a large area of flattish land is festooned with washing lines from which seem to flap enough bed linen for all Bengal. Then come the refuse dumps of an area known as the Dhapa Square Mile. Outsiders are not particularly welcome here, but we scrambled up to the top of one mountainous heap of compressed garbage. Fifty feet below us six teenage girls, each armed with an iron prong, extricated electrical wire from the rotting mass at their feet. Nearby a group of men shovelled the picked-over waste – all good fertile stuff – into a lorry. Gangs of pigs roamed the site; crows and kites wheeled above our heads. Half a mile down a rutted track we left these purgatorial dumping grounds and entered into an area of startling beauty. On either side of a canal carrying sewage water were fields of cabbage, cauliflower and pea. On the banks of the canal grew pawpaw, palm and flowering shrubs. Here and there were small plots of orange marigold and other flowers, many of which would be used in temple ceremonies. After a while this intimate landscape of small fields gave way to a broader, more watery world, and eventually we arrived at the Bantalla sewage works. Built by the British in 1943, they only worked for a couple of years. They were a colossal waste of money: the fishermen and vegetable farmers of the marshes – the 'natural ecologists', as Dr Ghosh calls them – had already developed a far cheaper, more efficacious and productive way of dealing with sewage.

'I first went to the marshes in 1980,' explained Dr Ghosh. 'The law-and-order situation was terrible then. Gangsters frequently looted fish, and they weren't the only ones who didn't want me there: the local political leaders were sometimes keen to keep the dishonest happenings quiet. In the early days I was frequently threatened and told, "We'll kill you if you come back".'

Dr Ghosh did keep coming back, and over the years he got to know many of the people working in the marshes – some 20,000 make a living there – and he began to understand how the system worked. The first of his many reports came out in 1981, and by 1985 he had mapped the entire area. He has persistently argued that the Calcutta system of sewage treatment is replicable in other Third World countries.

Dr Ghosh's championing of self-help sanitation has made him many enemies. Engineers are not in favour of a system which, as Dr Ghosh points out, they neither understand nor admire: 'Conventional sewage systems are invariably funded by multinationals or other highly financed groups – and they are prepared to pay engineers large sums of money to design and build them.' It has been the property speculators, however, who have been Dr Ghosh's most unsavoury adversaries. Over the years the wetlands have diminished in size.[4] During the 1960s a large chunk was lost to the Salt Lake housing scheme, and in 1969 many fisheries were drained and converted to rice paddy. The building of the Eastern Metropolitan Bypass during the 1980s subsequently brought the wetlands within closer reach of developers eager to turn the fishponds into homes for the wealthy. 'There was a time when I expected to be killed,' recalled Dr Ghosh. 'The real estate people are very unscrupulous fellows. They used to telephone my mother almost every day threatening to do terrible things to my family if I continued to oppose plans to develop the marshes.'

When we met Dr Ghosh, at the end of 1992, the abuse had stopped – temporarily, at least – and during the short period of less than a year there had been a great sea-change in the government's attitude towards the marshes. For almost ten years Dr Ghosh had fought a lone battle within the municipal administration calling for the authorities to recognize the marshes as a Waste Recycling Region. He was consistently opposed by his superiors, who at times indulged in petty retribution: for example, he was sacked as director of the Institute of Wetlands Management and Ecological Design, an organization which he himself had founded. 'Ever since 1985', he explained, 'my battle has been with the decision-makers, at every level in the country, and the battle has been to save the marshes and get the system of waste recycling in use elsewhere.' In late 1992, the Calcutta Metropolitan District Authority introduced new legislation in which it affirmed: 'It is necessary to preserve the entire [Calcutta] wetlands so that it may function as a waste recycling region. It is also necessary to control undesirable building activities in these areas.' For Dr Ghosh, this was a major triumph.

One afternoon we drove out to Panihati, a small town some 20 miles out of Calcutta and one of three sites chosen by Dr Ghosh for the installation of a low-cost, self-help sanitation scheme. Compared to the wetlands managed by the

Mudialy Fishermen's Cooperative Society – Dr Ghosh, incidentally, felt that their success had encouraged decision-makers to see the virtues of such schemes – the wetlands at Panihati were modest. An area of 21 hectares had been set aside to treat around 1 million litres of sewage a day. Dr Ghosh expected it to be operational within six months; all being well, it should yield 50 tonnes of fish a year. Gangs of labourers had been brought in to dig the ponds, and the government intended to rent these out to the former graziers of the land. 'This isn't a money-spending exercise,' said Dr Ghosh as we skirted around the newly dug ponds. 'It's money-saving, and we could do something similar almost anywhere in the world, and certainly anywhere in the tropics.'

While Dr Ghosh was establishing low-cost sanitation systems beyond the East Calcutta Marshes, Mukut Roy Choudhury was in the process of replicating his Mudialy experience at three other sites, one of which lay within the marshes. Impressed by the improvements he had brought to Mudialy, the West Bengal Fisheries Department had appointed him technical adviser to three other fisheries cooperatives, all of which leased their land from the state government. One of these was Purbakalikata Fishermen's Cooperative Society, which managed 70 hectares of land a mile or so from Calcutta's Chinatown, whose yellow-roofed Buddhist pagoda was one of the few interesting features on the skyline.

Mukut took us there one hot, sweaty morning and we were met by Gouranga Biswas, the society's secretary. A cheerful, bespectacled character in his early fifties, Gouranga led us round the fishponds which occupied over two-thirds of the leased land. The society, he explained, had begun life in 1989: 'We've now got 40 member families, and we set up the society because we felt we could do much to improve our standard of living. All of us used to struggle before – we were very badly paid at the things we did.' The families lived in several small villages scattered around the edge of the marshes. For the first six months of the society's life, everyone worked for free – digging and clearing ponds, cleaning away rubbish and so forth. 'Gradually, our income from fishing began to rise', explained Gouranga, 'and we were able to pay ourselves. At first we took 10 rupees each, then we increased it to 15, then 20.' The society's income rose steadily, from 74,000 rupees ($2,960) in 1989/90, to 297,000 rupees ($11,880) in 1990/1 and 336,000 rupees ($13,440) in 1991/2.

Today the wages are determined on the basis of seniority: those who joined in 1989 receive 35 rupees a day; those the year after 30 rupees, and so on down to the newcomers, who get 20 rupees a day.

For the first two and a half years of its existence, the society received no help whatsoever from outside sources. However, in early 1992 Mukut was appointed an adviser, and Gouranga and his colleagues, learning of the successes of the Mudialy fisheries, invited Shambhu Mondal and Ashok Patra, the Mudialy society's chairman and director, to visit Purbakalikata. Shambhu, Ashok and Mukut suggested, among other things, that the embankments between the ponds should be clothed with a variety of trees similar to those at Mudialy. Already thousands of saplings – fig, palm, *neem*, *subabul* – had been planted and we came across several society members watering them as we wandered around the ponds. 'We've also begun to grow vegetables,' said Gouranga, who felt that Mukut's advice was already bringing in tremendous benefits. In the first six months of the latest financial year the society had made 600,000 rupees ($24,000), almost double the profit for the previous twelve months. Mukut was characteristically modest: 'We can provide advice', he said, 'but they have to motivate themselves. The great thing is that there's no need for the government or anyone else to provide money – and this sort of thing certainly helps solve the unemployment problem.'

Beside one of the ponds at Purbakalikata was a stone house which lay roofless and ruined. 'We're going to rebuild it and turn it into a guest house,' said Gouranga. 'Next time you come, you can stay there!' As we climbed back into the car to head back across the city to Mudialy he said with a grin: 'In five years' time, we'll create something even better than Mudialy!'

Later that day we discussed the Mudialy fisheries with Dr Ghosh, who had been visiting the wetland there since 1985. He believed that there was still room for improvement in fisheries management, but he was impressed by the way in which the society was organized: 'It's more democratic than anything else I've come across,' he said. He found it difficult to see how the members handled internal conflicts, as they never discussed such matters with outsiders. 'But they conduct their affairs in a very participatory manner,' he concluded, 'although you always have to remember that not everyone wishes to participate.' He thought that around a fifth of the members played an active role in determining the society's future – 'the rest just chip in'. However, he did point out that it is the Mudialy *Fishermen's* Cooperative Society. The women have little or no say in the running of its affairs, and indeed, when we tried to talk to one of the members' wives, she steadfastly refused to discuss the work of the society, considering that to be her husband's business.

'I do feel that the women are well respected,' said Dr Ghosh, 'and I think that the men are beginning to realize that it's time that the women were more fully involved in the society. At present there are no activities specifically geared towards their needs.' A patriarchial society it may be, but at least the visitor does not get the impression – as in many parts of India – that the womenfolk are downtrodden. Nor are they all worn out by childbirth, as countless million others are throughout India. Most couples in the community practise some form of family planning, and family size is well below the national average.

During our days with the Mudialy fishermen, we were frequently struck by the scale of their ambitions, a clear manifestation of which was the five-storey centre which they were in the process of constructing within the wetlands. The concrete building, straddling a canal between two ponds, was already two and a half storeys high. Eventually it will house a conference room, audio-visual facilities, a cafeteria, a laboratory to test water quality, sleeping quarters for guests, lavatories and, on the top floor, an orchidarium. The society also plans to further refine the system of water purification, to install solar electricity and to generate bio-gas.

At the time of our visit – November 1992 – the fishermen's optimism about the future was tempered by a sense of unease. During the course of the year the Calcutta Port Trust, the landowner of the Mudialy wetlands, had made plain its intentions to evict the fishermen and fill in the wetlands to make way for warehouses, container parks, truck terminals and other dockland paraphernalia. In 1991 the landlords offered the society a three-year lease, the cost of which was to rise by 25 per cent each year. The society argued that such increases were grossly unfair and refused to pay them. Midway through 1992 the CPT issued an eviction notice which required the fishermen to leave the wetlands by 23 July. Somewhere in the region of 60 to 70 security guards turned up and tried to gain entry to the wetlands before the date of eviction. The fishermen and their families barred the entrance and there were some unpleasant skirmishes. The security staff retreated. On 22 July the state government, whose Fisheries Department had given strong backing to the Mudialy fishermen, applied to the high court for a stay order. The Fisheries Department even suggested that it should take the wetlands over from CPT. The judge granted the stay order, the fishermen continued to go about their daily business in the wetlands and the matter was still *sub judice* in November.

All this created a considerable stir in the local and national press. The CPT accused the fishermen of failing to pay the rents which were due and of preventing its staff from entering the wetlands. The CPT chairman, who was subsequently forced to resign, claimed that a report commissioned by the Trust had revealed that the fish caught and sold at Mudialy were contaminated by toxic chemicals and heavy metals and therefore unfit for human consumption. This was later shown to be untrue. The Trust also argued that the society had only been granted fishing rights; that it had no authority to construct buildings or create a nature park. In fact, the nature park is one of the features which attract some 2,000 visitors a day to Mudialy. A herd of spotted deer graze in a small enclosure beside the ponds at the entrance, and there are monkeys, waterfowl and several other creatures. The society spent over 9 million rupees ($360,000) creating embankments, planting trees and setting up the nature park. Its members, not surprisingly, took great exception to the CPT erecting a sign which read 'Calcutta Port Trust Ecological Park'. 'They were happy to claim credit for the nature park once, even though they hold it against us now,' said Shambhu.

In their dealings with the press, the Mudialy fishermen have shown themselves to be experts, and the majority of the public are impressed by their achievements. Curiously, that admirable band of campaigners – People United for Better Living in Calcutta – has refused to side with the Mudialy Society. Bonnari Kakkar felt that the society had behaved in a somewhat duplicitous manner. It had claimed to bring great benefits to nature – Shambhu said 77 species of bird had been recorded there – but in fact the area was much richer in birdlife before the fishermen cleared away scrub woodland and reorganized the ponds. Bonnari was also sceptical about the fishermen's claim that they had created a nature park for the benefit of the general public: 'There was a time earlier this year', she said, 'when the fishermen wouldn't let anyone into the park. It was only when the CPT sought their eviction that they let people in.' Presumably, to garner public support.

Whatever the truth in these assertions, and there undoubtedly is some, the fact remains that the Mudialy Fishermen's Cooperative Society has had a remarkable impact on one small area of Calcutta. Over a period of two generations a sizeable community has shuffled off the rags of poverty without any financial help from the outside world. Criminals have turned into honest men; the illiterate have learned to read; polluted water has been made clean.

Meanwhile, over on the other side of Calcutta, a much larger community of some 20,000 people continues the work of a century or more: the conversion of sewage and organic waste into fish and vegetables. The system has its imperfections, and Dr Ghosh and Mukut Roy Choudhury have played an important role in helping to refine the peasant technology. At the time of our visit Dr Ghosh was in the process of establishing low-cost sanitation schemes elsewhere in Bengal. He had no doubt that they would be successful, and that a system such as the one used by the fish and vegetable farmers in the East Calcutta Marshes could benefit cities and villages across the Third World, especially those with marshy backyards.

Six months after our visit to Calcutta, Dr Ghosh sent us an article from the *Indian Telegraph*, dated 6 May 1993 – 'I want to make you happy by going through the clippings,' he wrote. The newspaper recorded that central government was actively considering a West Bengal government 132-crore rupee ($40 million) action plan to conserve the 12,000 hectare East Calcutta Marshes. Under this 'Waste as Resource' scheme, most of the money would be spent restoring and upgrading the ageing system of canals which takes waste and water to the wetlands. Finance would also be made available for health and education projects, and the installation of a bio-gas plant. There was also talk of building a zoo, a bio-diversity park and a water sports facility. The work of the 'natural ecologists', as Dr Ghosh called them, was at last being appreciated by some of those in power.

2

NEPAL

Annapurna Conservation Area Project

'Looking after the forest is everyone's responsibility'

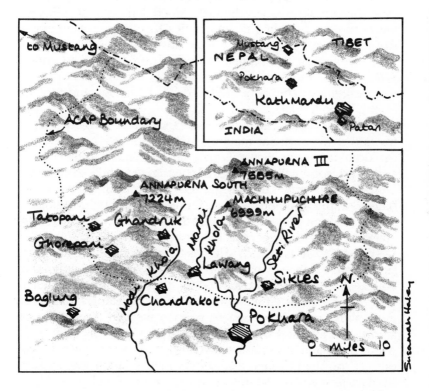

'Nowadays power lies with the people, not just with a few leaders!' Min Bahadur Gurung, the chairman of Ghandruk's Conservation and Development Committee, was a persuasive orator and the villagers listened attentively. 'We called a meeting of the mule owners before', he continued, wagging his right forefinger in anger, 'and none of them came. The more of us there are that agree to do something about the behaviour of the mule owners, the easier it'll be to implement our decisions.'

It was now midday and the meeting of the Conservation and Development Committee (CDC), which gathers on the first day of every Nepali month, had been in progress for two hours. It had begun calmly enough, with Min Gurung explaining to the fifteen-person committee, and the others who had decided to attend, the programme for building a new bridge which would link a remote village to the trail north of Ghandruk. The Annapurna Conservation Area Project (ACAP), beside whose headquarters we sat, had agreed to supply 145 bags of cement, iron rods and skilled labour. The villagers were expected to provide the mules to transport the cement from the roadhead a day's walk down the mountains from here; as part of the bargain they had also agreed to collect 450 bags of sand, which they would dig from the Modi Khola riverbed, gather the stone required for the bridge and provide all the unskilled labour.

While the committee discussed the bridge project, others trickled in to join the meeting. The majority were Gurungs, the dominant people in this part of the Himalaya: most wore colourful *topis*, the traditional headgear, and many wore Gurung *bhangras*, sack-like jackets which doubled as carrier bags. Some had come from as far as Chhomrong, a small village four hours' walk to the north of Ghandruk; others had clambered up the steep hillside from the rushing green waters of the Modi Khola. Away to our left, cascading down the hillside, were a score of handsome Gurung houses. Slate-roofed, with walls painted white and ochre, these dwellings were surrounded by thin terraces planted with vegetables and oats; each had a paved yard where women weaved, firewood was stored and livestock were tethered. Immediately in front of us was the village school and playing field, behind which was one of the many forest nurseries which had sprung up over the last few years. The rest of this substantial village – Ghandruk, the 'capital' of Gurung country, has a population of over 2,000 – lay out of sight over a jagged ridge.

The village was set in a landscape of astounding beauty, dominated by the snowy peaks of the Annapurnas and Machhupuchhre, the 'Fishtail'. The mountains were clearly visible when the CDC meeting began but by the time Min Gurung raised the subject of the mules, they were obscured by thunderous black clouds. The mule trains were a great nuisance, said Min Gurung. It was true that the people of the roadless Himalaya could not do without them: it was the mules which carried up to the hills everything from cement to corrugated iron, seeds for the farmers to Coca-Cola for the tourists. But they did much damage too. 'They break up the paths and shit everywhere,' he said. 'And they're always wandering into the farmers' fields and eating their crops. If we villagers made such a mess of the paths, we'd be punished – we'd have to clean up the mess. The mule owners never do!' Everyone agreed that something had to be done. But what? It was hard to put a pecuniary value to the damage and nuisance caused by the mules, and how should the mule-owners compensate farmers for crop losses? 'Perhaps we should punish them by making them provide voluntary labour,' suggested Min Gurung, sowing the seed of an idea whose time was soon to come. The mule owners would be arriving in the afternoon, he added, so they could resume their discussions then.

In the meantime the committee turned its attention to other business. During the course of the morning half a dozen individuals had drifted over to the meeting and handed in applications to the committee, each accompanied by a 1 rupee note. Prem Chandra Gurung, a young member of the ACAP staff who was translating the proceedings for us, picked up one of the applications and read us its contents. It was a request for permission to cut down two *chebar* trees 'for the maintenance and repair of my house in Ghandruk'. The applicant promised to follow the rules and regulations laid down by the committee. Some time later the committee discussed the application, agreed to it and specified which two trees could be cut down.

Shortly before the mule owners arrived, the committee held court over two men who were accused of illegally felling trees. It was now almost 2 o'clock, a chilly breeze presaged the forthcoming storm and 78 people, most of them men, now sat in an ever-enlarging circle listening to the deliberations of Min Gurung and his colleagues. The first of the accused was a small, lithe individual with a cocky manner. He smiled wryly as one of the committee members recounted his crime: the felling of a large bush without permission from the CDC, the villagers' organization responsible for all forestry matters. The miscreant claimed that he didn't know the bush was in a protected zone; he then suggested it was the fault of the forest guards for not being more vigilant. 'Looking after the forest is everyone's responsibility,' interjected another member of the committee. 'It's not just the responsibility of the forest guards – or even this committee – but everyone who lives here, the whole community!' The accused eventually accepted that he was in the wrong and the committee discussed how much to fine him. It decided on 50 rupees, the accused cheerfully paid up and the committee considered a further case of illegal felling. 'If he'd cut down a big tree', whispered Prem, 'he might have been fined anything up to 1,000 rupees.'

Around 3 o'clock four mule owners arrived. These were men of substance, owning some 200 mules between them, and they sat looking sullen and angry as the committee railed against their pack animals. One member suggested that the mule owners should be forced to stall-feed the animals; that, he said, would prevent them from raiding farmers' fields. A furious argument ensued: the mule owners denied that their animals caused any damage and claimed that it was impossible to stall-feed them. They even went on the offensive, arguing that they should be paid more for the loads they carried and pointing out, justifiably, that the hill people needed their services. Forked lightning added to the drama of the occasion and a black curtain of rain swept towards us. A heated discussion continued for half an hour and the mule owners, overwhelmed by the weight of public opinion, reluctantly agreed that their mules did cause some problems. Ideally, suggested Min Gurung, they should be fined, but as they wouldn't agree to that, there was only one thing for it: the mule owners should provide free labour and services for development activities which benefited the whole community. Listening to the committee discuss the virtues of the scheme was like watching a Greek tragedy: we knew its ending, and so did the mule owners. They agreed to give three days' free labour, enough to carry 145 bags of cement from the roadhead to the site of the new bridge. Power, as Min Gurung had asserted, really did lie with the people. And it was the people, encouraged and helped by the Annapurna Conservation Area Project, who were saving this magnificent part of the Himalaya from the destructive activities which, not long ago, threatened to ruin it for ever.[1]

The Annapurna Conservation Area Project (ACAP) had its genesis in a visit to the region by King Birendra in 1985. He witnessed a whole range of problems – from the destruction of forests to the unplanned proliferation of tourist lodges – and he issued a directive to reconcile the needs of nature conservation with those of tourism and economic development. The King Mahendra Trust for Nature Conservation (KMTNC), a leading non-governmental organization in Nepal, was given the task of implementing the directive and a three-man team was dispatched to the region to carry out a survey.

The team consisted of Mingma Norbu Sherpa, a national park warden who was to become the first director of ACAP; Brot Coburn, an American micro-hydro specialist who had spent many years working in Nepal; and Dr Chandra Prasad Gurung, a medical geographer who had been brought up in Sikles, a village a day's walk north of Pokhara, Nepal's second city.

At the time of our visit Dr Gurung was acting both as director of ACAP – he took over from Mingma Sherpa in 1990 – and as member secretary of the King Mahendra Trust. 'We went with very open minds,' he recalled when we met him in his office in Patan, Kathmandu's sister city. 'We spent four months in the field, walking all over the Annapurna region, sleeping in villages, talking to people about their way of life, the problems they had...We found that most of the 40,000 people living round Annapurna were very poor, that there were tremendous pressures from tourism and a lot of environmental destruction, especially of the forests.'

Since the late 1960s the Annapurna region had become increasingly popular with foreign tourists. This was understandable: geographically and culturally, it is one of the most fascinating areas in the world. Six ethnic groups inhabit an area which encompasses everything from rhododendron forests to alpine meadows, desert plateaus to terraced farmland. Some of the world's highest mountains are to be found here, and the western boundary of the Annapurna massif is defined by the Kali Gandaki valley, the deepest gorge in the world. This geographic diversity is reflected in the region's rich flora and fauna. In the remoter parts of the mountains can be found such rarities as musk deer, red panda, snow

21

leopard and blue sheep. The casual trekker is unlikely to see any of these, but will encounter a wealth of colourful birds and insects.

'The growth of tourism was really extraordinary,' explained Dr Gurung. 'In the early '70s you could count the numbers in hundreds, but by 1984 25,000 trekkers visited the area every year.' By the end of the 1980s the figure had risen to 35,000 and today it exceeds 43,000. When all the hired porters and guides are taken into consideration, around 80,000 outsiders come to the area each year, double its resident population. Tourism has been both enriching and destructive. 'Twenty-five years ago', continued Dr Gurung, 'there used to be just one cowshed at a place called Ghorepani. Now there are 32 lodges there. The whole area used to be covered by thick rhododendron forest – most of that's gone now.' Along the main trails – beside the Kali Gandaki, up the Modi Khola to the Annapurna Sanctuary, on the 21-day circuit round the Annapurna massif – lodges and tea-shops sprang up to serve the trekkers. To the owners of these establishments came new-found wealth, but while they prospered, the environment suffered. Forests were felled to provide both timber and fuelwood, which was used to cook the trekkers' meals and to supply hot water for showers. Most of the lodges lacked proper toilet facilities and sewage pollution became a serious problem along many popular trails. Tourism brought about insidious cultural changes too as Western visitors introduced to the hill villages standards of behaviour which were offensive to many members of these essentially conservative communities.[2]

During their four-month survey Dr Gurung and his companions had plenty of time to reflect on possible solutions. 'At that time', he explained, 'there were three types of designation for conservation in Nepal – national parks, wildlife reserves and hunting reserves. In places like Chitwan national park, conservation had been very successful if you assessed matters simply in terms of saving rhinos and tigers – but conservation was for wildlife, not for people. The local people were largely ignored and they were generally denied access to resources which by tradition had been theirs.' Approximately three-quarters of Nepal's expenditure on national parks – of which there were seven in 1985 – went on paying the military, whose task was to keep people *out* of the parks. Animosity towards wildlife conservation inevitably increased among the burgeoning populations living around the parks. 'We soon realized that we needed a new sort of designation,' explained Dr Gurung. 'If the wildlife and forests were to survive, the local people had to be involved. That was our starting point: conservation means human development; the living conditions of the hill people had to be upgraded.'

Hence the birth of a new designation – conservation area – which means, quite simply, conservation by the people for the people. In 1986 the Annapurna Conservation Area Project, encompassing an area of 4,633 square kilometres with its headquarters at Ghandruk, was officially launched. Dr Gurung hoped that ACAP would be self-financing and independent of outside aid by the mid-'90s. In 1989 the project began charging all trekkers an entry fee of 200 rupees (worth $10 then, around $4 now), and these fees have been put into a trust fund which, by 1993, was worth 35 million rupees. In 1993 the entry fee was increased to 650 rupees ($12). By 1996 the value of the trust fund should reach 50 million rupees; the interest from the fund, together with the annual tourist fees, should provide enough money for all the development projects in the area.

The Annapurna region was no stranger to outside aid. 'There had been plenty of multi-million dollar stuff', recounted Dr Gurung, 'and most of it had failed. What was obvious was that the small projects initiated by the locals and built for their participation were much more successful.' An important principle guiding ACAP's work has been that there should be no 'free lunches'. Experience has shown that whenever people have contributed to a project, they look after it. 'Let me give you an example', said Dr Gurung. 'Before ACAP was set up, a drinking water project was planned at a cost of 6.4 million rupees and a three-tap system was set up in Ghandruk. That work was paid for, planned and executed without any consultation with the locals, who were simply hired as casual labour. It wasn't long before all the taps were broken and the system fell into disuse.' Subsequently the villagers, with the help of ACAP staff, planned a five-tap scheme. This cost a mere 50,000 rupees, half of which was paid for by the locals themselves. The system is still in perfect working order.

Dr Gurung and his staff – ACAP now employs over 100 people – see themselves as *lamis*, or match-makers. 'Our job is to help the people identify the problems, to provide technical advice and to find sources of revenue and help.' To illustrate this Dr Gurung gave the example of the Ghandruk micro-hydro project, which since 1992 had provided 235 households with electric light and 17 lodges with energy for lighting and cooking. The Canadian Cooperation Office provided 900,000 rupees, ACAP contributed 350,000 rupees, the UK Committee for the King Mahendra Trust raised 200,000 rupees and the Intermediate Technology Development Group gave technical support. The Ghandruk Electricity Management Committee obtained a bank loan of 500,000 rupees and the villagers provided all the unskilled – and some of the skilled – labour, contributing 40 per cent of the costs to the scheme. Left to their own devices they could never have got such a project off the ground. ACAP, however, was able to approach a variety of organizations and coordinate the fund-raising.

Initially, ACAP confined its activities to a pilot area of 200 square kilometres encompassing the Upper Modi Khola Valley, the Annapurna Sanctuary and the popular trekking area between Ghandruk and Ghorepani. All of this fell within the compass of Ghandruk Village Development Committee (VDC).[3] The pilot programme was considered a success and in 1991 ACAP's area of operation was expanded to take in 1,500 square kilometres and 16 VDCs with a population of 20,000 people. In 1993 ACAP was given the responsibility of managing the Ministry of Tourism's Upper Mustang Conservation and Development Project, under which the 'forbidden kingdom' of Mustang was opened to the outside world for the first time.[4] ACAP now has four field offices, each with a different focus for its work: while Ghandruk concentrates on conservation and tourism, Lawang has its emphasis on agro-forestry and community development, Sikles has focused on agriculture and Mustang on tourism and the conservation of the cultural heritage. To say that everything is inter-related sounds like a truism, yet experience over the past seven years in Ghandruk seems to bear this out. The programme had its roots in the management of tourism, but managing tourists has led to a great diversity of activities, from the standardization of menus and the installation of toilets to the planting of forests and the introduction of solar power and hydro-electricity.

At the conclusion of the Conservation and Development Committee meeting, we returned to Himalayan Lodge, a small hotel on the edge of Ghandruk commanding magnificent views over the northern portion of the village and the mountains beyond. In the valley below a rainbow was etched against black clouds emptying themselves beneath the late-afternoon sun. Tek Bahadur Gurung, owner of Himalayan Lodge, returned from the meeting in high spirits. He had been one of those to criticize the mule-owners and he was delighted with the outcome of the meeting. 'Getting them to carry the cement is a sort of indirect fine,' he said, a broad grin creasing his weathered face. 'They'd never have stood for a direct fine, but they agreed to carry the cement as they could see that it was for the good of everyone.'

Tek Gurung was a man of great charm and gentleness, yet he conducted his affairs with the confidence and precision one would expect of a former British Gurkha soldier. He was an important figure in Ghandruk, being the present chairman of the Village Development Committee and the chairman of one of the two Lodge Management Committees (LMCs) within the area.[4] He had seen great changes during his lifetime. 'When I was young', he recalled, 'if I walked half an hour up the hill from here I was in thick jungle. Now people have to go two hours or more to collect firewood.' The forests had diminished for a variety of reasons. As the population in the hills increased, so did the demand for fuelwood. Immigration had also had a profound effect on the landscape. Tek pointed down the valley: 'Twenty years ago there used to be very thick jungle between Landrung and Chandrakot. Then some Magars from Baglung moved in and they cut all the forest. That's what happens when people migrate.' In recent times, however, tourism had been the principal slayer of the forests. 'When I returned from the army in 1967', explained Tek, 'one or two tourists used to come through here each year, but there were no hotels then.' The first lodge opened in 1972 and over the years more people decided to open up tea-shops and lodges as the flow of tourists increased. There are now 20 lodges in Ghandruk village – many converted from farm buildings – and over 50 lodges and tea-shops within the area administered by Ghandruk VDC. The development of the tourist industry was anarchic: 'Originally the lodge owners thought about making money above all else,' explained Tek. 'There were no proper toilets, rubbish was thrown everywhere and there were no standard charges, so trekkers were always bargaining and trying to knock prices down. In those days huge amounts of wood were used, often very wastefully.' Tek himself used to fill a drum with cold water at 10 am every day and make a fire beneath it to heat water for evening showers. On some days no trekkers came, so there was tremendous waste of wood. In any case, open fires such as these are highly inefficient.

The first Lodge Management Committee (LMC) was set up in Ghandruk in 1988 at the instigation of ACAP. It has proved to be highly influential in a variety of ways. At the most prosaic level it has ensured that lodge owners, whom the committee represents, keep their properties clean, serve 'good, clean food' as Tek put it, and provide adequate sanitation facilities. Prices are fixed, so there is no question of trekkers bargaining, and menus have been standardized. The LMC meets twice yearly and has the power to lay down rules – democratically decided upon – which all lodge owners must adhere to. For example, the LMC has decided that all lodges must have proper toilets. 'Sometimes', explained Tek, 'a lodge owner will say, "I don't have any money. I can't afford to build a toilet". It's probably not true – he just wants to spend his money on buying land or something else. So we say, "OK, we will give you 4,000 rupee loan and you *must* build a toilet".' The committee gets the money from ACAP, and the lodge owner pays the loan back with 5 per cent interest, the interest being retained by the committee. Within a few years all lodges in Ghandruk will have proper toilets.

ACAP has provided technical advice – though no funds – on the installation of back-boilers, which heat water during the cooking of meals, and solar panels. By late 1992 over 120 lodges within the ACAP area had installed back-boilers, and Tek estimated that by 1996 every lodge in Ghandruk would be using solar power. From an environmental point of view this has been highly beneficial. According to Anil Manandhar, ACAP's Conservation Officer in Ghandruk, a typical lodge in Ghorepani used to consume 250 kilos of wood a day. Since the introduction of back-boilers and space heaters, daily wood consumption has dropped to less than 80 kilos. A similar story can be told throughout the region.

ACAP has helped introduce other measures to reduce fuelwood consumption. At Chhomrong, further up the valley from Ghandruk, a kerosene depot has been established and all lodges and expeditions are now obliged to use kerosene rather than fuelwood. ACAP has also introduced schemes to improve the efficiency of domestic *chulos*, the clay ovens which most households cook with. It has laid on training courses for lodge owners – covering everything from toilet building to the efficient use of energy – and it has produced a 'Minimum Impact Code' leaflet telling visitors how they can help to reduce their consumption of energy and thus conserve forests.[5]

On a grander scale ACAP acted as *lami* to help the villagers to finance and build the Ghandruk community-owned micro-hydro electricity project which provides electricity for over 2,000 people. The committee responsible for managing the facility, for collecting charges and repaying the loan has been chosen by the villagers, who are understandably proud of their achievement. Unlike the inhabitants of Kathmandu, who are subjected to daily power cuts, the people of Ghandruk have electricity for 24 hours a day and it has been provided at a cost which makes some of the government's large-scale projects appear disgracefully profligate. For example, the World Bank-financed 69,000 kilowatt Marsayandi B scheme was built at a cost of $4,400 per kilowatt, whereas the 50 kilowatt Ghandruk scheme cost $1,400 per kilowatt.

Between them, all these energy-creating and energy-saving devices – the micro-hydro plant, back-boilers, solar heaters and improved *chulos* – have helped to reduce the demand for wood. However, with the help and encouragement of ACAP the communities have also taken practical steps to protect and enhance their forests. Prior to the 1957 Nationalization of Forests Act, Nepalese villagers had managed their own forests with minimal interference from the government. 'They'd developed their own systems of management', explained Dr Chandra Gurung, 'and in some of the remote regions these continued to work after the Act came into force.' In his home village of Sikles, for example, the forest was divided into ten parcels and villagers could collect fuelwood for just ten days each year from one particular parcel, which they would not touch again for another ten years. This system worked – and works – well. However, in most areas the villagers lost control of their forests to the Forestry Department, which was frequently dictatorial and invariably bureaucratic. Villages were fined and imprisoned for taking wood from forests which they considered ancestrally theirs, and they gradually came to view the forests as alien resources to be plundered, rather than communally owned resources to be sustainably managed. In recent years, the government has begun to see the error of its ways and in 1986 responsibility for the management of forests within the Annapurna Conservation Area was given to ACAP, which immediately devolved its powers to the Conservation and Development Committees (CDCs).[6]

The first CDC to be established – there were eight by February 1993 – was in Ghandruk. Getting the CDC off the ground was not an easy task, as its present chairman Min Bahadur Gurung recalled: 'A lot of people were against us at first, as they didn't understand what conservation meant. We knew we couldn't force things on people, so we went from village to village – we were a small group of villagers and ACAP staff – talking to them about their problems, about what they wanted. If the committee had only dealt with conservation it would have failed. But we combined it with development – that's very important.' This explains the CDC's involvement in many issues – such as bridge building and the control of mule trains – which are unrelated to forestry or conservation matters. Once the committee had gained the support of the population it introduced a ban on hunting – this was especially important for musk deer, which were heading for extinction – and a three-year moratorium on the cutting of trees in certain areas. 'The committee always consults the villagers,' said Min Gurung. 'Our members are chosen by the villagers and the rules and regulations are really made by the people – the committee just sees that they are carried out.' Under the old system, villagers had to go to the government Forest Range Office to get permission to cut trees. This was a lengthy process which many were inclined to ignore. Now, they can obtain permits direct from the CDC.

Within the project area, ACAP has established several forest nurseries which provide free seedlings for community and private planting, and fencing materials for community planting. Over the past couple of years private nurseries have also been established and ACAP hopes that all nurseries will eventually be privately run. A survey of planting schemes in Lawang, to the east of Ghandruk, revealed a 65–75 per cent seedling survival rate in private plantations and a 90 per cent survival rate in community plantations. These figures compare very favourably with government-run projects.

Between 1987 and 1993 Ghandruk nursery, the oldest in the project area, distributed over 250,000 seedlings, over half of which went to private individuals. Seeds are collected in the wild and sewn in a compost made of soil, leaf matter and manure. The nursery provides a wide variety of trees. Himalayan cherry and walnut are good all-purpose trees: their leaves are used for animal fodder and their wood for fuel and timber. The walnut has the added bonus of bearing fruit. Bamboo is used for fencing and making baskets, and deep-rooting willow are ideal for controlling soil erosion. The nurseries raise many other species of tree beside these and the communities and farmers choose according to their needs.

Communities living in difficult circumstances seldom survive without a strong spirit of cooperation. The hill people of Nepal are used to working together – for example, to build trails, manage their forests, set up irrigation schemes – and in Ghandruk the traditional *jhara* system, which determines the division of labour among households, has been put to good use. ACAP, as one of its staff put it, has simply added fuel to a vigorous fire. On the larger schemes villagers nearly always provide their share of costs by giving labour rather than cash. This was the case for the 3.4 million rupee micro-hydro scheme and the bridge which was being discussed at the CDC meeting. However, there have been many projects – especially the smaller ones – which have been supported by cash contributions. Take, for example, Ghandruk health clinic, the running costs for which are met by the interest on a 300,000 rupee fund. ACAP contributed 200,000 rupees, leaving the villagers to raise the remaining 100,000. This they did by collecting 150 rupees from each household.

One of the most impressive aspects of ACAP has been the involvement of women in community affairs. Before we left Ghandruk, we went to see the venerable Bhakti Kumari Gurung, who at that time was the only female member of the CDC.[7] An enormous woman with a wrinkled face, a fine collection of gold nose rings and a warm, open manner, she sat cross-legged spinning sheep's wool, the raw material for rugs she made to supplement her family's income. 'If you can't do much physical work', she said, 'then weaving is a big help.' She felt that life had improved considerably in recent years. 'In the old days', she recalled, 'we had to work very hard, both in the fields and collecting fuelwood. Now we have electricity we don't need much wood, so that's made life easier. And in the old days there were no vaccination programmes. Now there are, and the children are far healthier.' Within a couple of minute's walk of Bhakti's house was the health clinic, opened in 1987, the year-old day care centre, which looked after 29 children between the ages of two and five, and some beautifully paved trails.[8] The women had made significant contributions to all these projects. They were not the passive recipients of outside largesse, but active participants in their own betterment.

ACAP's Women's Development Section – run by two inspired young women, Dibya Gurung and Jagan Gurung – had played an important role in motivating and supporting the village women. We eventually caught up with Dibya Gurung in Lawang. It took us a couple of days to get there, although any self-respecting Nepalese could have walked it in six hours or so. On the first day we headed down the spectacular Modi Khola valley, then climbed sharply to the ridge town of Chandrakot, where we spent the night. It was late spring now: the silk-cotton trees were covered with red fleshy flowers; kingfishers, fantails and dippers nested by the river; bare-footed farmers followed ox and plough on the narrow terraces. We passed several mule trains and came across a group of villagers expertly slitting a pig's throat.

The next day it took us five hours to walk from Hyangjabesi to Lawang, a sprawling village populated by Buddhist-inclined Gurungs and various Hindu castes. It commanded spectacular views of the Mardi Khola valley. We were greeted by Dibya Gurung with garlands made of marigolds, tares and clover. As well as being the women's development officer, she was acting officer-in-charge at Lawang, where ACAP had a staff of twenty. A woman of remarkable intelligence and energy, Dibya seemed to transmit her enthusiasm to all around her.

ACAP, she explained, had arrived in Lawang in 1990 with the intention of focusing on agro-forestry. The staff had spent the first year convincing local people that there was a need for the programme. 'There was a lot of suspicion at first,' explained Dibya. 'People thought we were going to put restrictions on what they did, that we'd be dictatorial.' The staff travelled from village to village talking about the problems people faced – declining productivity of the land, illiteracy, lack of clean water and so forth. Sometimes they used street theatre to illustrate such things as the link between poor sanitation and disease. 'We backed this extension work with positive action', said Dibya, 'building small bridges, repairing trails, setting up tap-water schemes. We didn't want to create the impression that we'd come with lots of money, and the villages contributed on a 50–50 basis.'[9]

The need to focus on women's activities as well as agro-forestry immediately became apparent to ACAP staff. ACAP's Women's Development Programme began in Ghandruk in 1990; once that had been established, Dibya moved down to Lawang. 'Getting the women organized was relatively easy', explained Dibya, 'as there was a tradition of women gathering together in *Kacho Katara* groups.' These groups would sing and dance for passing travellers or visiting dignatories as a way of raising money. Profits were sometimes put to frivolous use – for example, to pay for picnics – but they were also used for more tangible purposes, such as buying the huge cooking utensils required for feeding large numbers of people at funerals, weddings and religious festivals. Dibya encouraged the women to set up Mothers' Groups – or *Ama Toli* – and there are now sixteen in Lawang and nine in Ghandruk. Like the old *Kacho Katara* groups, the Mothers' Groups raise money by dancing and singing. Before long the Lawang women had raised 40,000 rupees. 'They were keen to build a health post', recalled Dibya, 'but as there was one just half an hour's walk away, we were reluctant to encourage such an expensive undertaking.' So the women decided to rebuild the trail up to the village instead.

Trail-building has been a major preoccupation of the Mothers' Groups in Ghandruk too. One group spent two and a half years raising 16,800 rupees; ACAP added a further 6,000. The women collected the materials to build the trail and hired the skilled labour to dress the stone and do the work. Another Mothers' Group in Ghandruk raised 11,000 rupees to repair a battered trail; this time there was no contribution from ACAP. The Lawang trail – it climbs over 1,500 feet and snakes upwards from the valley bottom for 2 miles or more – is a magnificent creation, and involved several Mothers' Groups which had joined in cooperation. Some small stretches were individually sponsored in memory of dead relatives. Such a conspicuous sign of female industry helped to win the admiration of the menfolk, who at first viewed the women's activities with displeasure. 'They used to be very rude,' explained one elderly woman in Lawang. 'They'd say, "Why are you old hags going off to dance? It's disgusting!" Today they really appreciate what we're doing.' She added, with a broad smile, that the women now felt as though they had climbed to the summit of Machhupuchhre, the holy mountain which soared skywards behind us.

At first, the Mothers' Groups excluded the men. 'That was a bad mistake,' reflected Dibya. 'It really upset them.' Now the women invite men, especially the community leaders, to all their meetings, and this has helped to engender the spirit of cooperation. The Mothers' Groups meet once a month and in Lawang the women follow the meetings with a clean-up of their village. Cleanliness has become an important issue: 'I've seen big changes since I came,' said Dibya. 'People used to shit on the trails and around the villages then. There's hell to pay if they do now!' Indeed, in many villages, the Mothers' Groups have successfully mounted toilet-building campaigns. In Imu, for example, there used to be just three toilets, all belonging to ex-British Gurkhas. There are now over 35, all built at the instigation of the Mothers' Group. The benefits have been clearly felt by all: the incidence of diarrhoea and eye infection has dropped dramatically.

General health has also been improved by the introduction of better *chulos*, or ovens. In February 1991 ACAP trained two women from each village in Lawang and Riban VDCs to convert old-fashioned smoke-belching *chulos* into more efficient, smokeless ovens. The recipients of converted *chulos* must supply the material and be present while the women do the work; ACAP pays 80 rupees for each converted *chulo* to the women, and 10 rupees to the Mothers' Group. The converted *chulos* use 10–15 per cent less fuelwood than the old ovens, and the women in many areas have further reduced wood consumption by acquiring pressure cookers. In the three villages of Chhomrong, Kimrong and Tauhi – all in Ghandruk VDC – the Mothers' Groups distributed 44 pressure cookers in one year alone.

'Conservation', Dr Gurung said, 'means human development.' ACAP's first priority was to improve the standard of living of the hill people. In Ghandruk, tourism had brought wealth to a few, primarily to those who owned lodges and tea-shops. A certain amount of imported money had trickled down to other members of the community – the mule owners who brought goods up from the valley, farmers who sold fresh food to the lodges, porters who carried the trekkers' rucksacks – but the majority of the population had benefited not one jot. In fact, tourism had brought with it inflation, so locals now had to pay higher prices for goods and services. Well aware of the inequities which tourism had fostered, ACAP had sought to redress the balance by promoting other forms of economic development, and this has been especially important to the work of the Women's Development Section, which has set up adult literacy programmes – over 500 women took part in Ghandruk in 1992 – and training courses to develop a variety of skills.

Chij Kumari Gurung was fairly typical of the women who had benefited from ACAP's Developing Women's Entrepreneurship in Tourism programme. She was one of seventeen to take part in July 1992 in a course training women how to operate a business. She had learnt to weave seven years previously, but made little money from her skill. Since the ACAP training she had established a small weaving concern in a shop in Ghandruk. She was now selling enough carpets to passing tourists to make a reasonable living. Another woman had established a similar business under the name of Ama Carpet Centre. ACAP had given her an interest-free loan of 10,000 rupees and she was paying this off at the rate of 500 rupees a month. As well as making carpets from the local sheep's wool, she was weaving gunny sacks from nettle fibre.

Establishing income-generating schemes is a complicated business and Dibya Gurung felt that ACAP had to proceed cautiously: 'There's no point in training people to produce things which won't sell' she said. In non-touristic areas like Lawang, people were not particularly entrepreneurial. However, with the help of ACAP, women in the region were exploring a variety of options. In 1993 they had tried to rear Angora rabbits – there is a high demand for mohair in Kathmandu – but many of the rabbits died. 'Next year', said Dibya, 'we'll have a small training group on rabbit-rearing.' This part of the Himalaya has a long history of producing fibres from nettles, and some women were keen to pursue that. Others were already making money by knitting thick socks to sell to trekkers heading up to Annapurna Base Camp. On a more ambitious level, ACAP and the British-based Intermediate Technology Development Group were exploring the potential for producing hand-made paper from the bark of *lokta* trees, which grow prodigiously in this part of the Himalaya. *Lokta* paper sells well to tourists in the capital and some is even being exported to Europe.

It would be disingenuous to suggest that everything which ACAP has touched has turned to gold. There have been many teething problems and some conspicuous failures. For example, in March 1993 ACAP was trying to establish a Conservation and Development Committee in Dhampus, a large village across the valley from Lawang. A committee had been formed once; it had collapsed, re-formed and collapsed again. The political rifts between the ruling Congress Party and the opposition Panchayat Party ran so deep in this village that there seemed little hope of getting them to cooperate. In other places, certain powerful individuals were deeply antagonistic to ACAP. Perhaps this was inevitable: ACAP has attempted to make rural decision-making more democratic and it has also sought to help the least privileged, such as the landless lower castes. Then in the village of Riban the men have been deliberately obstructive – they resent ACAP staff even visiting – and they have given no support whatsoever to the Mothers' Group. All the more admirable, therefore, that the women have run such successful toilet and *chulo* campaigns.

It would be disingenuous, too, to suggest that ACAP and the villagers have it all their own within the Annapurna Conservation Area. A 1,000 kilowatt hydro-electric plant is being built at Taatopaani; Indian pharmaceutical companies have become increasingly active in the collection of medicinal plants; in some areas the unplanned proliferation of tourist lodges continues. ACAP has had little or no influence over these and various other development activities.

The failures, however, have been outweighed by the successes, especially in Ghandruk. Asked how he would measure ACAP's achievements in the future, Anil Manandhar, its conservation officer, replied: 'If we're successful, we'll be moving out of here in ten years' time because the villagers will be entirely in charge. That's our goal – that the people become self-reliant. And we know they can do it – provided they're given the responsibility.' It remains to be seen whether ACAP's achievements in Ghandruk can be replicated in other parts of the Annapurna region.

No one doubts that the presence of several highly intelligent – and some would say, philanthropic – leaders has been a crucial factor. 'Ten years ago', said Min Gurung when we met him at his house one morning – tethered buffaloes chomping in the shed, hens pecking around children eating rice and lentils, 'there was no high school, no health clinic, no electricity; the trails were dangerous and the bridges were poor. Now things are much better. Ten years ago, when the Gurkha soldiers retired from the army, they didn't want to come back here; they stayed in Pokhara. But now they're returning and buying land they sold before. They can see that Pokhara is polluted and Ghandruk is prospering. In material terms, we might not be a lot better off, but the facilities – health care, education, water – are far better than they were before.'

3

ZIMBABWE

CAMPFIRE

'A bureaucrat chasing cattle to make way for wildlife!'

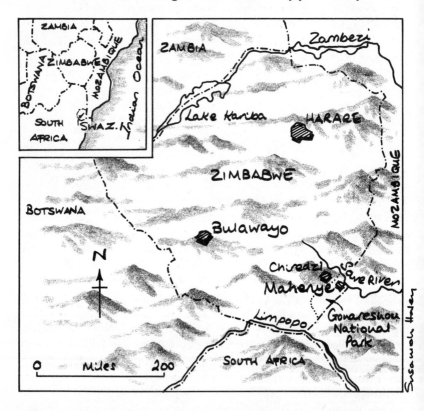

The chairman of Tongagara's village development committee, Phineas Chauke, was a small, stringy man with a quiet, cheerful manner. ·He rolled a cheroot-sized cigarette from some coarse tobacco and a shred of old newspaper, lit up and observed the gathering of villagers through a silky screen of blue-grey smoke. Behind him sat seven men, while off to one side a dozen women with children of various shapes and sizes clustered around the base of an acacia tree. It was cool for October and a grey sky arched across the monochrome landscape. 'Drought,' said Phineas, 'that's the great theme of our days. That's what we talk about at our meetings. That and wildlife. We always talk about how we can profit from wildlife.'

In a good year the farmers living in this low-lying region near the Mozambique border could expect some 16 inches of rain. The previous year they had received less than an inch, and the year before scarcely a drop. The ravages of drought – the worst in living memory – were everywhere to be seen. A stone's throw from Tongagara the Save River, fully half a mile wide in places, had been reduced to a sandy, waterless gash. Further south the Limpopo had dried up completely. The year before the farmers had failed to grow any maize or millet; crops had been sown in the autumn, at the start of what should have been the rainy season, but they wilted soon after. The thatched, mud-walled granaries were all empty, and in every village people were surviving on government food relief. At midday long queues of children, plates in hand, waited patiently for a dollop of mealie-meal made from maize imported from Argentina. The children would eat again in the evening, but adults were fortunate if they ate more than once a day, although shortly before our arrival many villages in this region had been given free meat from elephants culled in the nearby national park; this had been a welcome addition to their sparse and inadequate diet. The drought had wiped out tens of thousands of cattle – up to half had died in the worst-affected areas – and the wildlife had suffered too, though not so severely as domestic stock. In Gonarezhou national park, to the south of the Save River, we came across the carcass of a young elephant which had apparently starved to death, and large areas of woodland within the park had been devastated by hungry herds eager to squeeze moisture and sustenance from the dessicated land.

An atmosphere of despondency hovered over many of the places we passed through. A few miles north of Tongagara, in the village of Cobra Fungai, we talked to the women tending a vegetable garden. Some were energetically pumping water from deep wells; others were tending neat rows of beans and maize. 'Without the food relief, we'd never survive,' explained Kias Farmada, the mother of nine children. 'When we were young, we could plough, we could reap, there was rain. Now our children have nothing.' For Kias and the older people of Cobra, the past was another country and the future seemed bleak.

Times were tough in Tongagara too, yet Phineas Chauke and the other inhabitants of the village were guardedly optimistic; their salvation lay not in cattle, whose ownership had traditionally been seen as an index of wealth, but in wildlife, which, till recently, they had viewed with a mixture of animosity and fear. 'Ten years ago we were enemies of the national park,' explained Phineas. 'We used snares to catch impala, duiker and buffalo, and some people crossed the river to poach in the park.' The poachers were frequently caught and sometimes beaten by the guards. Then in 1984 the park authorities approached the villagers with a simple – and astonishing – message: 'They told us the wildlife was ours', recalled Phineas, 'and that if we refrained from poaching, we would gain from it.' Initially, the villagers were unclear how they would benefit from this truce with nature. 'The park people gave us the meat from the elephants they'd culled', said Phineas, 'but it wasn't until Campfire came here that we really saw how wildlife could help us.'

Zimbabwe's Communal Areas Management Programme for Indigenous Resources – Campfire for short – is a unusual venture whose purpose is to give the management of natural resources, and especially wildlife, back to the people to whom they really belong.[1] Before the European invasion of Zimbabwe, and the appropriation by the newcomers of the better and more fertile land, there was a beneficial partnership between the local people and wildlife. 'In the old days', explained a man with a blind eye sitting behind Phineas, 'the village chiefs would decide which animals could be killed and how to share out the meat and hides.' Hunting was controlled and, under the rules prevailing then, sustainable. With the arrival of the Europeans, the pattern of land use changed dramatically. Africans were herded into 'native reserves', or 'communal lands' as they were renamed after Independence, and the settlers set about turning large chunks of the country into profitable farmland.[2] In areas of reliable rainfall they planted crops like maize, tobacco and sugar; in the more arid regions they introduced vast herds of exotic cattle. Over much of the country wildlife was seen as a pest: in an attempt to prevent the spread of tsetse fly carried by wild animals, species such as kudu and buffalo were systematically slain and, as recently as the 1970s, over 6,000 buffalo were killed in the south-east in an attempt to prevent the spread of foot-and-mouth disease among cattle. Zimbabwe's wildlife was gradually pushed towards the country's periphery, and it is here, along the borders with Mozambique, Botswana and Zambia, that most of the national parks and hunting reserves are to be found today. During the colonial period Africans were estranged not only from much of their land, but from their wildlife too: creatures which once provided meat, ivory, skins and even medicines became forbidden fruit, the property of the state; meanwhile in many areas, especially those close to national parks, wild animals frequently raided crops, destroyed homes and killed people. Wildlife became an adversary, to be disposed of and exploited wherever possible.

During the 1970s it became increasingly obvious to government ecologists that beyond the boundaries of the national parks wild animals were unlikely to survive in appreciable numbers, and that the sanctity of the national parks themselves would be threatened, unless rural communities derived tangible benefits from their presence. It was this realization that led to the founding of Campfire, which seeks to promote the sustainable use – rather than the random abuse – of Zimbabwe's natural resources. By selling hunting quotas to safari operators, and by strictly controlling cropping and culling, the people of villages like Tongagara have been able to turn pests into providers. In some areas, particularly those prone to drought, wildlife is proving to be a much better ally than cattle in the perennial battle against poverty.

Before we left Tongagara, Phineas went into his *idhlo* – the traditional thatched hut – and reappeared with a tattered ledger which held records of animals killed during recent years in the surrounding forests:

Killed 1 elephant bull on 5/12/91. Client name J Dias Snr Spain.

12/6/92 Charged by Buffalo Cow on the Island. Realized it had a snare on the hind leg. Had to shoot it. Reported it to national parks. Meat to Wildlife Committee.

13/7/92 Culled 3 Adult Female Hippos in Dakata Pool. Meat shared between Fife's village and Mahohoma's village. Hides recovered to Mahenye Safari Camp for field curing.

Last year every household in the village received a dividend of Z$140 from the sale of hunting quotas.[3] 'We feel we have some power now,' said Phineas. 'Next year our ward is hoping to get Z$300,000 from the quotas – then we'll really feel our plans have come to fruition.' The villagers, explained Phineas, were thinking of building a school, or perhaps a small health clinic, from their earnings. This was precisely what had happened in Tongagara B, a larger village half an hour's drive down the Save River.

Most of the entries in Phineas's ledger had been signed by Clive Stockil, a white farmer and safari operator admired and trusted by the villagers. A thoughtful, heavy-built man in his mid-40s, he had an intimate knowledge of local language, customs and wildlife. He was an important figure in the Gazaland district, especially active in Mahenye Ward, which encompassed the two Tongagaras and Mahohoma. Other key players in the Campfire story included Robert Monro and Elliot Chauke, both of whom accompanied us on our tour of the region. Monro was a humorous and articulate white Zimbabwean. He had left the country during the War of Independence to attend the University of London, but returned afterwards to co-found the Zimbabwe Trust. In partnership with the Department of National Parks, the Multispecies Project of the World Wide Fund for Nature (WWF), the University of Zimbabwe's Centre for Applied Social Sciences (CASS) and the Campfire Association, which represents participating district councils, the Trust has played a prominent part in getting Campfire off the ground. While Robert Monro was able to paint for us a broad picture of Campfire's aims and achievements, Elliot Chauke, whom we first met over warthog fillets and cold beer in the district capital of Chiredzi, showed us how wildlife management worked in the villages. Elliot was the chairman of the district council's wildlife committee and vice-chairman of the Campfire Association. An imposing figure with feline eyes and powerful features, he knew this part of Zimbabwe like the back of his hand, having spent five years in the bush fighting with the Liberation Army, and he acted as both our guide and interpreter.

'You wouldn't believe the changes there have been in my short lifetime,' said Clive Stockil as we gathered one evening around the log fire at his tented camp. A nightjar called out from the towering trees behind us, and every now and then the clouds would part just long enough for a three-quarter moon to illuminate the Save's broad and empty riverbed. 'We've pressed the ecosystem way beyond its limits of endurance by years of mismanagement.' Grasslands had been so overgrazed by cattle that they had turned into barren wastes and many of the rivers in the region had begun to silt up. 'Twenty years ago there were plenty of deep pools here', explained Stockil, prodding towards the river with a slice of kudu biltong, 'and even in the driest of seasons they retained some water. Now they've all been filled in with sand. We've created a dust bowl by our stupidity.' As long ago as the mid-1970s Stockil argued that in many areas it would make better sense, both in environmental and economic terms, to abandon cattle and adopt a programme of what is cumbersomely termed multispecies ranching. At the time many people, especially government officials, scoffed at such ideas, but under provisions made in the Parks and Wild Life Act of 1975 commercial farmers – which is to say, white farmers – were given the opportunity to make use of the wildlife on their land, providing they did so in a sensible and sustainable manner. Over the years, growing numbers decided to forsake cattle. Of the country's 4,500 commercial farmers, getting on for 500 are now actively involved in wildlife production. Sports hunting, the production of meat from game and eco-tourism are the dominant land use on 2,700,000 hectares of commercial farmland.[4]

By the early 1980s relations between the Gonarezhou national park authority and the people living on the east bank of the Save River and on Nwachumeni – the island adjacent to Tongagara B – had reached an all-time low. Game from the park frequently trampled crops and injured people working in the fields, and the villagers retaliated. In 1982 Clive Stockil suggested to the villagers and the park authorities that there were two possible solutions. One was drastic: a fence could be built along the park boundary and the wildlife in the communal land outside eliminated. The second possibility, and the one which found favour, would involve the villagers managing the wildlife themselves. The national park agreed to provide a hunting quota of two elephants. The villagers, for their part, voluntarily decided to turn Nwachumeni Island into a wildlife reserve; they took down their huts and moved to the east bank of the river. Unfortunately, the existing legislation deprived the villagers of the revenue which accrued from selling the rights to shoot the elephants; it went from the

Department of National Parks straight to the Treasury. Over the next five years, the hunting quota gradually increased, but the people of Mahenye ward received nothing for their considerable sacrifices other than modest amounts of free game meat. Eventually, however, the Department of National Parks negotiated the release of funds from the Treasury for the construction of a grinding mill, some school buildings and a health clinic. 'Ten years ago', said Stockil, 'the attitude towards animals which crossed over the river from the national park was quite simple: "If it comes, we'll eat it". There was no incentive to look after the wildlife. But there's been a dramatic change in attitude. Now funds get back to the villagers, and we've now got over 200 elephants, lots of buffalo, kudu and other species living this side of the river.'

One morning Elliot Chauke and Robert Monro took us down to Mahenye school, many of whose classrooms had been constructed with the profits made from selling hunting quotas. Daniel Sibiya, a smartly dressed young man from Harare, was teaching a class of ten to eleven year olds. He invited us to ask them about Campfire. A young boy with a Barcelona Olympics T-shirt shot up: 'By looking after our wildlife we can develop the country,' he explained. A girl in a pink dress said her family had received some money from Campfire. Eight of the 39 children said they wanted to work as game guards – 'Catching poachers,' as one of them put it. Next door another teacher was holding a meeting of the school environmental club. The walls of the classroom were covered with paintings of animals and poems about nature, drought and farming.

According to their teacher, the children enjoyed seeing animals around the village, but they were scared of them. And with good reason: a wall chart in the nearby clinic – part-built from the proceeds from game hunting – showed that in Mahenye ward, which had a population of around 5,000, 36 people had been injured in April, 31 in May, 22 in June, 20 in July and 17 in August. Two-thirds of these injuries were caused by wild animals, with buffalo, elephant and crocodile being the principal culprits; most of the victims, it seems, were young men hunting for food, or hides. The nurse in charge said that three villagers had been trampled to death by elephants over the last year, but he felt this was a modest price to pay in return for the substantial benefits which had arisen from Campfire projects. The villagers obviously thought so too: when a government department proposed that a large area within Mahenye ward be given over to cattle, the villagers resisted the plans, arguing that the land should be left to wildlife.

Many of those we spoke to appreciated animals for their aesthetic value as well as their economic potential. Robert Monro recalled a colleagues's conversation with an old man in the Zambezi Valley who proclaimed: 'When we are hungry, the elephant is food; when we're full, the elephant is beautiful.' Kias Farmada, like many of her friends in Cobra Fungai, was hungry – she could no longer afford morning porridge and ate her only meal of the day in the evening – yet wild animals were more to her than cash. 'We want our children to appreciate wildlife when they grow up,' she said. 'When an elephant comes close to the village, I raise my child up and say to him – see, this is an elephant!' In a pool near the village they were nurturing five hippos, which they fed daily on a diet of hay. Indeed in many parts of the country where Campfire was in operation people were helping wild animals to make it through the drought: some provided fodder, others had dug deep into riverbeds to provide drinking water.

A curious and revealing incident occurred when we were on our way to Mahenye. We were accompanied by some inquisitive officials from the District Administrator's office when we came across a large pile of cane cuttings which had been provided for the elephants. Four half-starved cattle were munching away at the fodder. One of the DA's officers climbed out of his pickup and peppered the cows with stones. 'A bureaucrat chasing cattle to make way for wildlife!' exclaimed Elliot. 'That would have been unthinkable a few years ago.'

Campfire is often referred to as a wildlife conservation scheme. 'But it's not,' insisted Robert Monro. 'It's about people at the lowest level agitating for control of their resources. What we're talking about is land use – the appropriate and equitable use of resources – rather than conservation, or even bio-diversity.' Who owns the natural resources? Who should determine their fate? These are the great issues of the day in rural Zimbabwe.[5] Virtually everyone we talked to – from the highest echelons in the Department of National Parks, to local politicians, wildlife biologists and the villagers themselves –

saw the devolution of power as a crucial prerequisite for Campfire's success.

The 1975 Wild Life Act encouraged the 'owners and occupiers of alienated land' – virtually all of whom were white farmers – to put their wildlife resources to whatever use they saw fit, with the proviso that they did so in a sustainable manner.[6] This was highly discriminatory as similar opportunities were denied the black communities living on communal lands. Here the government, in the guise of the Department of National Parks, remained 'the appropriate authority' for wildlife management.[7] Profits derived from hunting safaris, game cropping and so forth went to the Treasury. In principle, these revenues should have returned to district councils to be used on community projects in the areas where the hunting or cropping had taken place. In practice, most of it never made it out of the Treasury. In any case, local communities had little or no say in the whole business and popular support for wildlife activities remained minimal or non-existent.

The controlled exploitation of wildlife on private lands did generate sizeable returns both for the landowners and the Treasury. It was also recognized that the switch from cattle ranching to mixed cattle/wildlife or pure wildlife regimes was often in the best interests of the environment. Encouraged by this, the government, following Independence, decided to broaden the scope of the Wild Life Act. A 1982 amendment paved the way for Campfire, whereby the Minister for Natural Resources was given the power to confer appropriate authority status on district councils. This would afford them the same rights and responsibilities as the owners and occupiers of alienated land. By December 1992, 22 of Zimbabwe's 55 district councils had been granted direct management authority over their wildlife resources.[8]

The first two districts to embark on the programme were Guruve and Nyaminyami in the Zambezi valley. Both developed Campfire projects which brought considerable benefits to their rural populations. In 1989, the first year of operation, Guruve's net revenue from wildlife activities came to over Z$330,000 and in one ward, Kanyurira, the revenues were sufficient to build a clinic, buy school furniture and provide a dividend of Z$200 to each household. (This was equivalent to over half the average gross income derived from cotton, the main cash crop.) 'The buffalo are our cattle', declared a spirit medium in Kanyurira ward after payment of the first household dividends. The revenues in Guruve were exclusively derived from safari hunting, whereas Nyaminyami combined hunting with a programme of impala culling (1,500 animals a year). In 1989, the district made Z$320,000 from its wildlife enterprises, of which Z$190,000 was distributed to local communities. Since then the district has expanded its activities to include tourist ventures.

According to Professor Murphree of the Centre for Applied Social Sciences (CASS) in Harare, there have so far been only three really successful community initatives under Campfire: those at Mahenye and Kanyurira, and one in the Chikwarakwara ward in Beitbridge district, in the south-east corner of the country. 'There may be others coming up', he suggested when we met him in his book-lined office at the University of Zimbabwe, 'but so far these three have been the obvious successes – and none of these has been perfect.' Professor Murphree became involved in the study of wildlife utilization in 1984 when the Department of National Parks sought his views on an early Campfire idea. As it happened, that particular venture never got off the ground, but CASS has since carried out detailed socio-economic studies of many Campfire areas. In the mid-80s CASS urged the Department to seek the assistance of non-governmental agencies. The Zimbabwe Trust has subsequently played a key role in helping local communities to establish the institutions – and infrastructure – necessary to manage Campfire, and WWF has provided ecological advice to district councils and the Campfire villages.

'Campfire is very dynamic,' reflected Professor Murphree. 'It's reasonably flexible and it's difficult to predict where it will work best.' Nevertheless, his research has identified a number of factors which contribute to a project's success. The first – amply borne out by our experiences in Mahenye ward – is that villagers are most inclined to manage their wildlife resources wisely if these resources are perceived as having a tangible value. Clive Stockil and other safari operators charge around US$1,000 a day to hunters who come in search of a bull elephant, and an additional US$7,500 trophy fee for the elephant itself; this trophy fee goes to the local community. With this sort of price tag, elephants are no longer seen as pests but as walking bank accounts.

On our way down to Stockil's camp, Elliot Chauke took us to see a deep well which had been dug for a herd of five elephants in a dried-up riverbed at Chingwedziva; the local game

45

guard said he didn't want the large bull elephant to go on a hunting quota as the villagers felt the animal would be worth more as an attraction to wildlife photographers. In Cobra Fungai, in contrast, the villagers had decided to tolerate a gang of crocodiles which prayed on their goats as they hoped to 'sell' the reptiles for their trophy value. Where local communities do derive benefits from wildlife – for example, in Mahenye ward and Kanyurira – poaching activity tends to decline. 'Every household is a policeman now,' Phineas Chauke of Tongagara told us.

It is quite clear that the communities which put up with the inconvenience of wildlife should be the principal beneficiaries of any exploitation. 'If people don't get the returns they deserve, or if they aren't empowered to use their wildlife', said David Cumming of WWF's Multispecies Project, 'then the wildlife will disappear. It's as simple as that.' Cumming gave an example of a ward, rich in wildlife, in the north of the country. In the early 1980s the community had been fired up by talk of tapping its wildlife resources, but by the time WWF arrived on the scene in 1988 disillusion had set in. 'As soon as we began discussing Campfire', explained Cumming, 'the chief said, "We've heard all this before. We haven't seen a cent. We don't even want to see a hare on our land now".' The villagers have since come round to the idea of Campfire, but instances such as this show the importance of people getting their just rewards.

There is much talk, especially among governments and aid agencies, about the need for grassroots participation. However, participatory projects often mean no more than using local labour to achieve ends determined by outside forces. 'There's been a lot of talk here about producer communities', said Cumming, 'but very few are managing or husbanding their resources in a direct, self-governing manner. We've still got a long way to go in getting locals fully in charge.' This is a vital issue, and one which will make or break Campfire in many areas.

Campfire accepted the structures of local government established at the time of Independence (1980). This was a sensible move as it helped ensure the support of local politicians and bureaucrats. However, there remains a fundamental discrepancy between the law – which delegates proprietorship of wildlife to district councils – and the principle which holds that the communities who produce wildlife should be the managers and main beneficiaries of Campfire projects.[9] All too often councils have been reluctant to allow the producer communities a full say in how their projects should be managed, and some have held on to a greater share of the revenues than they are entitled to. Official Campfire guidelines stipulate that district councils should keep no more than 15 per cent of the wildlife revenues, that a maximum of 35 per cent should go towards costs, with the remainder going to the producer communities.

The guidelines also entreat district councils to devolve decision-making on wildlife management to producer communities; virtually all the successful Campfire projects are found in districts where councils have willingly done this. In Gazaland district, for example the wards are left to work out annual quotas for safari hunting or cropping, though they must seek approval for their decisions from the district council and the Department of National Parks. This system is working well. However, even in those districts which have witnessed a progressive devolution of power, problems remain. 'The wards often have a population of 6,000 or so', said Professor Murphree, 'and that's far too large to allow the sort of face-to-face contact you need if community consensus is to be fairly achieved.'[10] There are exceptions: Masoka village in Kanyurira ward has a population of 1,000; Chikwarakwara, the same; Mahenye, around 3,000. These are the three great success stories so far and it seems that small communities which encourage a high degree of public participation are the ones where Campfire is most likely to flourish.

'It would be wrong', suggested Professor Murphree as he dragged on another menthol cigarette, 'to be completely populist, to say, "Let them cast off their fetters and get on with it!" The communities on the ground do need some inputs from outside, but what we have to avoid is a centrist, commandist approach.' It is particularly intriguing to see the way in which the collaborative group which supports national Campfire policy has dealt with its own internal power issues. In the early years this group consisted of the Zimbabwe Trust, WWF's Multispecies Project and CASS. After a while the Department of National Parks was drafted in and given the chair. Then came the Campfire Association, representing the participating district councils. By then it was recognized that the Department of National Parks should no longer be the lead organization – Campfire was supposed to be a community venture –

and the Campfire Association took the chair. In some people's eyes, the Association has been a 'black front' grafted on to a white-dominated power base, but such a criticism ignores the fact that the other players in the collaborative group are unswervingly dedicated to giving responsibility for wildlife management to the practitioners, all of whom are black. At a meeting of the group shortly before our visit, it was decided that the Campfire Association should throw its membership open to all the producer wards across the country. This should lead to further devolution of power. Many believe the next step should be legal provision to allow wards to receive appropriate authority status in their own right. Clive Stockil put the issue in graphic terms: 'What we should be saying to the villagers is, "Look, that elephant is worth Z$65,000; you do what you want with it – eat it, shoot it, whatever". It's a nonsense if we don't let them manage the whole project themselves. It's a learning process still – we've got to get everything down to the level of the community.'

Colonialism has left a legacy of unfairness in Zimbabwe which is especially apparent in the skewed pattern of land ownership. The president, Mr Robert Mugabe, recently described the land question as one of the main factors that encouraged his people to launch the war of national liberation, yet nearly a third of the country's land is still owned by a small number of wealthy – and predominantly white – farmers. It is true that there have been some efforts to redistribute land; in 1980, 42 per cent of the country was held by 6,000 white farmers, whereas nine years later 29 per cent was held by 4,300 farmers, not all of whom were white. But the majority of the rural population still resides in the communal lands, many of which are overcrowded and overgrazed. As a result, thousands of families have streamed northwards, from the degraded communal lands in the south, towards the less populous Zambezi valley. The reactions of Campfire communities in the valley have been instructive. Several years ago the people of Masoka, in Kanyurira ward, were happy to take in settlers from elsewhere as an increase in the population helped support their demands for better public services. Then came the Campfire project, and with it the sudden enrichment of the small community. Immigrants were attracted to the village by its prosperity, but the locals soon realized that they would have to share the spoils derived from their wildlife. They now scrutinize the potential newcomers much more rigorously than before, although they have been unable to prevent a rapid increase in the population, which has risen from some 60 families to well over 100.

Immigration poses a threat that goes far beyond the parochial. 'Many of the immigrants have a frontier mentality,' suggested David Cumming. 'They are often not in tune with nature, and they see the soils and the forests as ripe for exploitation. There's a real danger that in relatively unspoilt areas like the Zambezi valley we're passing up the options to use wildlife resources in a sustainable way.'

If immigration is one of the external pressures which threatens the success of Campfire in some areas, another – less obvious in its impact, perhaps – stems from the strictures of international environmental policy. Making sustainable use of nature, particularly through hunting and culling, has not enamoured the Zimbabwean government to conservationists in the outside world, and while their opprobrium may not appear to directly impinge on the workings of Campfire, it can certainly undermine it by depriving communities of a potential source of revenue. The Convention on International Trade in Endangered Species (CITES) has banned international trade in a whole range of animal products such as ivory and rhino horn. The thinking behind the policy is simple: endangered species have a greater chance of survival if trade in their derivatives is proscribed. Yet many Zimbabwean conservationists believe that blanket bans are seriously counterproductive. 'The problem with CITES', suggested Roy Martin, the head of research in the Department of National Parks, 'is that it's twenty years out of date and it only deals in negatives. It doesn't embody any concept of sustainable use and it sets ridiculous population thresholds below which it is presumed that species will become extinct.' Martin believes that a limited trade in crocodile products has worked well, and indeed helped to conserve the species in the wild.

'There's no record of a single species having become extinct as a result of international trade', argued Robert Monro, 'and the present bans have done nothing to prevent the decline in many species.' He cited the case of the rhinoceros. Since a ban on the trade of rhino horn was introduced in 1976, the animals have become progressively rarer, even in

Zimbabwe, which has operated an expensive and merciless shoot-to-kill policy against poachers. At present three teams of experts are permanently employed dehorning rhinoceroses in an attempt to deter poaching, and 3 tons of horn is sitting in a warehouse in Harare. 'If there was a limited trade in rhino horn', claimed Monro, 'then the money could be ploughed back into conservation.'[11]

The Zimbabweans have persistently (and less controversially, perhaps) argued for a limited trade in ivory. The overall population of African elephants may have declined from over a million to around 600,000, but in some countries – for example, Zimbabwe, Botswana and South Africa – the population has steadily risen. There were probably fewer than 5,000 elephants in Zimbabwe at the turn of the century; there are now well over 70,000. Many of the country's forests have been devastated by elephants and the Department of National Parks wishes to reduce the population to around 40,000. This would mean an annual cull of 5,000 animals for the next fourteen years. However, the resources to carry out such a programme simply do not exist, though they would if the country were allowed to sell its ivory abroad. Revenues from such a trade would not only help the government to fund its conservation activities – it already spends US$100 per square kilometre a year in its protected areas – they would also provide benefits for the rural poor, in other words for the very people who suffer most from the depredations of wild animals. Opponents of Zimbabwe's pro-trade stance point out that the revenues earned from the sale of ivory would probably end up with the Treasury. In recent years the Treasury has reduced its allocation of funds to the Department of National Parks; consequently, the claim that ivory-generated revenues would be ploughed back into conservation is specious.[12] Critics are also sceptical about Zimbabwe's claim that it has an elephant population of 77,000.

The workings of CITES are largely determined by the dominant conservation agencies of the developed world. Many Zimbabweans feel that these agencies and their supporters are more concerned with sentiment than sense; they also question their right to impose trading bans which profoundly affect the lives of other people. When Robert Monro, Elliot Chauke and Clive Stockil attended the CITES meeting in Switzerland in 1989, they were shunned by the press and reviled by many of the participants, but Monro detected a distinct change in attitude when he attended the 1992 CITES meeting in Kyoto, Japan. Zimbabwe's arguments were at least being heard and many organizations now tacitly admit that a policy of sustainable use may make far better conservation sense than the retention of blanket bans. Certainly, the Campfire experience supports such a view.

Whatever the arguments for or against the resumption of a limited trade in ivory, there can be no denying that Campfire has been remarkably influential in changing village people's perceptions about wildlife. At a time when the country was experiencing its worst drought in living memory, the villagers in Mahenye were providing fodder and protection for their hippos and digging deep holes to supply elephants with drinking water. We came across two of these on our last afternoon as Elliot and one of Clive Stockil's trackers led us down the bed of the Save River. The holes were some 15 feet deep and 30 feet across; they had cost Z$7,000 and taken many hours of hard labour to dig. The bare sand surrounding the water was pocked with dinner-plate-sized footprints and trails of fresh dung led towards the thick forests on the far bank. The elephants, like humans, explained Elliot, were exceedingly fussy about drinking water and every two or three days the villagers would come out here to clear the scum off the water.

Before we left Harare David Cumming of WWF had told us: 'I have a sense that the people in the south are really looking for new ways to better their lives. They've been right to the bottom of the barrel ...' Yes, agreed Elliot as we continued down the riverbed, the people here were used to misfortune and hardship. Three years ago a marauding band of Renamo guerillas had crossed over the border from Mozambique, murdered 50-odd people in Tongagara, stolen their food supplies, and vandalized the villages' meagre infrastructure, destroying the health clinic and other buildings. Then came the drought, crop failure and the inevitable food shortages.

A couple of miles south of Stockil's camp we came to a small island in the river. The tracker pointed out the spores of lion and elephant; monkeys chattered in the trees above us. Stockil had purchased from the villagers the right to build a sixteen-bed camp here. He was intending to move away from what he called 'consumptive tourism' – safari hunting – to 'eco-tourism'. With an experienced ornithologist as guide, visitors will be able to see 150 different species of bird in a day. By now the sinking sun was casting a burnished glaze across the ocean of forest-fringed sand which stretched south to Nwachumeni Island. 'Stockil was nearly killed near here the other week,' announced Elliot in a very matter-of-fact tone. Apparently a buffalo had pinned him to the ground and would have finished him off had another buffalo not charged it out of the way. Six weeks previously a wounded buffalo cow had killed a professional hunter and his client in another Campfire area. By the time we reached Nwachumeni even the tracker was betraying his nerves; a colourful flock of bee-eaters swooped for insects from a high bank of sand, but we encountered no buffalo.

Back at camp, the sun long since set and the nightjars calling once again in the woods, Elliot talked about the war of liberation. For five years he had lived in the bush; for five years he never once saw his wife and children, nor heard news of them. He had witnessed many terrible things and he attributed his survival to his religious beliefs: he quoted frequently from the Bible – the present drought, he suggested, had been prophesied in Micah – but he also had a liking for James Hadley Chase and Perry Mason. Elliot had a small and beautifully kept farm about an hour's drive south-west of Stockil's camp. He and a friend had spent two months digging a 50-foot well, the water from which irrigated a fine garden. Elliot's job as chairman of the district council's wildlife committee and his work as vice-chairman of the Campfire Association meant that he spent a good deal of time away from his wife, his six daughters and small son. His civic duties were voluntary, and his income was derived entirely from his smallholding. 'We fought the war', said Elliot, 'because we wanted freedom. We were fighting for the freedom to determine how we lived.'

Campfire is about freedom; about the rights of communities to work out their own destiny and manage the resources around them. The people of Mahenye have been to the 'bottom of the barrel'; that they are now in a position to view the future with optimism is almost entirely due to Campfire and the inspirational leadership of men like Elliot Chauke.

4

UGANDA

Pallisa Community Development Trust

'Show us and we will give you our support!'

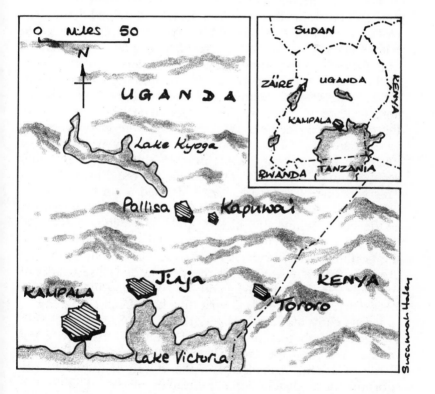

'When the Karamojong came', said Stanley Okurut, the chairman of the Pallisa Community Development Trust (PACODET), 'they took virtually everything we had – cattle, goats, pigs, hens, groundnuts...They killed many people, they raped some women and kidnapped others, and as they left they burned our homes and granaries. When the Karamojong came on a raid, they absolutely devastated the area.'

Stanley was a slender young man with an intelligent, open face; his manner was studious and undemonstrative, and he weighed his thoughts carefully before speaking. Most of the people living in Pallisa district, he explained, belonged to the Teso tribe, and most made their living as peasant farmers. There had never been any love lost between the Iteso people and the nomadic Karamojong, who occupied the drier land to the north, but in the distant past skirmishes had been few and unspectacular. However, following the fall of Idi Amin in 1979 and the subsequent retreat of his army, the Karamojong had broken into some abandoned barracks and helped themselves to large quantities of modern weaponry. 'When they came with spears in earlier times', recalled Stanley, 'the villagers organized themselves and resisted the raiders – but there was nothing they could do once the Karamojong armed themselves with AK-47s.' During 1987 and 1988 gangs of Karamojong repeatedly plundered the region. The Iteso appealed to the government for help, but their pleas were ignored; in any case, there was clear evidence that the army was colluding with the Karamojong and helping to shift the stolen cattle south, to markets in Jinja and elsewhere around Lake Victoria. This was one of several factors which led to an armed uprising by some Iteso in 1987. Compared to the lengthy traumas of the past – during the rules of Amin and Milton Obote over a million Ugandan citizens were murdered – the rebellion in the north-east was relatively short lived: peace returned to the area in 1989. It was time for the people of Pallisa district to rebuild their shattered lives and, by organizing themselves in PACODET, that is precisely what they have been doing.

It was early morning in late January and Stanley had gathered together thirteen members of PACODET's executive committee to discuss the great issues of the day. We sat in the shade of a large mango tree in the village of Kapuwai. The morning dew glistened on the leaves of the cassava crop beside us and a flock of yellow weaver birds celebrated the arrival of a new day by screeching noisily from their pendulous nests in a nearby palm. Ducks and hens pecked around the base of a mud and wattle granary; orange-throated agama lizards scuttered across the scuffed grass of the compound;

CALCUTTA

People from Mudialy Fishermen's Cooperative Society hauling in the morning catch.

Mudialy town, where profits from fishing have been used to give interest-free loans to members. A new concrete house – built with a loan – looms above the cramped dwellings of earlier and poorer times. Another new house is being constructed on the left.

Outdoor fish market in the East Calcutta marshes.

Auctioning off the catch at the Mudialy ponds. On this day it took less than two hours to auction a ton of fish.

Mukut Roy Choudhury, the ecologist from the West Bengal Fisheries Department who has helped the Mudialy fishermen refine their pond system.

NEPAL

Ghandruk, capital of Gurung county. The daycare centre, set up with ACAP's help, is on the far right.

ACAP has encouraged mothers' groups to convert old-fashioned smoke-belching chulos *into more efficient, smokeless ovens. This one is in Lawang village.*

Chij Kumari weaving a small carpet on her loom in Ghandruk. She was one of the 17 women who took part in an ACAP course training them how to operate a business.

Ghandruk's Conservation and Development Committee meets on the first day of every Nepali month. Chairman Miu Bahadur Gurung (third from right) makes his views known to the man behind.

A mule train heading through Chandrakot on its way to Ghandruk. Many of Chandrakot's houses have been turned into tourist lodges.

ZIMBABWE

In Mahenye ward profits from wildlife have been used to build classrooms in the local school. Here, children show off their pottery at the school's environmental club.

Elliot Chauke stands beside a well dug by villagers in an empty river bed. At night the villagers remove the logs to let the elephants drink.

Many villages in the drought-stricken south of Zimbabwe have had to rely on government food relief.

UGANDA

This boy was one of half a dozen who spent the whole day waist-deep in water. By the end of the day he had caught only a handful of small fish.

Teenagers ploughing in Kapuwai.

The PACODET committee. Front row, from left: VV, Filder, Anne, Lawrence, James, Stanley, Amos.

A family group at its shamba *near Kapuwai.*

LOS ANGELES

Demonstrators marching past the Texaco plant in the Wilmington suburb of Los Angeles, which was rocked by explosions. The marchers are drawing attention to safety issues, pollution and workers' rights.

Carlos Molina pointing to the chimney stacks of some of the industrial plants in Wilmington.

two women laboriously raised water from a well with a tin can and carried it back to their thatched huts.

Over the course of the next week the same group would gather every day beneath the mango tree; strange faces soon became familiar, and before long we began to understand the views and foibles of each individual. Stanley was very much the leader of PACODET, but without the support of the others he would have achieved little. A prominent member of the association was Lawrence, the headmaster of the local primary school; an upright, talkative man with an explosive laugh, on two occasions during the 'bad times' he had narrowly escaped an enforced visit to the army barracks – and certain death. James and Amos were teachers too. Handsome, intelligent and soft spoken, James had assumed the role of scribe and continuously took notes. With his broad smile and jug ears, Amos brought a touch of levity to the meetings and was especially astute when discussing his own subject, which was geography.

Several of those who came to the meetings lived in villages beyond Kapuwai. Vincent Okurut – or VV, as he was known – was from Kobuin, a settlement 6 miles to the north, beyond the great outcrops of granite which straddled the landscape like whales. He was employed by the government as an agricultural extension officer and could discourse freely on any matter related to farming. It took him an hour by bike to reach the meetings, and another hour to return home, often late at night. Then there was Simeon Osire, a retired public health inspector from Kagoli. The world he saw today was profoundly different from that of his childhood, when food was plentiful, forests were large and luxuriant, and lions, leopards and giraffes roamed the countryside. Most of the wild beasts have gone, and so too have Simeon's livestock, which were stolen by raiders – Iteso, in this instance – during the armed uprising of the late 1980s. There were many fewer women at these daily meetings then men, and only two attended regularly. Stanley's wife Ann was a young, quiet woman of singular beauty, while Filder, who was married to Lawrence, was more forceful and forthcoming. She had seven children, the youngest of whom, a two-month old boy called Job, came along to the meetings.

We had come to Pallisa district – a six-hour drive from the capital Kampala – in the company of two health experts from Makerere University. John Arube-Wani, the son of a former Anglican archbishop, had had almost twenty years' experience in hospital social work; since 1985 he had spent much of his time studying health issues in the countryside, where 90 per cent of the Ugandan population resides. This was his fourth visit to Pallisa. Dr Tom Barton, an American physician-turned-anthropologist, arrived in Uganda in 1989; an expert on sexually transmitted diseases – a tenth of Uganda's population is HIV positive and destined to die of AIDS – he was a technical adviser to the Child Health and Development Centre at the University. Tom was a keen supporter of PACODET's approach to primary health care and was also helping Stanley and his colleagues think about the ways in which they could tackle the district's environmental problems.

'When we first decided to do something', recalled Stanley, who returned to Pallisa district in 1989 having completed his studies in zoology at Makerere University, 'we saw that the most pressing problem was ill-health. Malaria was rampant and women sometimes died in childbirth. Many of the children died too. Not a week passed without deaths in every village. Then one day an old woman died just down there.' He pointed towards the cart track which led to the primary school. 'We decided to count the number of deaths and look at the diseases which were killing people. We knew the government wouldn't do anything – we had to act ourselves.' So PACODET set to work and over the past three years it has made great strides in delivering primary health care to the population. 'Now', said Stanley, 'it's time we look at other issues.'

PACODET's history offers a good insight into the way in which a dedicated group of people can shape their own destiny. In 1986 half a dozen students born in the Kapuwai parish of Pallisa district decided to work out ways of improving their community's standard of living. They founded the Kapuwai Students' Progressive Association (KSPA), but before they could start work the armed rebellion began in 1987. For the next couple of years Stanley and his friends stayed away from the area – young men of their age were likely to be killed by the army – but they returned soon after the conclusion of the troubles. KSPA reconvened in 1989 as the Pallisa Community Development Trust (PACODET). 'Student associations exist all over Uganda', explained Stanley, 'but they tend to spend much of their time organizing discos; we decided to do things differently – we wanted to serve the community.' The students talked to the elders about the health problems in the villages and the elders said: 'You tell us that something can be done. Show us that what you say is true, and we will give you our support!"[1]

The students called a meeting. Over a hundred people turned up and together they discussed ways in which they might improve health. Funds were obviously required, and each individual who wanted to join PACODET contributed 100 shillings (approximately $0.50 in those days).[2] Four hundred people attended the next meeting; before long PACODET had raised 40,000 shillings and its work could begin. 'Malaria was a major problem', said Stanley, 'so one of the first things we did was buy chloroquine to treat the sufferers. People still get malaria, but now we can cure it quickly.' Another major killer – especially of young children – was measles and PACODET saw that there was an urgent need for a vaccination programme. The association approached Pallisa's district medical officer and requested that the government help train some of the villagers in basic health care. Since 1989, 40 community health workers and 15 traditional birth attendants have been trained in and around Kapuwai. The vaccination programme began beneath a mango tree near the primary school and PACODET's health workers were soon vaccinating 700 children a month – against measles, TB, tetanus, polio, diphtheria and whooping cough – and immunizing 300 mothers a month against tetanus. Since 1989 a temporary health centre has also been treating around 4,000 people a month for various ailments.

The programme has been a resounding success. Child mortality has fallen dramatically and the health of the adult population has also improved. Prior to the PACODET initiative, several members of the community had received some health care training. However, lack of government support meant that they remained idle until PACODET began its health programme. Others – like VV – had gained their experience in health care while working. VV was now in charge of the Kobuin Health Clinic.

During the past year John Arube-Wani had carried out a qualitative survey of five 'successful' primary health projects around the country. 'This is the only one which was initiated by the community itself', he said, 'and you really notice the difference. Here the villagers can discuss the concepts thoroughly; they feel in control and they know that they will continue to be successful. The other groups I've seen are much more fearful about their futures as they're so dependent on outside help.' Tom Barton thought it significant that none of PACODET's key members had had any medical training. Stanley was a zoologist; Amos a geographer; Filder a teacher. 'They read the World Health Organization booklets on primary health care and actually believed them!' he suggested. 'Most doctors and nurses are much more cynical than that.' The Ministry of Health has recognized the Pallisa Community Development Health Care Project as one of the best in Uganda. The Ministry, incidentally, has supplied a fridge, vaccine carriers and bicycles, and given training when requested to do so. However, most of the input, whether financial or technical, comes from PACODET, whose members now pay an annual subscription of 500 shillings per household and an enrolment fee of 3,500 shillings.

In January 1993, PACODET was midway through its most ambitious project to date: the construction of a health centre which would eventually serve around 100,000 people. The association bought 10 acres of land near the primary school in 1989, and work began on the dispensary block – which was almost complete at the time of our visit in autumn 1992. The European Development Fund (EDF) Micro-Projects Programme has contributed $49,140 towards the health centre; the local contribution has amounted to $17,055. While the EDF provided manufactured goods such as window frames, corrugated iron roofing and cement, the local people made and fired all the bricks, and felled and hewed the timber. Once the dispensary is complete, PACODET intends to build a community hall for lectures and meetings, a maternity ward, a hostel, staff quarters and a dormitory for disabled people. In the meantime PACODET'S staff – all of whom are volunteers – will continue to vaccinate children, deliver babies and offer health advice on such matters as breast-feeding and household hygiene.[3]

The human population was conspicuously healthier now to local eyes than it had been in 1989, but the same, apparently, could not be said for the environment. Stanley, VV, Lawrence, James and most of PACODET's executive committee were eager to tackle the area's environmental problems, yet they seemed unclear about their precise nature. Tom suggested that they conduct a simple exercise which would help to clarify their thoughts, and they spent the whole of one afternoon drawing up two lists. One described all the features of the environment – and the aspects of their lives – which they appreciated and enjoyed; the other concentrated on their dislikes and grievances.

'I like the leafy environment,' said Lawrence, who was first to speak. 'We have plenty of rain and good soil – that helps us to grow our food.' Stanley followed with an observation in keeping with his zoological training: 'This area is rich in birds and insects', he said, 'and some of them contribute to our farming.' Bees and various other insects, for example, were important crop pollinators. He also praised the rocky hills, as they provided a home for wild animals and stone with which to build. The swamps were appreciated for the fresh water they supplied; certain herbs for their medicinal properties; the rains for their predictability; the termites for providing a good source of protein and the fine-particled mounds which made an excellent brick-clay. Filder expressed great attachment to the thatched dwellings in which people lived – they were simple to construct and cool in the hot months – and Ann said she liked the trees: some were beautiful in their own right; others provided building materials and fruit. Within a few yards of the group was a bread-fruit tree, two mangos, an oil palm, a couple of pawpaw trees and a flowering frangipani. According to Stanley, everyone could be counted on to come together and share resources during times of difficulty. People tended to trust one another and their leaders, and local customs were widely respected.

Nature had been kind to the people of Pallisa district, and they knew it. When it came to discussing dislikes, nature was only occasionally accused of making their lives difficult: monkeys raided crops, especially around their granitic hideaways; termites occasionally caused crop damage too, but at least they were edible; and mosaic disease had had a serious impact on cassava yields in recent years. And, of course, there was the mosquito, the vector of the malaria parasite and the scourge of the tropics.

However, it was the human condition – and the improprieties and weaknesses of the people themselves – which dominated the group's list of grievances. 'Education standards are very poor,' said Lawrence, the headmaster. 'Many parents won't send their children to school as they either don't appreciate education or they can't afford to. And there's no money to look after the classrooms or buy equipment.' James, teacher in a neighbouring school, said it was difficult to convince people that education was useful, and yet many of their problems stemmed from ignorance. Alcoholism was seen as a problem, and so was the contamination of water sources and poor sanitation, even though over half the homes in the area now had their own pit latrines. Cooking stoves were inefficient and filled the huts with smoke; apart from posing a health hazard to those breathing the smoky air, the stoves were often responsible for children getting accidentally burnt. Women spent much of their time collecting and transporting water. Domestic refuse left to rot in the open attracted rats and many people lacked proper storage facilities and regularly lost part of their crops to pests and decay. Some crops appeared to be succumbing to diseases and pests which had become resistant to sprays, and many members of PACODET were worried about the ways in which pesticides were sold in the market. The shopkeepers often stored dangerous chemicals beside foodstuffs and they failed to provide proper instructions as to their use. Local children had recently painted white ants with a crop-dressing used for groundnuts; hundreds of birds – bulbuls, flycatchers, guinea fowl, weavers – had died after eating the poisoned ants. Indeed, nature seemed to be suffering on all fronts: for some time women had been cutting green wood to burn at home, thus damaging the local forests; fishing was no longer profitable and even the commonest wild creatures such as monkeys and snakes were becoming rarer. There were other familiar grouses such as you would hear in rural areas throughout the developing world: roads were poor or non-existent; there was no electricity or power; security was a problem, especially for women at night.

It took some time before anyone mentioned what many agreed to be the most complex and pressing problem: the rapidly rising population which was inevitably having an impact on the land. 'Talk to any of the elders', said VV, 'and they'll tell you that the productivity of the fields is falling. In the old days, people used to rest their land to allow it to recover. Now, they simply can't afford to leave it lying idle and the soils are becoming exhausted.' The loss of cattle – providers of draught power, meat, milk and manure – has made matters worse. 'Family planning is long overdue,' suggested Simeon. 'We're reproducing much too fast. If there's a calamity in the future, we'll all die off. I've got fifteen children and I'm beginning to realize the scale of the problem. I own 30 acres of land, which is a lot round here, but that won't be enough to support my children when they grow up – no, 30 acres doesn't go far.'

'Population growth really is a big problem,' agreed Stanley. 'It's not just the men who want lots of children, but the women too. It's very hard on the women in this society: if a child dies, she'll always get the blame; and if a couple is having trouble producing children, the woman also gets the blame.'[4]

In fact, the women in this part of Uganda are exceedingly downtrodden. If you were to pass through Pallisa district on a fleeting visit, or have the good fortune to spend an evening at one of their vibrant dancing sessions, you might well be deceived by outward appearances. The women present a generally cheery front, although one or two customs might cause you to raise your eyebrows: when approaching a man – say, with a cup of tea, or when introducing themselves – women of all ages sink to their knees; when men and women are together, the latter always behave with exaggerated deference.

During our meetings under the mango tree in Kapuwai, the men talked with surprising candour about the failings of their own sex. 'Men want to drink every day', said Lawrence, 'even if they don't have the money. Sometimes you see the father spending all the family money on himself – and that can lead to malnutrition of the children.' The dowry system, whereby men pay a bride-price for their future spouses, means that men often regard their wives – and most have two – as little more than a form of economic investment. 'You are going to grow rich out of that wife!' is a common saying in this area. 'Even if the marriage turns sour', said Amos, 'the woman's parents won't take her back as they'll already have spent the dowry money.' Women are relatively powerless, even though, as VV pointed out, they are the most productive members of the community: they do most of the farmwork, look after the home, fetch water and fuel, cook meals and take care of children and the sick. Wife-beating is a widespread problem in Pallisa district.

During the previous year a Womens' Association had been formed – with Filder and Ann at the forefront – and a small group of women met to discuss pertinent issues every Saturday. Half the executive committee and over two-thirds of PACODET's 400 dues-paying members are women, and female emancipation is one of the organization's most significant tasks. 'Men are by nature extravagant, and they never consult women when they make decisions about spending cash,' said Stanley. 'Yet women are more prudent, and they think far more about the future. It's very important – not just for them, but for all of us – that they assert themselves and participate fully in the development of this area.'

'Lack of capital, lack of income.' The phrase was like a refrain, repeated at regular intervals throughout the week. Without income, there was no money to pay for school fees, no money to buy seeds and fertilizer, no money to buy food during times of want, no money to buy clothes or anything else. We heard of many disappointments in the recent past. During the last season, many local farmers had grown cotton, a cash crop which the government had promised to buy at a fixed price. But the cotton bolls lay rotting in the field as corrupt cooperatives had failed to take the cotton off the farmers' hands. In 1989 many of the men had grown maize, as the government had said it could export it to Cuba. But the deal fell through and no income could be derived from corn.

PACODET had recently set up a revolving fund credit scheme; this was proving a modest success. At the beginning of the planting season PACODET gives small interest-free loans to farmers; with these they can purchase seeds, or perhaps spray pumps or hoes. Once the harvest is in, the farmers pay back their loans either in cash or kind. So far nobody had defaulted, though Stanley admitted that up to now the scale of the credit scheme had been quite small.[5]

On our second evening in Kapuwai the villagers decided to go on a series of walks in the surrounding countryside. This would enable them to make a thorough, if empirical, assessment of the key environmental issues. We began by walking through a patch of woodland. In the old days, commented one farmer, there used to be some fine woods here, with big trees and plenty of game. Today the only large animals to be seen were monkeys and the occasional antelope, and this particular wood had been heavily degraded by cutting – for fuelwood and building materials. Each year farmers nibbled away at its periphery. 'It'll all be gone if we carry on doing this,' explained Stanley, waving his hands at the recently ploughed furrows which ran up to a plot of burnt scrub. 'But if you challenge people who do this, they'll say: "How else can we make a living?" If someone encroached into the woods like this 30 years ago, people would have said: "What are you doing – this is madness!" But not now.'

Over the past few years many marshy areas have been converted to rice paddy. Rice farming is certainly a good way of making money: rice grows well, keeps well and sells well. However, the conversion of marshes into paddy had caused much controversy. Elderly women have to walk much further now to find suitable wetlands in which to fish, and the catfish habitat has been virtually eliminated in Pallisa district. 'Apart from the fact that the fish provided protein for many people,' said VV, 'they also ate the larvae of mosquitoes – now we get many more mosquitoes than we used to.'[6]

To some members of the executive committee these walks were revelatory. One morning we clambered up to the rocky, bolder-strewn summit of the highest hill. Monkeys chattered angrily in a thicket of acacia; vultures wheeled overhead. From here our companions could see quite clearly that their woods had shrunk. Dotted around the cultivated landscape were a few statuesque *mivuli* trees. In the old days, said one of the more senior members of the committee, these trees were far more common. 'Do you know', said Lawrence later, 'I've lived here all my life, but I've never been up this hill before today. Now I realize I've been depriving myself and my children of knowledge about the environment.'

The following morning the group of thirteen attempted to introduce some order into the chaos of likes and dislikes which they had drawn up on the first day. This was a lengthy process, occupying the best part of a day. By the time the sun had set the group had ranked, in order of importance, the main areas of concern. Top of the list came 'Lack of knowledge', followed by 'Population issue', 'Income generation', 'Water and sanitation', 'Energy, transport and housing', and finally 'Food security'. The clusters, or categories, were rather broad, and the problems not exhaustively defined, but the exercise was instructive nevertheless. 'It shocks me', said Stanley, reflecting on their findings, 'that what we agreed we most lack – and most urgently need – is knowledge.'

That evening the PACODET committee sent word round the area that on the following afternoon there would be a large meeting, open to everyone, to discuss Pallisa's environmental problems. Around a hundred people turned up at the primary school and split into six groups. Each group had as chairperson and rapporteur two members of the PACODET committee and spent several hours discussing a specific topic: while one looked at the issue of pesticide use and abuse, another discussed the population issue, another the encroachment of swamps and forests. Each group sat in a circle on the ground. Filder chaired one group with Job resting naked on her lap. Lawrence, her husband, chaired another. At first he wanted to sit on a bench which he had fetched from the school and the others had to convince him that he should forego his schoolmasterly attitude and join everyone else on the ground. Afterwards, he said he was glad he had done that; he felt his attitude changed dramatically when he sat at the same level as the others. After an hour or so a violent squall of rain drove everyone inside the dilapidated, mud-walled classrooms. At the end of the group work, reports were given by the rapporteurs and then the women sang religious songs and some folk melodies.

At the start of the afternoon a young community health worker had led 30-odd children to the far side of the playground and for a long time their singing and chanting echoed around the countryside. These children were lucky: they were receiving some form of education, which was more than could be said for the seven boys who accompanied one of us on the walk back to the house where we were staying. We had first seen these children early in the morning, standing waist-deep in a shallow lake. Each had a small fishing rod in one hand and two coconut calabashes floating by his waist, fish-bait in one, caught fish in the other. Now, some ten hours later, having gone the entire day without food, they were making the 5 mile walk back to their homes. None had caught more than a couple of ounces of anchovy-sized fish; one little boy – he couldn't have been more than five years old – had caught just four tiny fish. As they passed the school they stopped for a while and wistfully watched the group of children singing beneath the mango tree. Walking back beside us they seemed to recover their good humour and they laughed and chattered their way home.

On our final day in Kapuwai we observed Stanley, Filder, Amos and the others from a distance. They sat all morning in a tight huddle discussing the previous day's meetings and the week's work. At lunchtime we ate some millet porridge, chicken stew and rice; we convened for the last time in the afternoon. It was now time to draw up a Plan of Action. It would be untrue to say that the discussion went smoothly, that the group had reached a consensus about the action it could – or should – take. There was still a good deal of confusion, not just about the nature of Pallisa's environmental problems, but about their severity and significance. Stanley began by saying that the conservation of the swamps was a high priority, as was the protection of the woodlands from further encroachment. At present, he didn't think pesticide use was widespread enough to constitute a serious problem – 'but we must get proper knowledge about how much they are used', he concluded. Indeed, everyone agreed that ignorance contributed to poor land use practices, the mistreatment of women, the rapid growth of population and many other perceived ills. A variety of specific income-generating projects were mooted. The idea of trying to gain an income while improving the environmental conditions was suggested; many found this appealing. Stanley and others expressed interest in fish farming as a possible alternative to rice growing in the swamps. Others mentioned setting up a grinding mill – they already had a suitable building – and the women in the committee discussed the local manufacture of mosquito nets and latrine slabs. There were some ventures, such as tree planting, which the villagers could undertake themselves at little or no cost. In fact, they had already set up a small nursery. There was talk too of setting up a vegetable garden at the primary school.

Yet again, ignorance was identified as a major problem. The villagers had no idea how to make mosquito nets, or where to get the materials; they had little experience in forestry matters, and none in fish farming. PACODET's Plan of Action was mostly devoted to gathering information about training opportunities, funding sources and a variety of technologies, as well as about themselves and their surroundings. Over the next few months they intended to map their resources and carry out a survey of agricultural practices; they hoped to find out who was taking trees and who was encroaching the swamps. They also intended to look at a range of concerns from family planning to household hygiene, from dietary habits to the use of pesticides. It was an ambitious programme and the faces of those gathered below the mango tree expressed both excitement and apprehension. Time, they knew, would test their commitment, their ability and their luck.

Four months later the PACODET committee gathered once again in the shade of the mango tree at Kapuwai. The old hands who had attended the planning workshop in February

– Stanley, Amos, Filder, James, VV – were all there, but they had now been joined by many new faces, among them several women. It was early morning and pleasantly cool still. Crowing cocks strutted among the thatched granaries, and from a little further away came the sound of boys hitting sticks together next to a termite mound – by mimicking the sound of rain, they hoped to entice the edible occupants into the open. Nearby, in a small field, young men were training a team of oxen, goading them with yelps and shouts to plough in a straight line.

PACODET had become more structured in the past few months and various sub-committees had been formed to take charge of specific interests and activities; each was headed by a man and a woman. During the course of the day the sub-committees reported on the progress they had made since February. James and Filder began by discussing family planning, the promotion of which had been virtually non-existent in this part of Uganda. Realizing that it was impossible to get help from local officials without paying for their services, Filder and Ann had gone to Kampala in search of training and resources. It had been Filder's third trip to the capital; Ann's first. For a few days, explained Filder, they had slogged around Kampala, mostly on foot, visiting national and international agencies. They gathered huge amounts of information and ideas – folders were passed around as they spoke – and talked to many people. Gradually, they had become more confident, not just in their dealings with officialdom but in discussing matters among themselves and with their families. Now they were working out plans to introduce a family planning programme, plans which had been boosted by the recent news that Florence – a slender young woman who had been one of PACODET's first health workers – was to receive midwifery training. This would undoubtedly help any family planning initiative, as would the expertise which Stanley was about to gain as a newly appointed short-term consultant to CARE-Uganda. Stanley's main task for this aid agency was to assess family planning needs in three eastern districts, including Pallisa.

Amos was the next to speak and he presented to the gathering a small sample of the many maps which he and friends had made to illustrate the results of the health and environment surveys. The maps showing land use patterns – swamps, forests, cultivated areas – were complemented by photographs taken by Tom Barton from the top of the rocky hill which the group had first climbed during the February workshop. Since then many of them had returned to the hill (Lawrence, who still laughed at the memory of descending on all fives – hands, feet and buttocks – was a great enthusiast) and they felt that this high vantage point gave them a fine overview of Kapuwai and its surroundings; from there they could see how sparse the natural vegetation had become. 'We've measured the rice paddies', said Stanley at one point, 'and we found that they create stagnant pools where very few fish survive but mosquito larvae thrive. We're still analysing the data, but we know for sure that the fields have encroached on stands of papyrus in an important way.'

Ann then discussed the preliminary results of the health and environment surveys, which had involved field visits, group meetings and the distribution of a questionnaire to hundreds of local people. It seemed, she said, that the immunization programme was working well, that the incidence of diarrhoea and other preventable diseases was low and that children were reasonably well nourished. However, the subcommittee was particularly concerned about the dangerous use of pesticides and PACODET planned to launch an education campaign to address this matter. VV said that a new regulation would prohibit the use of Dimicron pesticide, which was used for the control of insects and birds. Offenders would be punished by whipping with a cane, and this could be supplemented by a fine. A more positive (and non-violent) step to reduce pesticide use had involved the purchase of a lorry load of cassava which was resistant to mosaic disease; this had been planted in a community plot and rootstock would later be distributed in the district. VV reported that some people had begun to use animal manure to fertilize their fields and to select seeds for their pest-resistant qualities. He had also helped Lawrence to set up a tree nursery in the school garden, and here the children would learn how to plant and tend trees.

Not that everything was going well. Someone mentioned that monkeys had begun to steal chickens; as there was so little forest left for them to hunt in, no one was particularly surprised by this. One person complained about the increase in rats around the villagers' homes, and another said there seemed to be fewer herons than in the past. As herons often prey on rodents, their decline might have had something to do with the increase in rats. Several committee members wondered whether the widespread use of persistent pesticides had led to the decline in herons; perhaps the drainage of wetlands had been a factor too. 'We're all learning basic ecology the hard way', said Amos, 'but we are surely learning it!'

During the spring, PACODET had decided that it wanted to set up a library/community centre. 'We need books for the children, for the health workers and everyone who wishes to know more about a particular activity or technology,' Lawrence had said. 'The library will become an inspiring place; we'll use the space in front of it for community meetings; we'll have drama and music, so even the illiterate will gain from it.' Lawrence and several other committee members drew up a proposal for funding, which was submitted to the Netherlands Embassy in Kampala. Stanley told the meeting that the proposal was still being considered, but that there was a good chance that it would be approved.

Outsiders might find it odd that a poor rural community should consider the creation of a community library a top priority. They would probably be even more bemused to find such a community turning down an offer of money, yet that was precisely what PACODET had done. A couple of years previously, PACODET sent in an application for the financing of a diesel grinding mill to USAID, the United States Agency for International Development. During their visit to Kampala Filder and Ann had discussed the proposal with USAID officials, who offered PACODET a considerable sum of money. At first the women were delighted, but after they had discussed the matter with Tom Barton and the PACODET committee, everyone began to have second thoughts. For one thing, they realized that there were now several mills in the area which were operating at a loss. There were also the environmental arguments against a diesel mill, which would emit noxious gases, fill the air with dust and introduce an unappealingly noisy element into an otherwise peaceful and largely machineless setting.

The PACODET committee eventually decided to ask USAID to shift the grant from the mill project to another one which would establish a sewing and carpentry workshop. 'So far we have no commitment from USAID', Filder told the committee, 'but they've agreed to hold on to the money until we present more detailed plans for the workshop. Perhaps they'll help us to get the tools we need to start working.' The women were eager to produce quilts, mosquito nets and clothes, and they wanted to use scraps of fabric, unwoven cotton, and anything else they could find. The workshop would also become a useful meeting place.[7]

It was now late afternoon and an orange sun was sinking fast in the west. Two teenagers got to their feet and announced that a group of some 30 young men and women had recently organized a band to hire out at weddings, village celebrations and other events. They were also offering their services as farm labourers. After dark their musician friends arrived: six of them sat in front of a giant xylophone, an *ababairen*, while many others gathered round with a variety of string instruments and thumb-pianos. It was a warm, humid night: fireflies blinked in the darkness and the smell of woodsmoke drifted over the gathering crowd. As soon as the music started, everyone – including a dozen children in ragged clothes – began to dance. They sang religious songs; they sang songs about AIDS, about past tragedies and future hopes. The people of Kapuwai had come a long way since their region was plundered by the Karamojong in the late '80s: they had every reason to celebrate.

5

MAURITANIA

Second Livestock Project

'Oy, you're stealing our hay!'

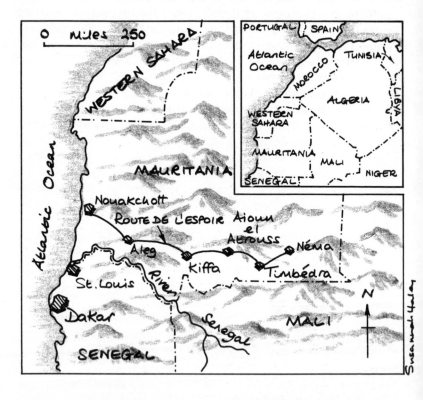

It took us a day and a half to cover the 600 miles between the capital Nouakchott and Timbedra. The two were joined by the Route de l'Espoir, the Road of Hope, a thin strip of tarmac which sliced through the south of Mauritania, linking the remote interior to the Atlantic coast. It was a sticky, wearisome journey through a harsh landscape of sand

and rock, rolling dunes and craggy mountains. Occasionally we passed a *campement* with cud-chewing camels and small flocks of goats and sheep; now and again we came across women and children lifting water from a well with leather buckets. We ate a lunch of fresh dates, goat meat and camel milk at an oasis – a rare splash of green in a world dominated by beige and brown – and we spent the night in the small town of Ayoun-el-Atrous with friends of our guide and translator, Mohamed el Moktar Ould Mohamed Ahmed. Overnight rain washed the dust from the air and we awoke to blue skies and the sound of a *muezzin* calling from a nearby mosque. Some time after midday we arrived in Timbedra and paid our respects to the police and the *préfet*. A hot dust-laden wind eddied around the town's sandy streets, and by the time we found Mohamed Mahmod Ould Beya and his colleagues the sun had almost disappeared and the sky was a crepuscular nicotine-yellow.

'The droughts of the 1970s changed everything,' said Mohamed Mahmod, the secretary-general of Timbedra-est Pastoral Association. 'Most people lost well over half their herds and some families lost all their animals.' It was now approaching 3 o'clock in the afternoon and Mohamed and ten fellow-members of the association decided to break for prayers. 'Looking back', he said as he wrapped a white turban round his head, 'some positive things came out of the droughts. They strengthened our resolve, made us eager to work hard. They also made us think more about looking after the environment.'

Wiry, light-skinned and sharp-featured, typically Moorish in both appearance and dress, Mohamed rose from the brightly patterned carpet, adjusted the sleeves of his blue *boubou* – the flowing robe worn by Mauritania's pastoralists – and joined the others as they filed through the door. Outside the temperature was nudging 110 degrees Fahrenheit and the sun was a blurred disc barely visible through a haze of dust. The men faced towards Mecca, knelt in the sand and prayed.

When the pastoralists returned from their prayers, we sat around two large platters of beef and cous-cous. While they chatted among themselves in Arabic – the Moors, the dominant group in Mauritania, speak the Hassaniya dialect – our guide, Mohamed el Moktar, a young sociologist working with the Ministry of Rural Development, talked about the fateful *années soixante-dix*. The great drought of 1973/4 had had a devastating effect on millions of pastoralists living in Africa's Sahelian region. The failure of the rains, explained Mohamed, led to colossal livestock losses; many remote regions experienced famine and tens of thousands of Mauritanian families made their way to Nouakchott, whose population doubled as the refugees erected their tented slums around its outskirts. In the 1960s some 60 per cent of Mauritania's population had been nomadic pastoralists; now, largely as a result of the droughts of the early '70s and mid-'80s, less than 10 per cent fell into this category, although the majority of the million or so people who lived in rural areas were still involved in some form of livestock rearing.

Once we'd finished the meal, Ahmado Ould Aly, a tall man with a piratical black beard, began to reminisce. 'I came here in 1974, at the time of the first big drought', he said, 'and the way of life changed dramatically within a very short space of time. Before then people thought about nothing except their animals. But the animals died and people had to think of other ways of surviving. They took on jobs they'd never have dreamt of doing before.' He paused just long enough to slurp down a glass of sickly-sweet mint tea. 'In some ways the traditional way of life – the old way – was very good,' he continued. 'People didn't need much – they had milk from their animals; occasionally they'd kill a goat or a cow so they could buy some salt and tea and flour. But they were self-sufficient. Those days are gone now. Life has changed – it's no use mourning the past. We have to take advantage of new opportunities; we'll keep the good things from our traditional way of life and blend them with the best of the modern world.'

What, we enquired, was the best of the modern world? 'Better animal health, more productive livestock, better pasture management,' replied Ahmado, adding that by joining the market economy the pastoralists were able to buy carpets, radios, medicines and other things which their forebears might not have had. It was true, he said, that one could still find some nomads, no more than a day's walk from here, who had had so little to do with the material world that they could scarcely tell the difference between a 1,000-ougiya note and a 100-ougiya note (a wry smile suggested that this was something of an exaggeration), but most pastoralists were now more open to outside influences.[1] For a people living in such a remote part of the Sahara, they were surprisingly well informed about world affairs, and wherever we went the pastoralists were tuning into the BBC World Service. One of the most significant events in recent years, according to Mohamed Mahmod, had been the formation of Timbedra-est Pastoral Association. This was one of 39 such groups which had been set up under Mauritania's Second Livestock Project, a World Bank funded scheme designed to inject new life and energy into the ailing livestock sector.[2]

Mauritania is one of the world's most sparsely populated countries. Twice the size of France, it has a mere two million inhabitants. Bordered to the north by Algeria and the disputed territory of Western Sahara, and to the south and east by Senegal and Mali, it is little known and much maligned. It is the country's tragedies and tribulations which make fleeting headlines in the outside world rather than its achievements. In the minds of most people Mauritania is associated with chronic droughts, racial tension – in 1960 it became the last country to officially abolish slavery – and disputes with its neighbours. Mauritania was briefly at war in the late 1970s with the Polisario Front fighting for the independence of Western Sahara, and a series of clashes between pastoralists and settled cultivators along the Senegal River in 1990 led to the closure of the border and outbursts of lynching in both the Senegalese capital Dakar, where several hundred Moor traders were murdered, and in Nouakchott, where many Senegalese suffered a similar fate. During the Gulf War, Mauritania supported Saddam Hussein: this gave the country a bad press in the West and led to massive cuts in the foreign aid budget, with major donors like Saudi Arabia and Kuwait withdrawing all support. The bald statistics suggest a country in crisis, dogged by perennial uncertainty: life expectancy is 46, infant mortality stands at 127 per 1,000 live births (compared with 87 in Senegal) and Nouakchott is full of 'drought refugees' who, in the words of one livestock expert, 'have nothing to do except dream of their lost herds'.[3]

Despite all this, many Mauritanians view the future with refreshing optimism. 'This is a very young country,' said Mohamed Ould Zeidane before we headed into the interior. 'There are lots of opportunities and people here are prepared to learn and experiment. This really gives me hope – though that's tempered by my fears for the environment.' Mohamed had spent several years working with the Second Livestock

Project – he was now an advisor in the Prime Minister's Office – and he took us to see Cheik Ould Dih, who had recently taken over the post of director of Agro-Pastoral Development and the day-to-day running of the Livestock Project. 'The key trend now', explained the director, 'is for the government to pull back, to be less interventionist. We want to let people do more for themselves. To some extent, this push towards privatization is a political decision by the government. But it's also been forced on us by the cut in the aid budget. We simply can't afford to finance everything.' At the World Bank offices on the other side of town, Sow Souleimane, also a relative newcomer to the project, applauded this loosening of state control, which was very much in line with World Bank thinking. It was also vital for the successful operation of the Second Livestock Project. '*L'idée du projet est formidable*,' he suggested. 'The idea of the project is tremendous – to trust the pastoralists themselves to look after the environment – the trees, the grass, the soil, the water.'

The World Bank, like virtually every other institution which has attempted to work in the pastoralist sector, has had its fingers burnt in the past. The drylands of Africa are littered with abandoned machinery, half-dug irrigation schemes, crumbling buildings and other memorials to good intentions and poor planning. All too often, projects funded by the Bank and others have failed to take account of the complex cultural and ecological peculiarities of pastoral life; rather than working through traditional organizations, they have tended to focus more on animal production (frequently, and with disastrous consequences, promoting American-style ranching) than on the pastoralists themselves. Seldom has any attention been paid to strengthening existing local institutions or to encouraging the pastoralists to improve the management of their herds and rangelands through their own endeavours. Fortunately, the World Bank has recognized the poor performance of many past projects and has begun to rethink its approach to Africa's drylands.

The main objectives of the Second Livestock Project – the first, which ran from 1972 to 1978, was primarily concerned with the rehabilitation of wells and animal health – are to boost livestock productivity and slow down the deterioration of the grazing lands. Where the project differs markedly from its predecessor is in its explicit aim of making groups of pastoralists – *associations pastorales* or pastoral associations –

responsible for managing their own resources. At present the project area encompasses some 130,000 square kilometres of Southern Mauritania; the beneficiaries are 180,000 Moors and a smaller number of Peuls, a nomadic group whose range stretches from Mauritania south to Northern Nigeria. The project officially began in 1987 with a small team of agricultural experts and sociologists – *l'équipe du volet associations pastorales* – identifying and helping to establish fifteen pilot pastoral associations (PAs). During the course of a year the team visited all villages and camps – collectively known as *localités* – and within two years fourteen of the fifteen pilot PAs had been established.

There are three types of PA in Mauritania. Along the bank of the River Senegal, where the majority of the population is involved in settled cultivation, are the *associations pastorales villageoises*. These tend to be small in area and livestock rearing is of secondary importance to crop cultivation. At the other end of the spectrum are the *associations pastorales nomades*, which occupy the most inhospitable territory. Here people practise the purest form of pastoralism, being on the move for much of the year and relying entirely on their livestock. Midway between the *AP villageoises* and the *AP nomades* – both geographically and in character – is the third group, known simply as *associations pastorales*, whose members can best be described as semi-nomadic agro-pastoralists. Their lives are dominated by their livestock, but they grow small amounts of grain such as millet and maize. Timbedra-est falls into this category.

The population living within each PA ranges from 3,000 to 25,000 with an average of 13,700. Timbedra-est and its neighbour Timbedra-ouest both have a population of 16,000. The average number of livestock within each PA is estimated at 12,500 cattle, 36,000 sheep and goats, 5,000 camels and 4,000 horses and donkeys. These averages don't tell us very much: *AP nomades* obviously have far greater animal populations than *AP villageoises* or *associations pastorales*. In any case, counting animals which spend much of their time on the move is obviously difficult. Mohamed Mahmod put the number of cattle (valued primarily for their milk) and camels in Timbedra-est at 40,000 and 25,000 respectively, and the number of sheep and goats at 60,000. Ahmado Ould Aly disagreed: he claimed that there were well over 100,000 sheep and goats belonging to people in the PA.

'Setting up the pastoral associations was a complicated affair,' recalled Mohamed el Moktar when we began to discuss the founding of Timbedra-est with its members. 'Obviously, the *équipe du volet* had to look at all sorts of factors and make sure that the boundaries between PAs made sense.' As a general rule, each PA encompasses communities which use the same pasture and the same water sources. 'Ideally', added Mohamed, who had visited every PA so far in existence, 'members should come from the same tribe to ensure the homogeneity of the association, but if two tribes have been living and working together, then that's OK – they can form a PA together if they want to.' The *équipe du volet* spent an average of twenty days helping to establish each pilot PA. During this period the team visited each *localité* – 47 in the case of Timbedra-est – and explained the aims of the project and the importance of setting up democratically elected committees. Each *localité*, consisting of fifteen to twenty families, elected one or two delegates, who then attended a general assembly whose function was to adopt a formal statute for the association and to set up a management committee. Mohamed Mahmod, Timbedra-est's secretary-general, felt that this had worked smoothly, although here, as elsewhere, the process tended to reinforce traditional power structures, with the nobility and clan leaders assuming key positions within the association while the lower classes – for example, the Harratins, or freed slaves – remained in the background.[4]

The first task of the pilot PAs was to set up a revolving fund – *un fond de roulement* – to which all members contributed. The amount collected varied from 150,000 ougiya ($1,250) in Ayoun-est PA to 675,390 ougiya ($5,600) in Rossonord PA. Once the committees had established their revolving funds, their presidents headed to Nouakchott where the Second Livestock Project gave as a grant a sum of money double the amount raised: hence the project added a million ougiya to the 500,000 raised by Timbedra-est. Each PA spent its revolving fund on livestock medicines, sold by the government at 20 per cent discount, and these were taken back to the home base to be sold to members.

Late in the afternoon, the temperature sinking towards 100 degrees Fahrenheit, we made our way into the centre of Timbedra with Mohamed Mahmod and half a dozen other committee members. A few yards from the market was Timbedra-est PA's animal pharmacy. The pharmacy was run by Mohamed Lemme Ould Khatty, a handsome young man whose grandfather – presently in Nouakchott buying more drugs – was president of the association. Mohamed took a bottle of anti-parasite serum from the neatly arranged shelves behind the counter: 'In Nouakchott we pay 800 ougiya for this', he said, 'and we'll sell it for 900 here. Generally the association makes a profit of around 10 per cent on the drugs.' With its revolving fund, the PA had set up and stocked a central pharmacy here and six smaller ones in remoter parts of the PA's territory. From the pastoralists' point of view, this aspect of the PA's work had been a success. 'We've seen a great improvement in the health of our animals,' said Mohamed Mahmod. 'In the old days, drugs may have been free, but the treatment was very hit and miss. Pastoralists who were a long way from the towns simply couldn't get the drugs they needed, and when they did they often didn't know how much to use and how to treat their animals. Now everyone is within reach of one of the pharmacies, and they can get expert advice on how to treat their animals.'

The Second Livestock Project is building on the achievements of its predecessor, which had ensured, through the offices of the Livestock Department, that all major animal diseases were brought under control with an annual programme of vaccination. For many years the government had provided an extension service as part of its animal health programme, but many pastoralists, spending most of their lives in remote regions, were unable to take full advantage of it. The Second Livestock Project has financed a new programme for training extension staff – or *encadreurs* – at the Kaedi School of Agriculture, and students are now trained not only in animal health matters as before, but in all aspects of resource managements and animal, crop and tree production. By July 1993, 39 PAs had been established – the pilot programme having been considered a success – and of these, 24 had benefited from the services of 19 *encadreurs*. A second batch of 20 *encadreurs* were shortly to finish training at Kaedi.

'In many ways', suggested Mohamed el Moktar as we left the pharmacy, 'the work of the *encadreurs* has been one of the best features of the project. Admittedly, you get good and bad, but a good one can have a very positive effect on an association's activities.' When the project officially ends in 1995 the *encadreurs*, will leave, but by then each association will have a small number of *auxiliaires* trained by the *encadreurs* to provide technical support and advice to members.

The *auxiliaires* are paid by the PAs out of their revolving funds. By mid-1993 Timbedra-est had eight *auxiliaires*, all of whom were local people chosen by the PA. Two, including the pharmacist Mohamed Lemme, were based in Timbedra, while the other six worked in the *campements* and villages in the desert. Six of the *auxiliaires* had been trained in animal health care and helped to run the pharmacies; two in environmental protection.

One of the principal aims of the Second Livestock Project is to help pastoralists look after their environment. Severe drought, a seemingly permanent decline in rainfall (in a good year now Timbedra gets 250 millimetres rather than the 400 millimetres it used to), a steady increase in human population in some areas and changes in herding and agricultural practice have conspired to turn once exploitable areas into barren wastes.[5] 'Twenty years ago', said one woman we spoke to at Zem-Zem, a village two hours' drive east of Nouakchott along the Route de l'Espoir, 'all this was forest and we had plenty of wild animals.' Today Zem-Zem sits in an ocean of sand sparsely punctuated with a few scruffy acacia bushes. 'In the '60s', said one of Timbedra's pastoralists, 'we had plenty of good pasture, more than enough, and plenty of trees too.' Now most of the trees have gone and the only ones to survive are those with spiny leaves, which seem to resist drought better than the others. The droughts not only led to the death of many animals, but to their concentration, as more and more animals competed for less and less pasture.[6]

Unfortunately, government policies have frequently done more harm than good. During the First Livestock Project the government built many public wells. This may have appeared philanthropic, but it led to a breakdown in traditional systems of pasture management. Previously, the desert communities had established over the course of many generations a complex system of access to water sources. If not owned by individuals, the wells were the property of groups of pastoralists or a community also in charge of its maintenance. By building public wells the government effectively created a free for all, and this encouraged overgrazing immediately round the wells, while no one took responsibility for maintenance and repairs.

Under the Second Livestock Project, wells owned by the state are to be given back to the pastoral associations, which will have the right to determine who uses the wells, when and at what cost.

Timbedra-est had adopted a variety of strategies to counter the degradation of its pastures and in each of its 47 *localités* the pastoralists had elected a *comité de gestion de la nature et du paturage*, a committee for the management of nature and pasture. One of the committees' tasks is to prevent bush fires, which can be a serious problem in October and November. 'Each committee', explained Mohamed Mahmod, 'goes out to talk to the nomads coming through our region and tells them that they'll be reported and arrested if through carelessness they start any fires.' This seemed to work: there had been no bush fires at all since the committees were set up.

In future, these committees will regulate grazing and manage the wells. This will be a complicated business reflecting the complexities of pastoral life. Pastoralism is a strategy for survival, its precise nature being determined by the availability and distribution of such key resources as fodder and water. There are two distinct seasons in the Sahel: the long dry season and the short rainy season. One of the trickiest tasks for the pastoralists is to ensure that adequate resources exist to get their animals through the period of want, known as *la soudure*, between April and July, when the rains come. During the rainy season grass is plentiful throughout most of Mauritania; animals are evenly dispersed and notions of territoriality are weak. Once the rains cease the nutritional value of the grasses swiftly declines and fodder becomes progressively scarcer: tenure now becomes a key issue and it is during this period that conflicts tend to occur between competing groups of pastoralists. When we visited Timbedra – at the height of the *Soudure* – there were few animals to be seen: most were still in Mali, though they were expected to return soon.

For the pastoralists in Timbedra-est PA, the better management of grazing lands meant two things: increasing their productivity by making hay at a time when the grass was at its most nutritious, and formulating ways of controlling grazing by members' herds as well as those passing through. The haymaking programme had begun in 1991 when 2,300 bales were cut and mechanically baled 40 miles to the north of Timbedra. The hay came from an area which had no wells and consequently the PA was utilizing a resource which otherwise would have been wasted. Half the bales were taken as payment by the people involved in the hay-making and the rest were sold for over a million ougiya, which went into the PA's revolving fund. The hay is especially valuable during the *soudure*, when there tends to be a shortage of fodder in certain regions, though in 1993 Timbedra-est PA still had a large stock which it had failed to sell.[7] A former director of the project, Eli Ould Ahmedou, felt that the hay-making had made people more aware of the value of the resources at their disposal. 'In the past', he said when we met in Nouakchott, 'if a lorry driver stopped and cut some hay to take to the capital, no one thought anything of it. But now they say, "Oy, you're stealing our hay!" and they'll stop him.'

Timbedra-est, like many other PAs, was in the process of working out a strategy to protect its pastures from overgrazing. 'We're going to fence off small enclosures beside the *localités*', explained Mohamed Mahmod, 'and we'll keep animals out of them for at least six months each year – that way we'll be able to get better fodder for the *soudure*.' On a grander scale, Timbedra was going to participate in the Second Livestock Project's programme of establishing *périmètres pilots pastoraux* (PPP), large plots of land which would be reserved for the use of communally owned herds of cattle. The PA will identify the pasture and provide the animals and labour, while the project will give technical advice and some financial support.[8]

Controlling the grazing behaviour of livestock belonging to the members of a PA is one thing; regulating that of outsiders quite another. One of the conditions of the project loan, laid down by the World Bank, was that the government would grant usufruct rights (in other words the use and profits though not the ownership) of grazing lands to the PAs. The relevant ministry finally issued a circular in 1990 acknowledging the PAs' rights to determining the use of water and pasture within their areas, but there seemed to be some uncertainty in the minds of the pastoralists as to whether or not this granted them the usufruct rights which they wanted and the Bank envisaged. 'If we have absolute rights to manage our territory', said Mohamed Mahmod, 'then we'll look after everything and we'll do it well.' The committee members anticipated the day – and they expected it to come shortly – when they would be able to charge usage fees to pastoralists from outside, or at least use their own resources as bargaining counters in determining reciprocal rights to graze their live-stock in areas managed by other PAs. The pastoralists in Timbedra were keen to think proprietorially and they were confident that an umbrella organization recently established in Nouakchott – *Le Bureau des Associations Pastorales* – would be able to coordinate the activities of all the PAs and help them reach mutually beneficial agreements.

The Second Livestock Project still has two years to run, during which time a further 80 PAs will be formed. It is too early to make any definite judgments: like the curate's egg, the project has been good in parts. It has certainly had some teething problems, some of which have been a reflection of discord between the World Bank and the government. One of the project's aims is to provide each of the pilot PAs with one new well and to repair and renovate four existing wells. The programme should have begun several years ago but the World Bank, keen to foster private enterprise, refused to release funds to the government, which wished to do the work itself. A private Mauritanian company with the relevant expertise was eventually formed in 1992. The PAs were unimpressed by this lengthy period of inaction, having set aside the 10 per cent of costs they were expected to contribute themselves some time before. However, by mid-1993 fourteen of the pilot PAs had signed contracts with the new well-building company and work was due to begin shortly.[9]

At a local level, efforts by the PAs to launch commercial ventures – known as *mini-projets* – had had mixed results. Timbedra-est's dairy scheme got off to a poor start during its first season when many of the calves perished. In neighbouring Timbedra-ouest the dairy scheme had fared better, and the PA was expecting its small herd of milkers to provide reasonable quantities of milk, which they could sell for 100 ougiya a litre. Although Timbedra-est had baled large quantities of good quality hay, it had yet to work out ways of getting this potentially valuable crop to the parts of the country where it was most needed and could command a good price. 'We need transport,' explained Mohamed Mahmod. 'We need to get the hay to Nouakchott, where we could get 500 ougiya a bale.' The PA was contemplating buying a secondhand lorry, which might cost 100,000 ougiya. As there was over a million ougiya in its revolving fund, buying a lorry was not beyond the PA's means.

As far as the pastoralists in Timbedra-est were concerned, the successes of the project outweighed its failures. Animal health had improved, the skills acquired by eight *auxiliaires* were being put to good use, and the committee members felt that people now had a much greater awareness than before of environmental problems. Lack of water had meant that the PA's tree-planting efforts had met with limited success, but bush fires were no longer a problem. Mohamed Mahmod argued that better animal health meant higher productivity: 'What matters now is not the number of animals we have, but their productivity. We want our members to increase the number of productive animals they have and get rid of the unproductive ones.' Eventually, he suggested, this would lead to a decline in animal numbers; combined with better grassland management, this would all be for the good of the environment. Others disputed this, but everyone we met agreed that the formation of the PAs had engendered a new spirit of cooperation. 'We're much better organized than we were before,' said one pastoralist in Timbedra-ouest PA. 'Now we have a common purpose and we can act as one.'

There is much talk among those involved with the administration of the Second Livestock Project about 'changing the attitudes' of the pastoralists. 'If they are going to prosper', said one official, 'they'll have to change some of their strategies. The government can't change attitudes; the pastoralists will have to realize what's needed themselves.' Eli Ould Ahmedou, a former director of the project, put it more bluntly: 'For a long time no one has taken responsibility for looking after the water sources, the pastures and the trees. That's what the pastoralists must do now – they must be collectively responsible for the land. They're the ones who must make the decisions in the future, not the government.' In short, the Second Livestock Project is about the devolution of power, and it is in this respect that it differs markedly from most other livestock projects. 'People have to participate in shaping their lives,' said Sow Souleimane of the World Bank. 'They have to be responsible. We shouldn't be treating people like babies. People need help, but they must do things themselves. And I think they want to do things themselves.'

On our journey back to the capital from Timbedra we stopped at three places where community activities bore out Sow Souleimane's belief that the people of Mauritania were eager to improve their lives. Following the drought and the loss of virtually all their livestock, most of the men of Zem-Zem village were forced to go to Nouakchott and elsewhere in search of work. The young women who were left behind decided they had to act: they founded a cooperative with 200 members in 1990 and set up a 1 hectare market garden. They were now self-sufficient in vegetables and had a surplus to sell to passing travellers and in Nouakchott's market. They had also set up a literacy class and a workshop for knitting clothes. All this they had done without any outside help.

Further south, on the banks of the Senegal River, 160 women's cooperatives have emerged over the past ten years. One group of Peul women had set up a superbly run 2 hectare market garden and small enterprises manufacturing iron fencing and children's clothes. Another small cooperative of Moor women had cultivated a 1 hectare garden. Three years ago these women had had to work away from their families as domestic servants in Nouakchott. Now the income from the sale of vegetables meant that they could stay at home. Their children were better nourished, and like many other women in the area they had taken advantage of adult literacy classes. The women's cooperatives had received advice, though no financial support, from an admirable government initiative, *Le centre de formation cooperatives du Boghé*.

Two hundred miles or so to the west of Timbedra we came to the village of Um-Lehbal, around three sides of which were well-established plantations. 'People first settled here in 1968,' explained Mohamed Val Ould Essayed, a small nomad with pop-eyes. 'I have to admit we neglected the environment around the village and it got worse and worse. By 1988 the dunes were so bare that you couldn't see from here to that house, there was so much sand in the air.' He motioned to a small cube-shaped building no more than 20 yards away from where we sat. 'That's when we decided we had to do something.' In 1988 the villagers set up a reforestation committee, *un comité chargé de la gestion de reboissement*, whose six elected members have overseen the reforestation programme. In 1988 the villagers planted 12,000 tree seedlings; in 1989 and 1990, 8,000 each year; in 1991, 4,000. 'We did it all ourselves,' said Mohamed. 'In the first year the Forest Department gave us some seeds – but that's all the help we've had.'

The villagers had set up a small nursery next to a well and once the first rains arrive every able-bodied person among the population of 200 helps in the planting and watering of the new seedlings. So far they have only lost 5 per cent of the planted trees. 'If we go to all this trouble', said Mohamed gruffly as we wandered through a plantation whose trees were now over 15 feet high, 'we're certainly not going to let them die.' The plantations had helped to stabilize the dunes and reduce the amount of wind-blown dust; they also provided fodder for domestic animals.

'We could do with a bit of help,' suggested one of the villagers. 'The water in the well by the nursery has turned salty. We need another well with good water and then we could grow vegetables and sell them. We want to fence the plantations too – then we could have fruit trees and grow gum arabic.' From time to time, he said, outsiders had come and promised all sorts of help: a new well, a diesel pump to lift water, fencing materials. 'But then we never hear from them again,' he said with a weary shrug.

'The great thing about these people', said Mohamed el Moktar, who had helped to set up the pastoral association for this area, 'is that when they have an idea, they pursue it. They work hard; they're determined. They'll carry on planting trees even if no one does help them.' We climbed into our vehicle and headed off down the Route de l'Espoir.

6
KRAKOW
The Green Federation

'Waste makes people think about the world around them'

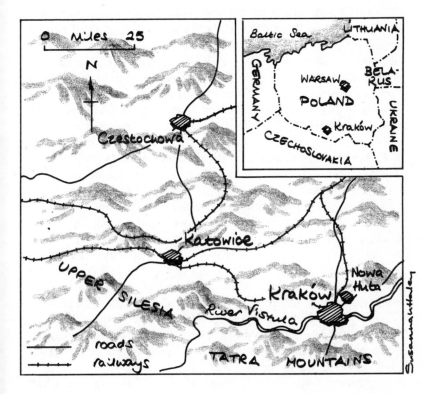

Our tram clattered along the broad avenue which led
from the centre of Krakow to the steelworks at Nowa
Huta. On a clear day this 10,000 acre complex of coke
ovens, blast furnaces and rolling mills – the workplace of
some 25,000 people – presents an awesome spectacle with its
great plumes of glutinous, nicotine-coloured smoke rising

from a thick forest of chimneys. But on this particular day, a week before Christmas, a dense, chilly fog with the unmistakable tang of sulphurous coal-smoke hung across the Vistula valley; there was little to see from the tram windows save endless rows of grey tenements and tower blocks, the living quarters for the steelworkers and their families.

'In the old days there was just one enemy', explained Darek Szwed, 'and that was communism. Now, for many people, there are dozens of small, diffuse enemies and they're mostly economic. How can I get a vacuum cleaner? How can I afford clothes for the children? How can we buy this or that?'

In this bleak world the tram passengers appeared as forlorn as their surroundings. 'There's a tremendous feeling of powerlessness,' continued Darek. 'In industrial areas like this many people are financially worse off than they were under the communists. There's a feeling of failure and hopelessness, especially among men in their 40s and 50s – they fear they'll lose their jobs soon. People dreamt that things would instantly change for the better when the communist era ended. But you can't change society overnight.'

However, for Darek, a fifth-year economics student, the dawn of democracy – the communists were ousted in 1989 – has brought real opportunities. 'I can now pursue the things which I think really matter,' he said. A small, wiry man in his early 20s with frizzy hair and close-shaved beard, Darek is a leading figure in the Green Federation and the inspiration behind a new waste recycling initiative. 'In Eastern Europe', he explained, 'you're generally either for the environment and against people, or vice versa. An environmental victory often means a human tragedy. If you close down a factory and say, "That's good, we've got less pollution now", you're ignoring the fact that workers have lost their jobs. But recycling doesn't drive people apart – it brings them together: it's good for the environment; it also creates jobs.'

Compared with the recycling culture of Calcutta (see Chapter 1), Krakow's adventures in this field may seem modest, but Darek's story, and his efforts to instil in both government and individuals an awareness about their environment, touches on many things: on the problem of transforming a planned economy to one led by market forces; on the difficulty of convincing people who have never been allowed to shape their own destiny that at last they have a chance to do so; on the complex nature of consumerism and its inevitable by-product – waste. But first, a few words about the waste-generator itself, the ancient city of Krakow.

According to one of the Hindu myths, God was left with seven stones once he had created the universe. He flung these across the world and where each landed sprang up a city which would never die. Rome, Jerusalem, Delphi, Delhi and Mecca seem obvious candidates for immortality. But Krakow? The choice seems absurd when you wander around places like Nowa Huta, but cocooned within this world of belching factories and shabby suburbs is a city of startling beauty. At its heart lies a vast cobbled square lined with magnificent Renaissance and baroque town-houses; there are a dozen fine churches, many with imposing statuary, and one, the Mariacki, with a clocktower from which the hours are signalled by a lone trumpeter, a tradition which stretches back to a Tartar siege some 700 years ago. The imposing bulk of Wawel Castle, former home of Poland's kings, is perched high above the River Vistula, and there are eleven universities, several of which were founded in medieval times.[1]

Krakow has had a turbulent past: it has suffered 5 earthquakes, 13 floods, 25 major fires and 17 sieges. Yet it survives, as the Hindu myth foretold – though only just. During the 1950s the communists build the Lenin steelworks on the edge of the city at Nowa Huta. Their choice of Krakow was deliberate. This was a city of the aristocracy and intelligentsia and by introducing a large proletarian workforce the new rulers sought to lessen the formers' influence. In the long run the project failed, not just economically – the works were, and still are, desperately inefficient – but socially too: Nowa Huta's steelworkers were as prominent as Gdansk's shipbuilders in supporting Solidarity's revolt against the communist regime.

Nowa Huta may have failed to weaken the intelligentsia, but it has certainly done much to damage the fabric of the city and the health of her inhabitants. The air pollution is so severe that many of Krakow's buildings are rotting away. The statues of the twelve apostles which stood unblemished for 300 years outside St Peter and Paul's Church were reduced to featureless lumps of stone within living memory, and newly painted buildings are transformed, in a matter of a couple of years, from bright strawberry and yellow to dirty shades of grey.[2] By the end of the 1980s Nowa Huta was producing startling levels of pollutants: 170 tonnes of lead, 7 tonnes of cadmium, 470 tonnes of zinc and 18 tonnes of iron a year: this fell as dust on and around Krakow, together with all the other pollutants spewing out of 200,000 domestic chimneys and wafting down from the industrial region of Upper Silesia.[3]

Steel production at Nowa Huta has fallen over the past few years, so air pollution has declined, but it is still severe enough to inflict a sore throat on the visitor within a day or so of arrival.[4] Unofficial estimates suggest that over half of the food produced in the Krakow region is unfit for human consumption. Infant mortality is well above the Polish average and four times greater than in Sweden, while life expectancy is some eight years less than in Western Europe. Krakow and Upper Silesia also suffer very high incidences of cancer, and many observers believe this can be attributed to the high levels of pollution. Even Krakow's sewer-rats have found living conditions intolerable. A few years ago the authorities reported that none were to be found in the city: optimists suggested that this was a triumph for the vermin-control squads; most, however, believed that pollution had driven them out.[5]

We climbed down from the tram once we reached Nowa Huta's main square and Darek led the way to the offices of the city government's Municipal Services Department. Mr Janusz Kala, the department's deputy-director, was a solidly built, ashen-faced man with a pleasant, open manner. 'In the past', he began, 'when the country was under communist rule, protection of the environment simply wasn't an issue of importance. Even when the environmental problems were very severe, we'd only act if the local community created a big fuss.' During the communist era, Krakow's waste management programme was chaotic and, at times, dangerous: toxic waste was disposed of in a most casual manner and the city landfill was poorly run. There was a certain amount of recycling, especially of scrap metal, but waste was generally seen as a nuisance rather than an opportunity.

Since 1989 Mr Kala's department has devoted considerable thought to such issues as waste management and pollution abatement. 'We have more power now', he said, 'but less money than before, and everyone agrees that the costs of improving the environmental situation are colossal.' The city, he explained, had contacted several foreign companies with a view to creating joint ventures and raising capital, and the World Bank had given $25 million in credit to help with the atmospheric clean-up campaign.

A third of the 850,000 cubic metres of waste disposed of each year in the city's landfill at Barycz consisted of paper. This, according to Mr Kala, was not only a waste of a resource which could be recycled; it was also a waste of space – the landfill was virtually full up, and the city government anticipated its closure in 1997. 'Paper recycling', explained Mr Kala, 'is now an important feature in our waste management strategy.' During the two months before our visit, children from around one hundred schools had collected over 120 tonnes of waste paper; this generated cash for the schools and work for half a dozen collection companies. Credit must go to many people and organizations, most especially to Darek Szwed and his colleagues in the Green Federation, an environmental pressure group set up in 1989.[6]

'I started to look at the waste problem in the summer of 1991,' explained Darek. 'During communist times the waste collection schemes seldom made sense, either economically or environmentally. For a while schools were coerced into collecting paper, but they soon became disillusioned. The authorities often failed to collect on time, and when they did they took it to the landfill and buried it. You could hardly call that recycling.'

Darek decided there was little point in approaching the city government with vague plans. 'What we needed was concrete evidence that recycling could pay for itself or generate cash.' During the summer and autumn of 1991 Darek and his friends visited many factories in the Krakow region and established which companies could take which waste products, and what prices they were prepared to pay for them. The Green Federation was particularly impressed by a paper mill at Czestochowa, an industrial town 140 kilometres north-west of Krakow; the mill was prepared to buy waste from Krakow and it was capable of producing 100 per cent recycled paper. Before approaching the city government, the Green Federation and its business arm, the Foundation for the Support of Ecological Initiatives, decided to put their ideas into practice. They produced a leaflet explaining the aims of recycling and distributed it in a residential suburb of Krakow. A week later they hired a lorry and gathered up the paper which local people had deposited at advertised collection points. The paper was delivered to the mill at Czestochowa and sold there. A fortnight later the exercise was repeated. On both occasions the Green Federation made a profit.

Darek then approached the city government and suggested a scheme which would enlist the support of schools. Many schools, he argued, were desperately short of money; if they encouraged their pupils to collect waste paper, they could earn much-needed cash and at the same time do something positive for the environment. The city's Education Commission supported the idea and it was agreed that the scheme should begin in the winter term of 1992. 'In a sense', reflected Darek, 'we were simply acting as a catalyst, convincing the local authorities, schools and individuals that recycling made sense.' He listed the more obvious environmental reasons: making new paper from old requires less water and energy than making paper from wood-pulp, the raw material commonly used in Poland; it also generates less in the way of air and water pollution. And by reducing the amount of paper waste, the city should be able to increase the life expectancy of its landfill. 'These things matter', suggested Darek, 'but we simply can't expect to get a good recycling system going unless it makes economic sense.' The 120 tonnes of paper collected during the winter term raised some 60 million zloties for the schools, the equivalent of $4,000. As far as Darek was concerned, this was just a beginning. 'We're well aware that good things can spring up one year and disappear the next. If recycling is going to work, it's absolutely essential that people buy the recycled products.' The Green Federation had recently bought 300 kilos of recycled paper from the Czestochowa mill and sold it at a profit. 'Our next step', said Darek, 'is to establish a good market for recycled goods.'

At its most prosaic, the recycling initiative meant the saving of natural resources: of timber, of water, of energy. Material formerly destined for a mucky burial in the city's landfill was now being transformed into reams of paper, which, in turn, could be recycled at a later date. But for Darek Szwed, the significance of Krakow's recycling scheme went far beyond its modest practical achievements. 'When I think about waste', he said one evening, 'it seems to touch almost every aspect of life. It touches on politics: on who makes decisions and why. It touches on social matters – on the ability of individuals and groups to cooperate. It makes people think about the world around them, and what they are doing to it.' If Poland is to solve its problems, he suggested, then it must usher in a new age of enlightenment. 'What we're trying to do in the Green Federation', explained Darek, 'is make people creative. We're very different from those environmental groups which want to capture people's minds. We want to make people think for themselves. Educating them about waste and recycling helps us to do that.'

Eighteen months earlier one of us had visited Krakow and spent time with Grzegorz Peszko, a professor at the Krakow Academy of Economics and the founder of the Green Federation. The Green Federation has fought various battles – sometimes alone, sometimes in partnership with other pressure groups – but from the outset one of its principal aims was to raise public awareness about environmental issues. Two years after founding the Green Federation, Peszko was somewhat gloomy: 'You see', he said, 'during the last ten years of communist rule, ecological awareness in Poland rose significantly. But over the past couple of years, it seems to have diminished. It's very depressing. I get the impression that under the communists environmental activity was often an ersatz for political action.' According to Peszko, the majority of people believed that once Poland sorted out its economic problems and become more prosperous, it could repair its damaged environment. 'But that doesn't take into account that while you can restore the architectural ruins, you will never restore many functions of the environment: the changes are often irreversible.' Hope for the future, suggested Peszko, lay with the young people of Poland: 'It's very difficult to influence the way the old generation – the ones in power – think. But the young are far more aware of our environmental problems.'

Widespread apathy about the state of the environment, especially among the older generations, is to some extent understandable. For one thing, the problems in places like Krakow can seem so overwhelming that it is hardly surprising if individuals feel that it is beyond their power to influence things for the better. For another, half a century of communist rule has weakened the spirit. One of the city's green councillors had this to say when we met him: 'Until recently people have been used to the state doing everything for them, and it's very hard convincing them that they too can play a role in improving the environment. Very few people understand that it's not just the big factories like Nowa Huta that affect the environment, but that their individual actions also matter. We have to make people more responsible for the way they live and behave.' All too often, as Darek pointed out, the arguments are confrontational, with the economic interests in direct conflict with the environmental. This was borne out by a recent strike at the Nowa Huta steelworks. Following a proposal to modernize parts of the plant, and thus reduce levels of air pollution, a group of workers went on hunger strike to protest against the loss of jobs which would follow. For those living near the breadline, a filthy and unhealthy environment is preferable to a clean one if a job goes with the former but not the latter.[7]

In spite of the apathy and the ignorance of the older generation, the young were present in vast numbers on the day we visited a waste conference in Katowice. Katowice is the largest city in Upper Silesia, the region to the west of Krakow. It is one of the world's most polluted cities – it even has a steelworks within sniffing distance of the main station – and one of the ugliest. The two-day conference was organized by the Information Centre for Air Protection, a branch of the highly respected Polish Ecological Club, and held in the aptly named Palace of Youth. The first day was devoted to children's activities; the second, attended by academics, environmentalists and industrialists, to seminars and lectures. Many organizations had set up stands to promote their goods and ideas. Far more impressive, however, were the 600 paintings and collages dealing with the subject of waste and pollution, submitted by schoolchildren in Upper Silesia. The children depicted jettisoned waste as dirty and chaotic; the harbinger of death, of a world cast in black and grey. Recycling, on the other hand, was associated in the children's imagination with order and cleanliness, with bright colours and fertile nature.

'We must start with the young,' declared Aleksandra Chodasewicz, a chemist working for the Polish Ecological Club. 'The older generation is lost to the environment.' She felt that the future for Upper Silesia was exceedingly bleak, but she was heartened by the enthusiastic response of the region's children to their educational campaigns. The local authority in Katowice had recently introduced a recycling scheme which relied on individual householders separating their waste into different components – glass, paper, organic matter – and Aleksandra felt that this was functioning well.

Among the foreign participants at the conference was Ton van Eck of Milieukontakt, a Dutch foundation which gives financial help and advice to environmental groups in Eastern

Europe. He thought that the environmental 'sub-culture' was much stronger among young people in Poland than in many parts of Western Europe, and he was impressed by the sophistication of groups like the Green Federation: 'They've learnt that they can achieve the most by concentrating on certain issues – such as waste and recycling. They really have managed to motivate the young.'

Not that anyone expects to change the world overnight. 'It's very important that we make the whole economy environmentally friendly,' Darek maintained. 'But that'll take 20 to 30 years.' Mr Kala of Krakow's Municipal Services Department agreed: 'Yes, we have to be realistic: we will get a recycling culture, but it'll take time. A generation, perhaps; say, 20 years to really change society's attitude to the environment.'

In Krakow the Green Federation has produced a variety of educational materials dealing with the waste issue: these have been distributed to schools and in some they now form a component of class work. The city government has also played a part in educating the general public; it has run off posters about recycling and distributed boxes for the collection of waste paper in public buildings, universities and government offices.

The city government realized that exhorting people to recycle their waste was only part of the solution. 'The Polish law on waste disposal is very unhelpful', said Mr Kala, 'so Krakow decided to draft its own. We're the first city in the country to introduce statutory waste management regulations.' A regulation 'Protecting the Environment from Waste and Sewage' came into force on 1 October 1992. Its aim, explained Mr Kala, was fivefold: to clean up the city; to control the landfills; to ensure the safe disposal of toxic waste; to compost organic matter wherever possible; and to encourage recycling. The city government was in the process of creating a database in which it intended to enlist all industries, enterprises and households, with details of the nature and amount of solid waste produced by each. A key element in the recycling programme was the separation of different wastes. At present each household pays 40,000 zloties a year (approximately $3) for waste collection; in future the charges will be waived for those households which separate their wastes into its different constituents.

Recycling is a tricky business, as many countries wealthier and more practised in the art of waste disposal than Poland have already discovered.[8] Darek was investigating the possibility of setting up recycling schemes for glass, plastic and other waste materials beside paper, but he had yet to make his figures work. Mr Kala was optimistic about the possibilities of increasing the amount of paper waste sent for recycling – 'There's money in it,' he said – but so far the city government had found that the prices obtainable for scrap glass and metal were often too low to make recycling economically feasible. Plastic waste also posed a problem. In Poland there were four companies dealing with plastic, but these were only capable of recycling polyethylene and polystyrene; the city intended to continue the practice of disposing of its plastic waste in the landfill.

In the context of Poland's environmental crisis, the paper recycling initiative in Krakow is barely scratching the surface of a colossal problem. Yet it may well be seen, a few years hence, as an important venture. The recycling initiative has undoubtedly brought together people and institutions who had previously been strangers to one another. 'This cooperation between local authorities, individuals and environmental groups is something quite new,' said Darek. 'Recycling is encouraging people to cooperate – and that's very important.' The idea that individuals are responsible for their own actions, and that everyone can take positive steps to help improve the environment, is at last beginning to take hold in Krakow, especially among the young, many of whom have helped in the recycling scheme. Rubbish, it seems, can be inspirational stuff.

7

LOS ANGELES

WATCHDOG

'ten years from now we will all breathe clean air...'

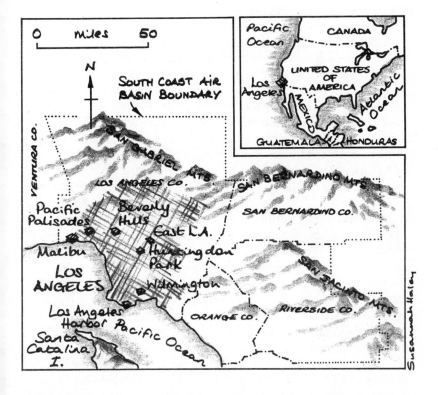

In 1973 Carlos Molina left his job and lodgings in Arizona. He packed his bags, climbed into his car and headed for Los Angeles. 'When I reached the San Bernardino mountains', he recalled, 'I looked down on a huge brown cloud covering the whole city. I had a strong impulse to turn back, but there was no place to make a U-turn, so I just kept on driving and driving. That is how I ended up in Los Angeles. It was hot and very smoggy down there, but there were plenty of jobs around. I said to myself: "If the others can keep on breathing, then so can I".'

Carlos had moved to the United States from his native Guatemala several years earlier, when he was 21 years old. He joined his father, and when his father died he moved in with his sister. He worked for a while in Indianapolis, Florida and Arizona before finally making his way into LA. During his first couple of years he lived in various suburbs, working mostly in factories. In 1974 he met his wife; two years later they married and had the first of their two children, a girl called Sara. 'In the beginning', explained Carlos, 'we lived in a very noisy, very smoggy part of LA, but as soon as we could afford it we bought this place in Wilmington.'

We were sitting on white metal chairs in the narrow strip of green between Carlos's house and his neighbour's. Beside us, in a porch bowered with green creepers, stood a large, colourfully painted Madonna and child. It was a pleasant, if ordinary house: one storey with a small lawn at the back, like so many in the neighbourhood. Short, roundish and heavily moustached, Carlos seemed as far removed from the conventional image of a Californian environmentalist as Wilmington was from the affluent suburbs of Beverly Hills and Bel Air. Ten years ago, the environmental movement in America's richest and most glamorous state was dominated by white, middle-class professionals. Times, however, had changed. Especially in the big cities, many poor and lower-class communities were becoming increasingly aware of being confined to polluted, unsafe and unpleasant environments. People who must breathe the most polluted air; people who must live besides waste dumps, prisons and industries processing toxic chemicals – people like Carlos – had now become key players in many environmental struggles.

Wilmington is an unremarkable suburb 20 miles south of downtown LA. Large cars and pickup trucks drive slowly past fast-food restaurants, giant hoardings and houses that all look alike; you seldom see anyone walking. To get there you must head down the Harbor Freeway, which is sometimes referred to by its users as the world's longest parking lot. Riding LA's freeways is like watching a panorama of the city gradually unwind: you slide by great affluence and considerable dereliction; past distinguished architecture or, more usually, a preponderance of the mundane. The Harbor Freeway traverses the crime-ridden South Central LA before running into the industrial landscape which stretches along the city's southern coast. Wilmington sprawls behind Los Angeles Harbor, midway between the freeway and Long Beach. Within an area of some 4 square miles are 7 of the 36 oil refineries in California. There are many other industries too: some manufacture chemicals, others serve the nearby port. Industry means jobs, which was one of the attractions for Carlos. Industry also means pollution and pollution means low house prices, another attraction.[1]

When the Molinas settled in Wilmington they gave little thought to the dirty air. 'For several years', reminisced Carlos as we sat drinking tea from flowery cups, 'I led a regular sort of life. I'd go to work, come home, have dinner, watch TV, sleep, wake up, go to work again. I never paid much attention to the fact that the oil refineries and other industries were right in our neighbourhood. They gave out a lot of smoke, and when I drove by in the car I could smell the stench, but I never truly paid attention to them.' Then one day Carlos began accompanying Sara to her school, which was opposite one of Wilmington's oil refineries, a short distance from a fertiliser plant and a sewerage treatment works. 'Every day I took her to school', continued Carlos, 'and every day I smelt the stench of pollution.' Sara told Carlos that some the children suffered from nausea, skin rashes and headaches; at times a green and black dust coated the playground and the classroom.

For a while, Carlos just worried about all this. Then, one day, he woke up determined to do something. He began by talking to officials at the school: they told him that the school had been there *before* the refinery. 'I became really mad!' Carlos recalled 'How could this have been allowed?' He then called the principal of the school and asked what was *he* doing about the pollution. The principal said that he was in touch with the directors of the refinery and the other plants – but Carlos soon realized that nothing was moving there. Some of the teachers were keen to do something about the pollution – they kept a catalogue of the ailments of the children and made phone calls to governmental agencies – but they had not enough time to follow up matters as they deserved. Carlos tried to organize other parents, but he encountered more scepticism than support.

One day, the school magazine published an article which told of the gift from the refinery of some saplings to be planted in front of the school. To mark this great event, the school was having a celebration, a band was being laid on, but no mention was made of the air pollution. Carlos was furious: 'Here they were, telling us they were tackling the problem when they were actually selling our children's health for a few branches and leaves!' Carlos stormed over to the school and demanded a meeting with the principal, who refused to see him. He had to make do with the vice-principal, who acceded to his demand to speak at the next parents-teachers' meeting. 'But he said that I had to submit my speech in advance', said Carlos, fulminating at the memory of it, 'and that they'd tell me what I could or could not say. Do you understand? I was censored! At that point I refused to speak. My case with the school was closed. I saw that it was impossible to organize round there!'

The years dragged by; the pollution continued. The children – Sara was now fourteen, Carlos Junior eleven – made steady progress at school. Carlos Senior continued to agitate against the pollution but it was often a dispiriting business. He contacted churches and community groups; spoke at public meetings. He even founded an organisation called Parents against Pollution. 'Here you are really nobody if you don't belong to an association', he explained with a broad grin. 'Once you're part of an association, you have a voice. I even got interviewed on a private TV channel! My kids used to make fun of me, saying that I shouldn't call it Parents Against Pollution, but *A Parent* Against Pollution!'

In the summer of 1991, Carlos received an invitation to participate in a meeting organised by the South Coast Air Quality Management District (AQMD); there he met some members of a campaigning organisation called the Labor/Community Strategy Center. This meeting was to change his life: he was no longer alone and isolated in his struggle to clean up Wilmington's air.

To understand the nature and severity of environmental problems in Los Angeles, one needs to appreciate its unique geographic setting and socio-economic might. The county of Los Angeles faces the Pacific Ocean and is bordered by the San Gabriel, San Bernardino and San Jacinto mountains in the

North, East and South. These angelic mountains and the celebrated California sunshine create an atmospheric cul de sac where the air tends to remain inert for long periods. The Shoshone Indians, who lived there long before the first white people arrived, called Los Angeles the 'valley of smoke', as the smoke from their campfires simply hung about their heads. In those days it didn't much matter, but today it surely does. Instead of fragrant wood smoke, the air of Los Angeles is permeated by the exhaust products of 8 million vehicles, the pollutants released by the largest industrial concentration in the USA – 900,000 manufacturing jobs, 35,000 plants – and the emissions from chemicals in consumer products used daily by 14 million people.

Pollution affects the whole city, but not in equal measure. Maps of pollutants' concentration unfailingly show the hot spots far from the ocean and near industrial agglomerates, the areas where people of lower social class – Latino (many, like Carlos, from Central America), black, recent immigrants from Asia – tend to live. Certainly, in places like East LA, Watts and Huntington Park, you find more unemployed youth than high rank executives. The LA upper and middle class – the majority of whom are white – seldom if ever venture into the great swathes of territory occupied by the poor. They remain close to the ocean – in places like Bel Air, Malibu, Pacific Palisades – where the air is still breathable and industrial activity non-existent. One can thus speak of 'local' problems in Los Angeles, although their severity and the number of people they affect make their solution more formidable than dealing with national problems in many small countries.

The primary pollutants emitted and trapped in LA's atmosphere include toxic and carcinogenic substances – like hydrocarbons, carbon monoxide, nitrogen oxides, heavy metals, organic compounds, asbestos, dioxins and all sorts of dust and soot.[2] When this rich cocktail is baked by the sunshine, it generates the secondary pollutants of photochemical smog[3] – more than 100 compounds, dominated by ozone – for which Los Angeles maintains a number of US (and world) records.[4] The effects of breathing such polluted air range from acute poisoning to chronically diminished lung capacity, from blood abnormalities to cancer, from respiratory disease to birth defects. In the late 1980s scientists from the University of Southern California performed autopsies on 100 inner city youths (most of whom were coloured) who had died from unnatural causes – car accidents, murder, drug overdose, and so on. Eighty per cent had 'notable abnormalities in lung tissue', 27 per cent had severe lesions; many apparently were 'running out of lung'.[5] The agency in charge of air quality matters (AQMD) has estimated that the cost of pollution-related health care in the region amounts to around $10 billion a year.

The AQMD was established in 1977, and it set itself the task of creating a smog-free Los Angeles by the year 2010. With a budget of nearly $100 million a year, this regional agency has the authority to research, plan and implement strategies to control air pollution in the four counties of Los Angeles, Orange, Riverside and San Bernardino. These make up the South Coast Air Basin, an area of 13,500 square miles and home to 12 million people. The AQMD is a formidable power in LA: it can ban polluting consumer products, establish traffic regulations, impose tax on polluters and block commercial developments. Its supporters point to its considerable success in reducing ozone pollution.[6] Its detractors suggest that the links between the board of the agency and local corporate polluters are too close to allow free and effective action. They stress that virtually nothing has been done to eliminate a whole range of toxic and carcinogenic pollutants besides ozone. Several organizations have periodically felt obliged to remind the AQMD that its mandate does not include any responsibility to protect commercial and industrial interests; rather, it is supposed to improve the quality of the air that people breathe. The most vocal and successful of such organizations is the clumsily named Labor/Community Strategy Center, whose WATCHDOG coalition has been at the forefront of the struggle to improve LA's environment.

With its vigilante overtone, the name WATCHDOG conjures up the image of a bunch of angry campaigners, which indeed they are. This is not to say that they lack sophistication. For one thing, the coalition intentionally gathers multiracial and diverse components. It unites civil rights movements, environmental associations, labour unions, women's groups and community associations from all corners of the immense territory of LA. Most 'environmental' action involves pressuring regulatory agencies, but the coalition does not shy away from any direct confrontation with corporate polluters.

One of the least shy figures in the movement is Eric Mann, director of the Labor/Community Strategy Center. A charismatic and tough-talking character, Eric moved from New York to

LA in the 1970s and worked for many years in the General Motors Van Nuys plant, in northern LA. As a labour organizer, he was a key campaigner in the fight to prevent the closure of the plant in 1982. The campaign was successful, the plant remained open and Eric became a full-time political activist. Today, for him and his colleagues at the Strategy Center, the struggle against pollution goes hand in hand with the struggle against poverty, racism and the exploitation of labour. With a simple but powerful expression they say they fight for 'environmental equity'.

Can LA – or for that matter, any modern, industrial city – have both jobs and clean air? Can industrial production be reconciled with a safe environment? These are, indeed, the crucial questions in the mind of many concerned people. The answer to them has often been a resounding 'no', not just from the captains of industry – who see pollution control as profit-limiting[7] – but also from trade unionists who value jobs above cleanliness and safety and from environmentalists who value cleanliness and safety above jobs. Fortunately, this is not the answer of the Labor/Community Strategy Center. 'Our movement began as a campaign to protect workers' jobs,' explained Eric Mann one morning, as we sat down for breakfast in our hotel, 'and, since then, we have not changed our mind in the least.' Eric was in a no-nonsense mood: he managed to get the restaurant TV turned off, which is no minor achievement in LA. 'When people confront us on our environmental stand we can say that we want jobs and we work for jobs – as our roots testify. But we want to take a closer look at them. What are we producing? What are the health effects of production on workers and the community? The workers and the community – not just capital – should have a voice in our industrial future.'

Many people argue that a cleaner environment is all very well, but forcing industry to forgo dirty technologies and install clean ones is costly, and may lead to the closure of plants and the loss of jobs. 'As an ex-auto worker', said Eric, 'you can be sure that I understand the dilemma. Some time ago there were 1.1 million people employed in the US automobile manufacturing industry; now it's below 700,000 and the number is still falling. It's all about trade-offs – such as the health of people versus capital investments in obsolete and dangerous technology. But trade-offs are rarely made explicit, and certainly not decided upon in a democratic way.'

According to Eric, many workers are frightened; they have a vested interest in believing that environmentalists adopt scare tactics, as their employers often claim. They know that some pollutants cause cancer, but they cannot afford to give up the only good thing they have: their job. Fear of losing one's job is very stressful. 'Do you know,' asked Eric, 'that child abuse is on the rise in areas close by defence contractors' plants, where workers expect to be laid off from one day to the next? You do not hear much about it because it does not fit the usual racist stereotype: most defence contractors' workers are white, and not Latino or black.'

The Labor/Community Strategy Center has devoted much time to investigating environmentally sound industrial practices and their potential contribution to the jobs market. It has calculated that in the United States some 2 million new jobs are 'waiting to become effective' in environmental businesses – for example energy-efficiency enterprises, clean-up operations, the manufacture of anti-pollution technologies and so forth. Eric and his colleagues believed that this would happen if the government adopted 'a progressive social agenda for energy policy'. They are well aware that blanket bans on dangerous pollutants would lead to the closure of many industrial plants; left to their own capitalistic rationale, private industries would adapt by dispensing with labour or shifting operations to countries with laxer pollution controls. The loss of jobs would soon turn workers against the environmental movement. 'If we are to have an environmental revolution,' concluded Eric, 'two things are needed. First, massive governmental intervention. There's no way the private sector will amend its ways on its own. Second, a great expansion in democracy. There are innumerable complicated choices to be made, radical technological change is going to create massive dislocations, and people have a right to be informed and directly involved.'[8]

Los Angeles. Too much of everything. Buildings, factories, roads, parking lots and cars... no end in sight. Our hotel was immense, pretentious and crummy. The toilets leaked and the bedside lamps did not work, but there were three different locks on the doors. Too much food on the plate – we regularly sent back half of it – and too expensive. You could choose a non-smoking area, but there were several TVs on every-

everywhere you went for food or drink. Outside, clusters of tower blocks interspersed by a few skinny palm trees. In the sky, more planes than birds. Hardly any walking hominids. LA is a hyper-reality of plastic, cement, grey tar and ribbons of bumper to bumper vehicles (ten lanes, five in each direction) gently rolling on low hills. Everything is fogged in a grey dust that in the evening becomes reddish, a sort of fire in the sky.

Finished our breakfast, it took us over an hour to cover the 15 mile drive south to WATCHDOG's office in Wilmington. LA was designed to suit transportation by private vehicles, a symbol of comfort and speed. Perpetual traffic jams and drive-by shootings have tarnished the image of car travel, yet LA's public transport services are so inadequate that most people – environmentalists included – are forced to travel to work by car. A number of metro rail and light rail projects are underway, but it is foreseen that even when they will be completed, 96 per cent of LA residents will still travel by car. We were left wondering how an unemployed person could possibly find a job – and maintain it – without a private vehicle.

The Labor/Community Strategy Center has built its campaign around a publication called *LA's Lethal Air*. 'We want people to understand that the air is killing them,' said Eric as we stuttered slowly southwards. 'They have many other problems, from poor schools to police violence, from drug pushing to AIDS. Why should they care about air pollution? Because it's slowly killing them, that's why!' We talked for a while about studies which suggested that smoking, alcoholism and road accidents killed far more people than pollution. 'I have no vested interest in overstating the case', countered Eric, 'but the health consequences of pollution are serious. Besides being toxic, the pollutants we breathe lower the immunological capacities of our bodies. People remain sick longer, illnesses are more serious and strike more often, and people develop allergies. All too often, the studies you've mentioned look at pollutants in isolation, as if people didn't smoke, have no other risk factors or didn't breathe a mix of pollutants, rather than one at a time. More studies are needed, but in the meantime we cannot pretend that everything is fine.'

Eric was right. The health effects of breathing polluted air day after day are in many ways unresolved. The most serious consequences often become apparent after long delays and (the latency period for cancer can be as long as several decades) or accumulate slowly into chronic conditions. The idea of a 'weakening of the immune system' is a poorly defined concept, difficult to measure. The epidemiological studies that could throw light on these problems require lengthy periods of awkward and expensive research. For example, it is difficult to estimate the absorbed doses of air pollutants or to separate the effects of one pollutant from another. But this should not justify a relaxed attitude. The severity of a public health problem depends on the seriousness of the effect *and* the number of people exposed. If the effects of air pollution are not yet precisely understood, the number of people exposed is enormous, enough to warrant the most conservative measures. Needless to say, exposure is especially severe for people who live and work in very polluted environments. Those concerned about air quality and those concerned about social justice have one more reason to ally.

By the time we reached Wilmington we were still musing on LA's urban dilemma. On the one hand the filthy air, the shallow breathing, the sense of being trapped in a hell of metal and asphalt, the time taxed away by traffic, the fear of serious health problems to come... On the other jobs, the stores open 24 hours a day, being able to pay the mortgage for a house and the instalments for the electronic appliances in the living room. The whole locked into a pervasive system in which an individual may feel utterly impotent. What can an angry WATCHDOG do? Is there more to it than growling?

Seemingly, there is. The young organizers we met at the office told us of workshops and meetings, door-to-door canvassing with a health questionnaire, and of a number of battles with the regulatory agencies – of which whey had won quite a few. *LA's Lethal Air* had proved an important tool in gathering support, as Kikanza Ramsey – known affectionately by her colleagues as the Queen of Canvassing – explained: 'For me, a black woman, and for oppressed communities in general, there's something powerful in campaigning on the basis of scientific information. In the US there is a prejudice that poor people, women and people of colour do not read or do not understand science. As part of the process of empowering ourselves, it is important that we organize around a book, around a well-articulated base of knowledge.'

Kikanza and the other organisers spend a good deal of time treading the streets and knocking on doors. It is a tough and at times thankless task. 'We start with a health questionnaire,' explained Kikanza, 'and we find out whether the family has any health problems related to air pollution'. This is not always straightforward. As Carlos told us, many people seem to take it for granted that their throat should feel raspy, that they should have difficulties breathing at night and their kids should be coughing all the time. 'We show them *LA's Lethal Air*,' continued Kikanza. 'If they want, we put them on our mailing list. We encourage them to write to elected officials and to the AQMD, and we show them how they can request specific information from companies that release pollutants close to their homes. And, of course, we encourage them to help WATCHDOG.' Once the organisers have completed door-to-door canvassing in problem areas, they arrange house and community meetings. These can be resoundingly successful, though not always: 'Sometimes we have hundreds of powerful conversations', sighed Kikanza. 'and we expect people to come *en masse* to the next meeting – but then we end up drinking the whole pot of coffee ourselves as no-one shows up.'

Many of the areas in which WATCHDOG campaigns are already served by existing associations. Some of them – such as associations of home owners – see air pollution mostly as an economic issue, lowering property values. 'These associations have no intention of mingling with the lower classes,' said Lisa Duran, another WATCHDOG organizer. 'They don't want to mix with Spanish-speaking people who need translators at the meetings and who see the problem in terms of health rather than property value.' Other groups, however, see the problems from a health and social justice perspective, and these tend to join WATCHDOG activities at the first occasion. One of the best known among such groups, active long before the founding of WATCHDOG, is the Mothers of East Los Angeles, an organisation of predominantly Latino and black women. Under the brilliant leadership of Juliana Gutierrez, the Mothers have successfully fought against plans to build a toxic waste incinerator in their area. It took innumerable protest marches, scores of meetings with city officials, press conferences, the help of lawyers who provided free services and – towards the end of the seven-year struggle – the support of WATCHDOG, before the authorities finally tore up the plans. The Mothers have achieved much else besides: they have stopped drug dealers from operating in many parts of East LA, they have successfully campaigned against a plan to build a new prison (prisons, like pollution, are a feature of impoverished neighbourhoods in California) and the monthly bulletin which they produce with the help of WATCHDOG has raised public awareness in East LA about pollution and other environmental issues.

Since its formation, WATCHDOG has exerted considerable reformist pressure on the AQMD and other agencies. Soon after our arrival at the Wilmington office, Lisa Hoyos Tweten produced a pile of newspaper cuttings recounting past battles with the authorities. 'The regulatory agencies should be accountable directly to the people', she insisted, 'but they are actually permeated with corporate interests. The key word in recent years has been "deregulation" and this has literally meant an attack on public health.' Another issue, according to Lisa, has been the internationalization of the struggle: 'If we manage to get better regulations here, the factories may move to another country. We need international solidarity to protect people in other countries as well as our own, but we also need regulations for trade and investments that protect the interests of US workers.'

Chris Mathis – a former autoworker with Eric Mann at the GM Van Nuys plant and today the chief organiser of the group – was quick to add: 'That is why we need organizing. We must stand up against the multimillion dollar corporations that run the city, own the factories, make the freeways, the cars and the parts that go into the cars. They are the ones who take the profits away and leave us with polluted air. It is by organizing and calling a boycott against GM that we won our labour battles ten years ago. We must do the same against pollution, we must educate people and provide leadership in the fight.'

As openly stated by Chris, there was 'a vision around this table' and the WATCHDOG organizers shared a strong commitment. Yet their emphasis on providing leadership had a familiar ring. Were they proposing a sort of 'vanguard of the proletariat'? Chris jumped to answer: 'Becoming conscious of problems is the basis of everything. All of us here received some input from outside – from a person, a book, an organised group – otherwise we would not be here today. I once heard about Frederick Douglas, an illiterate slave who inspired his people to freedom. That vision "ruined" me for life.'

'WATCHDOG tries to provide the best version of leadership: informing, inspiring, helping to achieve results,' said Lisa Duran. 'But we are not blank minds,' insisted Chris. 'We are not neutral and innocent outsiders who need to knock on 49 doors to form an opinion, and then at the 50th door say what the others have mentioned before. We do not glorify the community opinion *per se*. We knock on doors with a health questionnaire, lots of literature and our ideology, and it's all there to be discussed. Would you like us to say nothing when we hear all sorts of self-defeating assertions, like that the biggest urban problem is the lack of police, or that immigrants are the principal cause of our fiscal crisis?'

Lisa Hoyos believed that the environmental movement should learn from the history of the labour movement in the United States: 'The great battles for better living and better working conditions during the first half of the century came to a halt with the economic boom of the 50s. The companies managed to convince the workers that it was through a mutual alliance that they could all reap the greatest benefits. This is still the prevailing model. The unions do not present serious challenges to business... and still factories are closing down, occupational safety is neglected and the environment polluted.'

If the scale of problems in LA seems at times overwhelming, at least Lisa and her colleagues could take comfort from some notable victories. Many of the newspaper cuttings referred to the crucial role that WATCHDOG played in getting the 'Right to Know' law rewritten. The AQMD began drafting this law – its purpose was to determine how information about pollution-related health risks should be disseminated – without any community input whatsoever. WATCHDOG agitated for greater public participation and managed to set up discussion meetings in a variety of places. Before such public events, the WATCHDOG organizers went from house to house informing people about the health risks posed by pollution and the potential significance of the Right to Know law. 'Scores of people participated in these meetings,' recalled Lisa, 'and we achieved a great victory. Initially, the AQMD was only going to notify the public of risks affecting over one hundred people per million. We fought for one in a million, but finally settled for ten in a million. Initially, the notification was to consist of a small ad in a local newspaper. After our intervention, we got the agency to agree that everyone living within a certain area of cancer risk would get a letter at home explaining the risk in a clear and comprehensible way.' In addition, the Right to Know law, which was expected to come into force shortly, would ensure that information about environmental health risks will be available in local libraries and schools. Furthermore, the polluting companies would be obliged to hold local community meetings to discuss the issues.

Eric Mann recalled with some pride another significant victory. 'The AQMD wanted to discourage people from riding to work by car', he explained, 'and the way they were going to do this was by establishing higher parking fees at job sites where parking had customarily been free. We opposed this law, which essentially meant pushing the poor off the road. In appearance, we behaved in an anti-environmental way, but for us it is important not only to get fewer cars on the road, but *how* this is achieved and *who pays* for it.' On this issue, WATCHDOG did not go door to door; instead it called together a constituency of community groups and trade unions – for example, the union of hotel and restaurant employees and the 'Justice for Janitors' movement. The alliance agreed that the best way of reducing the number of cars on the road lay not in introducing disincentives which penalised the poor, but in offering a variety of positive incentives, such as the introduction of child care facilities at job sites so that parents didn't have to drive their children to child-minders. 'We raised a real stink', said Eric, 'and the law didn't get passed. This victory made it clear that our environmental demands are not to be met at the expense of the poor – that what we are campaigning for are not just environmental objectives *per se*, but environmental equity.'

During the night of 8 October 1992, a fortnight before our visit to LA, a loud explosion shook the slumbering suburb of Wilmington. Carlos Molina left his home and headed for the burning Texaco refinery with his camera. 'I decided to take some pictures', he explained, 'because I was worried that the company might deny that the explosion ever took place.' As it happened, the fire burned for four days. The pictures were spectacular: they showed a huge fire licking around the silhouetted containers and the stacks of the oil refinery. Before heading for the fire, Carlos telephoned other members of

WATCHDOG and they came to the site immediately. Some of the people living in houses near the refinery had to be evacuated and WATCHDOG members took their names; at one point police tried to stop them and threatened to arrest them on the grounds that they were agitators. Over the next few days they collected hundreds of testimonies from people who suffered nausea, headaches, vomiting, diarrhoea, shaking and disorientation.[9] Texaco's reaction to this disaster was far from exemplary. The company demanded to see the residence papers of those affected by the explosion who were claiming compensation for medical care. Many of the poor Latinos in LA are technically illegal immigrants.[10] 'They wanted to scare people into silence,' claimed Carlos. The company also suggested that installing stricter pollution controls and better safety procedures would inevitably lead to a reduction in the labour force. Despite all this, representatives of Texaco's management did agree to sit down and discuss matters with members of WATCHDOG. 'This was certainly a victory of sorts,' said Carlos. 'Some time ago, they did not even want to acknowledge our existence!'

Since Carlos's first encounter with WATCHDOG members and the subsequent opening of their office in Wilmington, much has happened to lift his spirits. He comes from a family of fighters and, back in Guatemala, one of his uncles had been almost beaten to death for his work upholding human rights. 'I have the same sort of character,' Carlos said as we were about to leave. 'For some reason I was destined to come here to LA; I have my task here, and I can already count my small victories.' One of these was when the AQMD – instead of holding the usual workdays meetings attended only by corporate lawyers – came to Wilmington on a Saturday to talk to the people about their pollution problems. Another was when Carlos convinced the director of his factory to find a benign substitute for a dangerous substance that was being used on the production lines. But the biggest victory still lay ahead. 'Ten years from now,' he asserted, 'there will be strong community groups linked together all over Los Angeles. By then we will have cheap mass transit. The industries will have cut toxic emissions. And we will all breathe clean air.'

8

COSTA RICA

San Miguel Association for Conservation and Development

'It's essential we maintain the biodiversity of the forest'

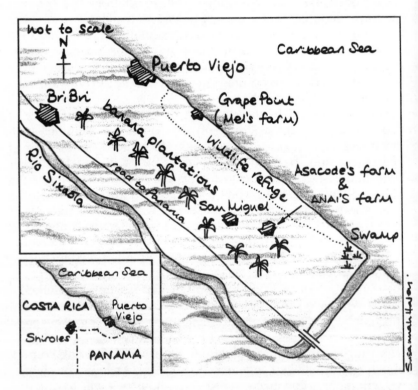

'If a *campesino* chops down a couple of acres of forest to plant rice, he might get sent to jail,' said Teodoro Lopez. 'But a banana company or the big loggers can devastate hundreds of acres – and do it quite legitimately!' Teodoro paused while we watched a coral snake glide through the leaf litter, mount a rotting log and disappear into the dank, frog-filled undergrowth. Hundreds of feet above us, in the dense forest canopy, a pair of fruit crows signalled their presence with excitable, fluty calls; lower down, a black woodpecker with a crimson crest drummed energetically against the towering trunk of an epiphyte-encrusted tree. 'There's simply no supportive framework to help artisanal wood-users like us,' continued Teodoro. 'All the laws in Costa Rica favour the industrial exploitation of tropical forest. If we had big machines and tractors and lorries to cart away the wood, then there'd be no problems – but that's not how we work.'

When it comes to discussing their achievements in the field of conservation, the Costa Rican authorities have never been shy. Certainly, the bare figures seem impressive: 12 per cent of the country is strictly protected, being designated as either national park or biological reserve, and a further 15 per cent falls within wildlife refuges, Indian reservations, forest reserves and other categories which confer some degree of protection. By safeguarding these areas, it is said that the survival of 95 per cent of Costa Rica's animal and plant species is assured. Tiny country it may be, but it harbours 5 per cent of the species known to exist on our planet, including 208 species of mammal, 850 species of bird, 160 species of amphibian, 200 species of reptile, 130 species of freshwater fish and over 25,000 species of insects. However, what the authorities generally fail to mention is that Costa Rica has the highest rate of deforestation in Central America and one of the highest in the world. This is a sad state of affairs for Costa Rica's wildlife and an impending disaster for many of the country's *campesinos*, the peasant farmers who are trying to make a living in or beside forested land.

Teodoro had brought us to a patch of primary rainforest near San Miguel village, just a few miles from the Sixaola River and the border with Panama. Copious quantities of sunshine and over 200 inches of rain a year had helped to create the lushest vegetation one could imagine. A little way to the east lay the Caribbean and to the west the Cordillera Talamanca, part of the craggy range of mountains which forms the backbone of the country. Talamanca was the last area in Costa Rica to be conquered by the Spaniards, although it was the United Fruit Company which established the first permanent white presence here; it still retains its frontier atmosphere. Thirty years ago the majority of the population in the hills were Bribri and Cabecar Indians, while the main inhabitants of the coast were the descendants of black immigrants from the coasts of Colombia and Nicaragua and the freed slaves who had arrived from the islands of the Caribbean in the second half of the nineteenth century. During recent years the region has seen some dramatic changes as a new wave of immigrants – *campesinos* from other parts of Costa Rica, refugees from war in Nicaragua and elsewhere, North Americans and Europeans in search of the good life – have descended on Talamanca and begun to carve out a living for themselves.

The small band of people who were accompanying us all called this place home, yet nearly every one of them had been born and brought up elsewhere. There was Melvin Baker, a humorous Texan who first came down this way in the early 1970s. He bought a horse and over a period of a year he rode and walked the entire Caribbean coastline of Costa Rica, thus gaining an intimate knowledge of the local ecology. Eventually he purchased 2 hectares of land south of Puerto Viejo. For eight years he worked as a cacao farmer, but then the *monilia* pod rot struck this part of Central America and soon after prices for cacao began to tumble. 'Nowadays', said Mel in his laconic drawl, 'I mostly just produce oxygen and let things grow for the wildlife.' He also worked all hours of the day for an organization called Asociacion ANAI, which was helping communities work out non-destructive ways of making a living from the forests.

A close associate of Mel's and a colleague in ANAI was Luis Rodriguez, a studious, stocky forester who lived near the provincial capital of Bri Bri, which boasted four telephones, a couple of bars, a town hall, a corrupt administration and not much else. We had first met Luis at Shiroles Experimental Farm in the Bri Bri Indian Reservation. 'I know it's shameful', he'd said, 'but in this country we can't say that there's a culture entirely based on forests, even though 80 per cent of this region is forested.' He added, however, that many *campesinos* and indigenous people had a good understanding of the value of the forest, although most were unaware of the potential cash value of the trees around them.

One group which had benefited from Luis's advice was ASACODE – la Asociacion San Migueleña de Conservacion y Desarrollo, the San Miguel Association for Conservation and Development – which had been founded in 1988 by Teodoro

Lopez and eleven other heads of household, two of whom were with us now. Teodoro was a rugged character with a wispy moustache, corkscrew curls and the physique of someone used to hard work. His father-in-law, Jose Luis Zuñiga, was of slighter build, but remarkably young looking for a man who already had seven grown-up children. 'I may have 47 hectares of land and forest', he said at one point, 'but divided among seven children, that won't go far. If they are going to stay, we'll have to work out ways of making a living from the forest.' The third member of ASACODE in our party was Felix Vasquez, a striking young man with a mane of black curls and arms like a blacksmith. 'People come here claiming to be experts on tropical forests', said Luis, 'but Felix knows far more than most scientists about how these forests work.'

Over four-fifth's of ASACODE's members – the original twelve has risen to twenty – had emigrated to Talamanca from Guanacaste, an arid grassland region in the north of Costa Rica. 'For poor people there', recounted José Luis, one of the few native Talamancans, 'life was very difficult. Guanacaste was dominated by cattle empires and to survive many people had to leave.' Those who journeyed south brought with them the cattle culture of the north. They squatted in the forests of Talamanca, cleared away trees and began to ranch cattle.[1] For a while this small-scale ranching seemed to work, but before long the soils lost their fertility and the amount of forage available for the cattle fell sharply. 'You won't find a single successful venture in the forests based on initiatives imported from other regions,' remarked Luis.

Unable to survive from cattle ranching, the *campesinos* were forced to look at alternatives. Cacao, the tree which provides chocolate beans, was no longer an option, and although banana cultivation was still profitable – witness the proliferation of plantations over the past few years – the *campesinos* could only grow bananas for home consumption or as pig feed. As a last resort, they decided to work with nature, rather than against it; to tap the resources of the forests, rather than ravage them, as was the wont of the banana barons and the logging companies.

On our first morning with ASACODE, we had made our way along a treacherous dirt track to an 80 hectare farm owned by Gregorio, a member of the association. The farm consisted of a patch of old cacao trees, recently abandoned and gone to scrub, several plots of maize and some fine tropical forest. At the foot of a long glade stood a silk-cotton tree of spectacular dimensions: the buttressed trunk was over 30 foot in diameter at the base and beside it we humans appeared as insignificant as Lilliputians. As we paused to admire it, Teodoro Lopez said: 'If one of the big industrial logging companies came to fell that, Gregorio would get about 3,000 colones.'[2] How much, we queried, would it be worth in the hands of ASACODE. Teodoro thought about this for a while: 'We haven't been going long enough to work out the exact economics', he replied, 'but to us I reckon that tree would be worth about 100,000 colones once it was felled and processed.'

We wandered across a flowery meadow, past a green iguana on a tree stump and through the derelict cacao plantation into dense jungle. A mature *Pilon* tree (*Hieronyma alchornoides*) was being cut into 4 inch thick planks by two members of ASACODE. The wood, a deep chestnut colour, was very tough and Luis pointed to the sparkling nodules of silica, a feature of *Pilon* which meant that it did not polish well. 'There are about twenty important trees around here', explained Luis, encompassing the surrounding forest with a broad sweep of his arms, 'and ASACODE are going to take out just two this year.' A few minutes' walk away from the *Pilon* was another tree – *Carapa guianensis* – which had been recently felled. 'If an industrial company had felled this', explained Luis, 'they'd have left it once they'd seen the middle was rotten, and Gregorio wouldn't have got anything for it.' ASACODE, in contrast, was making use of all the timber around the rotten core and would pay Gregorio accordingly.

The conventional or industrial system of forest exploitation is so profoundly different from the sort of 'low-tech', peasant system employed by ASACODE – symbiotic forestry, as Luis called it – that one is inclined to forget that the *campesinos* and the industrial loggers are dealing with the same resource. Had Gregorio invited an industrial company on to his land to tap the forest resources, it would have been the company, rather than Gregorio, which chose which trees to fell. The company would have taken timber up to the level of the first major branch of each tree and left the rest – in other words, at least half of the tree – to rot on the forest floor. Tractors would have been used to pull the timber out of the forest to the awaiting lorries; consequently, large swathes of forest would have been flattened, possibly eliminating some of the rarer species and undoubtedly retarding the process of regeneration.

Compare this brutal system of forest exploitation with the benign yet efficacious methods employed by ASACODE. Gregorio, the landowner, had a say in which trees to fell. 'There might be occasions', explained Teodoro, 'when the landowner's choice strikes us as ecologically unsound – in that case, we'll tell him why, and between us we'll choose a different tree.' In this instance, Gregorio's wishes had coincided with those of ASACODE. A chainsaw was used to fell the trees and an Alaska mill to cut the trunks into planks; every part was being taken, from the thick trunks to thin branches. Removal of timber from the forest was done by Indian water buffalo rather than tractors. This practice had many virtues: it caused minimal disturbance to young trees and the ground flora, and the only fuel required was fodder for the animals. ASACODE now had three buffalo and the members felt that their prodigious strength and general usefulness had justified a considerable financial outlay of some US$2,000 each.

By inviting ASACODE rather than one of the big industrial companies to extract timber, Gregorio was gaining in two distinct ways. ASACODE's system of forest use was geared towards sustainability; its competitors' was not. Under ASACODE's regime Gregorio will be able to make a living from his forests year after year. It also made better financial sense – even in the short term – to work with ASACODE. For one thing, ASACODE recovered a greater portion of each felled tree than the logging companies; for another, they paid better. 'At the very most', said Teodoro, 'the industrial companies will pay 6 or 7 colones per square foot to the landowner, whereas we pay at least 10.' According to Felix, the industrial companies nearly always cheated the landowners by underestimating the amount of timber they took. 'If you take that into account', he said, 'they're really paying 4 or 5 colones rather than 6 or 7 per square foot.' As a member of ASACODE, Gregorio also stood to gain a share of any profits which the group made from its timber activities.

The wasteful habits of the industrial companies were not confined to the forest, and over 50 per cent of extracted timber ended up as debris on the wood-yard floor. Obviously, this meant that even more trees had to be felled to meet demand. In ASACODE's small wood-yard, half an hour's drive from Gregorio's farm, great efforts were made to utilize as much of the timber as possible. 'The industrial companies hate the way we run this yard', said Teodoro as he showed us round, 'because it shows how wasteful they are.' It was here, he explained, that ASACODE really increased the value of the wood, and at present it was unable to satisfy demand. The ASACODE wood-yard was processing five trees a month (they had set themselves a maximum of 45 trees for 1993) and Teodoro was in no doubt that even if the quantities of wood produced doubled or tripled, they would have no problem selling it. One could see the attraction for the customers, whether local *campesinos* constructing houses for themselves, or furniture-makers from the capital, San Jose: ASACODE's wood was 15 per cent cheaper than wood sold in Bri Bri or San Jose and, being a small enterprise, ASACODE was able to cater for individual tastes and requirements. At present ASACODE had no plans to expand its wood-yard activities or increase the amount of timber it handled. 'We're not like the industrial companies,' explained Teodoro. 'Their policies are governed by market forces, and short-term ones at that. ASACODE's are governed by sustainability.'

Over the past few years ASACODE had expended considerable energy on investigating the best ways of planting and managing forests. Most reforestation programmes in Costa Rica have concentrated on establishing monocultures of fast-growing species like laurel and eucalyptus. Such plantations are easy to establish and easy to manage; they also satisfy the timber industry's demands for uniformity. However, from an ecological point of view such plantations are virtually without value and no substitute for the richness of natural tropical forest. By setting up a Native Species Project, ASACODE was bucking the prevailing trend. 'As a group, we've always been against monocultures,' explained Teodoro. 'Forests exist with a multitude of species and we want to keep them like that. We're not against planting species like laurel, but it's important to plant other species alongside it.'

The Native Species Project began in 1989 at *finca* ASACODE, or ASACODE farm, a 70 hectare mix of virgin rainforest and secondary growth acquired with financial help from ANAI and IUCN, the International Union for the Conservation of Nature and Natural Resources. The route to the farm from the main road gives the visitor a taste of the conflicting interests in Lower Talamanca. You journey first through mile upon mile of banana plantations, a monotonous green enlivened only by the blue of the pesticide-impregnated plastic bags wrapped around each bunch of ripening fruit. Occasionally you pass a warehouse where workers pack the bananas, and clusters of houses where they and their families are billeted.[3] You won't see any birds or wild animals; you'll hear little other than the clank of the iron cableways carrying the bananas to the warehouses, or the sound of the articulated lorries thundering by as they cart the bananas up the coast to the jetties at Puerto Limon, whence they make the long journey to the supermarkets of Europe and the United States. Blemished bananas or fruit the wrong size or shape is simply left to rot; from time to time the visitor catches a whiff of the fermenting fruit, a whiff so foul that expansionist banana companies have been known to dump their waste on the doorsteps of *campesinos* reluctant to sell their land.

Eventually you leave the dirt road and drive beside a cableway through a plantation. After a few hundred yards you reach a deep drainage ditch, beyond which lies a scene of great rustic charm: José Luis Zuñiga's 47 hectare farm. His house, a wooden affair painted various shades of pastel green and blue, stands on sturdy stilts a few yards from the ditch. Beside it is a small orchard and an enclosure where he is rearing some peccaries – the wild pigs of Costa Rica's forests. Behind his house are some open fields grazed by horses and cattle and beyond lies tall forest. A few years ago the land across the ditch from José Luis's farm was similar to this: a mosaic of orchards, fields and scattered forest. But the banana companies had bought out the *campesinos* and now they wanted to get their hands on José Luis's property too. He had refused to sell, but his proximity to the new plantations made life difficult: a ditch had replaced the road which once linked his farm to the outside world, and the planes that sprayed pesticide on the bananas once a month had a habit of overflying his house and spraying his land. This was probably a deliberate act calculated to scare him into selling his property to the banana company.[4]

We arrived at José Luis's farm in time for lunch: rice, beans, vegetables and cheese followed by a sticky pudding made of cacao. Among those who prepared lunch was a teenage daughter of José Luis; she was learning to speak English and hoped to guide tourists to *finca* ASACODE. Once we had eaten, we made our way to the *finca*, a 40 minute walk, much of it through good forest. On our way there we stopped to watch a three-toed sloth munching leaves in the forest canopy and we passed a family of howler monkeys dozing in the crest of a small tree.

'If we were simply interested in making quick money', said José Luis as we inspected ASACODE's tree nursery, 'then we'd just grow commercial species. But there are many other reasons why we want to save the forest – for wildlife, for the medicinal plants it yields, for educational purposes... When we founded ASACODE we could see that people were destroying the forests and that if things carried on that way, many species of tree would disappear altogether.' Fifteen years ago farmers opening up land for cattle ranching accounted for nine-tenths of the forest which was cleared in Costa Rica; the wood industry was responsible for the remaining 10 per cent. This situation has now been reversed, with the wood industry responsible for 90 per cent of the forest destruction today. Over a period of twenty years the amount of forest within San Miguel was reduced from 2,300 hectares to around 1,440 hectares; in other words, over a third of the forest was cleared between 1970 and 1990. Of the 1,440 hectares that remained, only 417 hectares was primary forest unaltered by human activity. 'The loggers always go for the trees that give the greatest profit', continued José Luis, 'and species like *Cativo*, the plywood tree, have virtually been eliminated. Now we see it as our task to grow *Cativo* and other threatened species in the nursery and reintroduce them to the forests.'

At first ASACODE's members planted native tree seeds in the wild, but after a while they decided that they needed to learn more about the processes of germination and the conditions under which seedlings thrived. Felix Vasquez was responsible for collecting the seeds and bringing them to ASACODE's small nursery. 'What we are trying to do', explained Felix, 'is to find out how to germinate the seeds using the simplest techniques possible – that way, it will be easy for *campesinos* to raise seedlings themselves.' Felix and his colleagues had already learnt much from the exercise. 'Take this species, for example,' said Jose Luis, pointing to a box of *Almendro* seedlings. 'We found that if you plant this in the forest when it still has its first leaves – the cotyledons – the rats will eat it. So that affects the time when you must plant it.' ANAI had paid for several forest biologists to give training courses to ASACODE. These had evidently been much appreciated, but Luis Rodriguez felt that the real experts now were the *campesinos*. Felix could identify over 60 species of tree in their seedling stage, an astonishing achievement far beyond the capabilities of most botanists, and over the past few years he had acquired a thorough knowledge of the reproductive behaviour of over a hundred species. At regular intervals he checked specific trees in *finca* ASACODE to establish when they flowered, fruited and seeded. Sometimes he collected seeds from the forest floor; sometimes he had to climb the trees to collect them. ASACODE was also learning more about the forest's animal life. 'It's important we maintain the habitats of birds,' said José Luis at one point. He talked about the large, colourful macaws and their dependence on the fast-disappearing *Cativo* tree. 'If the *Cativo* disappear', he concluded, 'then so will the macaws – it's essential we maintain the bio-diversity of the forest.'

A short distance from the nursery ASACODE was conducting a unique experiment whose purpose was to study the growth rates, flowering habits and seeding behaviour of 27 different species of native tree. Three plots of the same size, each with 64 individual trees, had been established around a small hillock: one in full sun, one in partial shade and another in full shade. Although these plantations were only two years old, the trees in the sunny plot were already over 30 feet high. 'The trees grow much faster in full light, as you'd expect', explained Luis, 'but you have to do a tremendous amount of weeding. In the shady plots, growth rates are slower, but the *campesinos* don't have to expend lots of energy weeding.' Over the years ASACODE will learn more about the trees as the plantations age. 'At least we know that in twenty years' time there will be some good specimens here,' suggested Teodoro. 'We don't know what's going to happen to other farms round here – they might all disappear!' For these experimental trials ASACODE had chosen a wide variety of species. Some bore edible fruit, others were important for the quality of their wood. They had even planted trees which had medicinal properties: *hombre grande*, explained Teodoro, provided a substance which reduced fever and cleansed the blood, ideal for malaria sufferers. Mel Baker, having used it frequently himself, also sang its praises.

Economic endeavour in Talamanca has followed a cycle of boom and bust. Since United Fruit carved out the first of the great banana estates at the turn of the century, bananas have gone in and out of fashion with what, in hindsight, looks like dreary regularity. Midway through this century prices plummeted and many of the big companies went, leaving their land to be squatted by ex-plantation workers, Indians and outsiders. Then in the late 1980s there was another period of expansion, partially encouraged by government subsidies. While the agribusiness people staked their future on bananas, the *campesinos* relied on cacao. Boom came in the mid-'70s. World supplies fell following the political upheavals in West Africa's cacao-growing countries, and Costa Rica's *campesinos* suddenly saw the value of their crop spiral up from 25 cents a kilo to over US$2. Then in 1978 *monilia* disease struck and yields began to fall. In 1982 prices dropped considerably and by 1987 cacao was worth so little that most *campesinos* simply gave up looking after their trees.

'There's been a constant tendency', said Teodoro, 'for people to specialize. Once something makes money – whether it's bananas or cacao or cattle – people go for that and nothing else. That's what we're trying to avoid in ASACODE.' During the brief life of the organization, ASACODE has dabbled in a range of activities. It has experimented with the farming of green iguanas – a popular source of protein, especially among the local Indians – and José Luis has successfully bred peccaries, both to return to the wild and for the table. A charcoal oven has been set up behind Felix's house and ASACODE was now selling sacks of charcoal for around 500 colones. ASACODE was also selling seed collected by Felix from the trees at *finca* ASACODE.

However, all these ventures were small beer compared to ASACODE's ambitious eco-tourism project, which was centred on José Luis's farm and *finca* ASACODE. 'Right at the outset', explained José Luis, 'we knew that we wouldn't make money quickly with our Native Species Project, and we thought eco-tourism would help.' By early 1992 ASACODE had constructed a two-storey wooden building on its farm. There was a kitchen upstairs besides a large meeting area and four rooms with two or three beds in each. The lower floor had dormitory accommodation and outside there were showers and toilets. CASACODE, as the building was known, had been designed by José Luis and a Dutch volunteer; virtually all the money required for construction had been donated. It was exceptionally handsome and beautifully situated at the heart of the jungle, though so far few tourists had come. Indeed, there seemed to be some confusion in the minds of ASACODE's members about whether they should encourage tourists to visit the farm and stay here, or whether – as had happened so far – they should concentrate on bringing academics, college students and educational parties.

The few groups of tourists which had visited the farm had been taken on a trip which began with lunch at José Luis's home and progressed along an impressive series of wooden walkways to *finca* ASACODE and the primary forest beyond. ASACODE's members were still debating the best way to proceed with the eco-tourism. There was no shortage of tourists down at the coast in towns like Puerto Viejo, but San Miguel was a two-hour drive away along rough tracks poorly served by public transport. If eco-tourism was to take off in any significant way, there was a feeling that a consortium of interests around Lower Talamanca would have to cooperate. On the one hand, a consortium would encompass a large area in which tourists could visit a variety of habitats. On the other, various communities were needed to agree upon the protection of 'biological corridors' where plants and animals could thrive and exchange genetic material.

In the meantime, ASACODE was using the building on its farm more as a study centre than a hotel. Over the past couple of years ASACODE had played host to the United Nation's Food and Agriculture Organization (FAO), CATIE and IUCN. Many colleges and schools had dispatched groups to see ASACODE's work and many villagers had come too. 'There are a couple of excellent forest research centres in Costa Rica', said Luis Rodriguez, the ANAI forester, 'but they're very expensive to visit and their research is oriented towards pure science. This is the only place in the country where a bunch of villagers can come and learn from the experiences of another bunch of villagers who are working out ways of sustainably harvesting the forest.'

Perhaps ASACODE's greatest achievement has been to show that tropical forests have a far greater value, both in pecuniary and ecological terms, when their bounty is sustainably tapped rather than indiscriminately plundered. The realization that forests are worth much more in the hands of a group like ASACODE than if conventionally exploited has meant that land values round San Miguel have risen. Paradoxically, this had worked against ASACODE, which was eager to buy the 18 hectare block of pristine forest which lay between *finca* ASACODE and another patch of forest belonging to ANAI. The owners of the land were asking around $25,000, several times more than they would have demanded a few years before.

Many environmental stories are cast in the mould of David against Goliath, and this is no exception, with Goliath's role being played by the industrial logging companies, the banana barons and, less obviously, by government legislation which discriminates against the *campesinos* of the forests. However, it would be wrong to think of ASACODE as a defenceless David working in isolation. ASACODE has received tremendous support from Asociacion ANAI and from organizations like IUCN. ANAI has not only helped ASACODE with grants and loans, it has also provided technical, scientific and administrative expertise, and brought the villagers of San Miguel into contact with others in Talamanca who are also trying to use the forests sustainably.

ANAI was founded in 1973 by Bill McLarney, an American biologist, with the specific goal of helping the *campesinos* to save the tropical forest in Talamanca. Its first venture focused on a 7 hectare plot of remote forest, but it now operates throughout the region. One of ANAI's initial objectives was to help the *campesinos* diversify away from the cacao monoculture; to do this it set up two experimental farms and helped some 25 villages establish community nurseries. 'Unfortunately, agriculture looks like a poorer and poorer option for the *campesinos*,' said Diego Lynch, ANAI's director, who joined us on our last evening in Talamanca. 'In the nurseries people have grown all sorts of crops – timber-bearing trees, fruit trees, vanilla, black pepper, cinnamon – but for many of these, as for cacao, the world market prices have gone through the floor recently.' An estimated 6,000 people – approximately one-fifth of Talamanca's population – have benefited from the nurseries, which have produced over a million seedlings.

Mel Baker had experienced at first hand the problems of relying on a single crop and for the past eight years he had been intimately involved with ANAI's work. 'In the early days', he recalled, 'we had great difficulty in convincing *campesinos* that they should try something other than cacao, and at first they just wanted better, higher-yielding hybrid varieties of the crop.' Although many villages had allowed their nurseries to run down, Mel felt that they had played a vital role in sensitizing people to the problems of growing monocultures. 'They have also played an important catalytic role,' continued Mel. 'The people here tended to be very individualistic; they had little tradition of working together. But the nurseries got community organization off the ground.'

According to Diego Lynch, ANAI had identified key individuals like Teodoro and José Luis at an early stage and worked patiently with them over a long period, encouraging them to take an interest in environmental problems and to work towards community-based solutions. 'We started with small, concrete activities and projects', explained Diego, 'and we concentrated our efforts on initiating things which would be successful.' Initially, the projects were heavily subsidized, but recently ANAI switched to giving loans at favourable terms. 'We were very wary at first,' recalled Diego. 'We didn't want our support to degenerate into paternalism. We'd get something started, and let them get on with it, being watchful for when they needed help. We tried to let them flounder for a while before providing what was needed. Their experience is probably one of constantly struggling to keep afloat, and feeling somewhat abandoned by us.'

Diego felt that a key element in ASACODE's success had been the combination of strong leaders like Teodoro Lopez and Armando Vasquez and steady followers like Felix Vasquez. 'They're all honest, committed people,' reflected Diego. 'The presence of a highly motivated family is the only common thread in all the communities where we see a high potential for creating initiatives like ASACODE's. Other communities which lack this element of a key family simply don't seem to have the same potential.'

ANAI has backed many other groups in Talamanca beside ASACODE. For instance, it has supported a variety of educational ventures, being a key player in Shiroles Experimental Farm in the Bribri Indian Reservation and the owner of two educational farms where *campesinos* can observe and discuss the management of a variety of crops from *platanos* to cassava, from pepper to vanilla. In 1987 it helped establish a regional association – APPTA – to coordinate the buying, processing and marketing of agricultural and forestry produce. It ANAI has also set up a programme to train 'barefoot agronomists', or community promoters, most of whom are Indians living and working in Indian communities. Under this scheme promoters trained by ANAI act as an unofficial agricultural extension service.[5]

This is all very admirable, but will it help to save the lowland tropical forests from further devastation? As Teodoro Lopez had said when we walked through the native species plantations at *finca* ASACODE, 'We don't know what's going to happen to other farms round here – they might all disppear!' By which he meant the landowners might sell out to the banana companies or allow the big logging companies to work out their forests. Sadly, Costa Rica's forest laws are highly discriminatory, making it ridiculously hard for *campesinos* to make a living from their trees but all too easy for the large companies. Wherever we went, we heard people complain about the laws that governed commercial activity in the forest. 'The laws are stacked against the small users in a whole range of ways,' explained Luis Rodriguez. 'You have to remember that most of the laws – and they're not always entirely clear – were made in the days when the forests were owned by the state; now all forested land outside protected areas is privately owned.' There is a basic presumption in Costa Rican law that the improvement of land is synonymous with the felling of forest for agriculture. For instance, while a farmer can use a pig or a cow as collateral to raise loans, he cannot use a tree, whose potential value might be far greater. Yet ASACODE is showing that the rosiest future in Talamanca lies not in traditional agricultural practices – whether corn-growing or cattle-ranching – but in the sustainable use of forests.

Another legal anomaly relates to the permission needed to fell trees. While the law encourages small groups such as ASACODE to reforest land, these groups cannot apply for permission to fell trees.[6] Permits are only given to individual landowners, which makes the collective management of forests all the more difficult. 'We have to do everything by guile', confirmed Teodoro, 'as the government refuses to support small groups like us.' Actually, getting a permit is no easy matter either; in Bribri Indian Reservation we met one individual who complained that he even had to seek permission to fell trees which he had planted himself, and to get permission he would have to make several long and expensive journeys to the forestry department in a distant town.

It may be hard for individual *campesinos* to get permission to cut a tree, but it is easy for the big logging companies. 'Things are getting worse, not better', argued Luis, 'and there's a lot of corruption, with the big companies paying the forest inspectors to turn a blind eye to some of their exploits.' In recent months, the industrial loggers had been arguing for the introduction of a law which would forbid the use of the chainsaw, the indispensable tool of the small producers like ASACODE. They had also been agitating to get ASACODE's wood-yard closed down.

The week before we visited San Miguel, a local landowner had reneged on a deal he had made to allow an industrial logging company to fell some of his trees. He had decided to work with ASACODE instead. The message was getting through: the symbiotic approach to forest management was not only better for the forest, it was better for the landowners too. Goliath may have the strength, and the political influence, but David has the guile.

9

ECUADOR

Licto and Salinas Communities

'The minga gives us land, the land gives us food!'

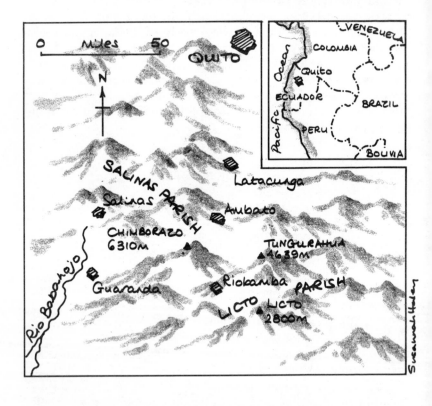

It was very early in the morning and the air was so cold that it hurt to breathe. The rising sun was gradually illuminating the lanes of Riobamba, revealing a few wood and stucco buildings, dating from the beginning of this century, amidst the drab cement faces of the newer constructions. A chain of mountains stood sharply against the sky, encircling the whole valley.

We went through a few squares, each with its pastel church facade, walked along a market buzzing with colourfully dressed peasants, and finally reached the outskirts of town. Our meeting was to take place in a flat building open to internal patios full of flower bushes. Several Indian peasants – each in hat and poncho – were sitting on the benches lining the patio, in stillness and silence. We had come to the provincial headquarters of the Ecuadorian Centre for Agricultural Services (CESA) – one of the largest non-governmental organizations supporting peasant farmers in Ecuador – to learn about the soil recuperation activities of some local communities.

'When we started working in Licto,[1] about four years ago, some people were using dynamite to break up the soil,' said Guillelmo Teran. 'The local name for such soil – it's as hard and unproductive as cement – is *cangahua*.' Guillelmo – the coordinator of the Licto programme of CESA – was an impressive looking character. Immaculately dressed, he had penetrating eyes and a mass of black hair which he often pushed off his forehead with a determined gesture. Everyone addressed him not as Guillelmo but as *Campeon*, or champion, and he later confessed to be proud of the nickname, which to him meant champion of the interests of the *Indios*[2] ... the one who fights hard for them and cannot be defeated.

The idea of using dynamite to break up the soils was imported by peasants doing temporary work for companies that dug tunnels, set up irrigation facilities and so forth. 'At first, we went along with it', recalled Campeon, 'and we offered advice on how to use the dynamite safely. To tell the truth, we actually bought dynamite to help two communities, but the results were not at all good. The soil was broken only slightly, and the risks for the peasants involved were too high.' CESA examined some alternatives, such as buying a tractor and rotavator, but that would have been very expensive and required skilled labour – soil recuperation would have become more a project of CESA than of the communities themselves. They finally decided to support traditional, pre-dynamite methods of soil recuperation by offering technical advice and tools. 'And even this was done sparingly,' concluded Campeon, 'only when there was a real necessity.'

'A real necessity' must be a hard predicament indeed for peasants in the High Andes, one of the most forbidding environments on earth. Most of such peasants – indigenous Indians who speak the Quechua language – were driven into the mountains by waves of colonizers and speculators who appropriated for themselves the lower, flatter, more easily irrigated and more fertile land. The Indian communities were left to cultivate rock-hard soils, on steep slopes and under extremes of temperature and rainfall. There, it is not uncommon for the lack of rain and the burning sun to leave the soil as dry as a hot stone for months; then, all of a sudden, a cloud may burst and wash away the seeds, or a summer hailstorm may shred the leaves off the plants. At other times the rains do not come at all and the ground remains barren, fully exposed to wind erosion.

CESA came to Licto, explained Campeon, as it was one of the poorest and most depressed areas of the whole Ecuador.[3] Some of his collaborators – till now they sat silently while Campeon talked – nodded and backed his assertion with bits of disturbing information. 'When we arrived, child mortality was over 50 per cent!' said one. 'There was hardly any firewood or timber to build houses,' added another. 'All the trees had been cut down and none were being planted.' The Indians paid taxes and provided soldiers, cheap labour and agricultural produce for the rest of the country, but the government scarcely offered any social services in return. Many families were unable to grow sufficient food to sustain themselves, especially those living in the villages at mid-elevation, where the ground is very steep and the soil particularly poor.

The High Andes can be subdivided into three relatively well distinguished ecological zones. Above 3,500 metres there are pastures for the grazing of animals and land where tubers can be cultivated. Between 2,300 and 3,500 metres, grains such as maize and *quinoa* are grown, and below 1,400 metres there are fruit trees and coca, as well as grains and vegetables.[4] A community living in one of these zones has a compelling necessity to relate to people in other zones in order to supplement its diet and decrease ecological risks, for example of crop failure. This takes place through relationships of solidarity within the *ayllu*, the clan that unites households from communities situated in different ecological zones. Among the people in the clan there is a constant circulation of products and a sense of obligation in time of adversity. Interestingly, women tend to marry within their *ayllu*. In contrast to crops and blood ties, however, services and reciprocities related to work are established within one's own village, the community of the same ecological zone.

In the last decades, parcelling among siblings, selling in extreme poverty and ecological degradation have created an alarming, progressive decrease in the size of plots owned by Indian families.[5] The Ecuadorian census of 1974 found that in the parish of Licto the average holding per family was about 2.75 hectares. By 1989, this had diminished to about 0.5 hectares. With less than half a hectare of land, a family cannot produce enough to eat and is forced to look for food and income in different ways from agriculture. Most men – the figure for Licto is 81.5 per cent – end up migrating to the towns, to large *haciendas* (farms) or to the sugar cane and banana plantations along the coast. Typically, they stay away several months and come back only for a few weeks, usually around the time of a religious festivity.

Scarcity of land per household, scarcity of good soil, scarcity of water, scarcity of trees and vegetable cover, scarcity of employment opportunities, scarcity of governmental services, scarcity of money... scarcity typifies the Andean Sierra – a severe and unforgiving border between earth and sky. Only by exercising their ingenuity and working extremely hard, do the local people manage to cope.

Rosario Auraucela, an Indian peasant active in soil recuperation, accompanied us to see a communal plot in Pungalbug, one of the 26 communities which made up the Licto parish. For the past ten years her husband had been forced to leave the parish to find work elsewhere. Her five children – the eldest was now twenty – helped her to work the small family plot. She talked swiftly, her eyes attentive and vaguely ironic, her speech full of diminutives, an ingratiating habit among Ecuadorians. We were her 'little friends'; she was happy to show us the 'little plot' where they now grew some 'little oats'. The blue shawl around her shoulders was held in place by a silvery pin; around her waist she wore a yellow band with orange embroidery. When we reached the communal 'little plot' she broke into a terrific smile, her brown teeth showing great satisfaction for the progress made so far.

'Do you see that plot?' she asked, pointing to an acre of terrace whose soil had been broken into large pieces. 'It was left idle for a long time because it was *cangahua*, hard as cement – not even eucalyptus would grow there. Among the "little women" in the community we talked for years about recuperating it, but nothing was done because many of us wanted to wait for the men to do the work. Finally, when CESA offered some "little tools" and "little seeds", the community decided to organize the *minga*.'

The *minga* is a central event in the lives of Indian communities, and a main avenue of people's solidarity.[6] It is communal work, decided upon and regulated by the community members themselves during their assembly at the end of each month. Every family sends a member for the *minga*, which can be called upon to maintain a road, open an irrigation channel, support people who are sick, cultivate the land and many other things. The *minga* usually happens once a week, from 9 in the morning till 3 in the afternoon. After work the people might eat together, or conclude their efforts with a drinking party. If a family does not fulfil its obligations, it will be subjected to heavy social pressure.[7]

The process of recuperating *cangahua* to productive use is extremely laborious and can take two to three years. Work begins after heavy rain, the wet soil (*cangahua* is 95 per cent impermeable to water) being broken up by hammering a sharp wedge into it. The peasants know about special textures and treads where they can insert the instruments to work more easily. Broken into large hard pieces, the soil is turned over in order to let the rain soften it further. Several months later the soil is broken into smaller pieces and mixed with whatever organic matter the peasants can collect from their animals. By the first winter, the soil is usually soft enough to be planted with lentils and oats, which are then cut and mixed into the ground as a green manure. After that, a crop of barley is generally sown. Finally, after some more manuring, the preferred crops of maize and potatoes are planted. The soil is now fully recuperated.

Rosario continued: 'Seventy-one families participated in the *minga* for this plot, and most of us, although not all – have to send women. It is now six months that every Thursday I come here and work. We break the soil, we rebuild old terraces, we dig channels for the water. The other plot there we have been working for more than two years, and now it produces lentils, oats and even some maize. We share these products among the community's households. The *minga* gives us land, the land gives us food!'

Three and a half years ago, when CESA first began to support the work of soil recuperation, the *minga* were nearly always called on to take care of communal plots. Now the practice was spreading to private land, with people working on the individual plots on a rotational basis (in this case the *minga* is called *prestamano*). Before leaving us – her blue shawl swinging right and left while she ran back to interrupted chores – Rosario told us that a *prestamano* was going on that very day in Laurel Gompueno, one of Licto's communities at a higher elevation.

It was now early afternoon and we decided to head for Laurel Gompueno. The air was unseasonably hot. In the far distance, high above us and across an unbroken mosaic of fields, we could make out a small plot crowded with colourfully dressed peasants. We arrived just as the day's work ended. Some people were cleaning their tools; others had already left, small dots of colour receding fast into the distant landscape. A well defined trapezium of land was neatly broken into medium-sized chunks of dark soil. A couple of dogs yapped around a few individuals who were sharing food, sitting and chatting among themselves. We sat down with some youngsters. There was plenty of teasing among the young men and women, and plenty of laughter too. None of them could have been older than twenty, but many of the men had already made several journeys to work far from Laurel Gompueno. They all said that life was better here than anywhere else, and that they came back to their village as soon as they managed to put aside a little money. The soil of the plot they had worked on today was very hard *cangahua* just a few months ago; soon they would plant it with oats and lentils. CESA had been helping them. It had sent a doctor to take care of the children, helped in the construction of some irrigation works and given them agricultural tools, including the hoes and shovels that some had used today.

CESA's aim is to support local initiatives without imposing its own agenda. For example, communities organize themselves as they see fit and CESA does not promote any new structure, not even a women's group, the great favourite among many other organizations working in the Andes. It is only because most men go elsewhere in search of jobs, that CESA inevitably ends up working with groups where women predominate. Increasingly, women in Andean communities take up activities that were a traditional male prerogative. For instance, today they play a more important role in decision-making. One often finds women voicing their family concerns and defending their interests during communal assemblies.[8] But they have also taken on the heaviest agricultural jobs and this is on top of their traditional roles. A woman must now till the land and plant seeds as well as decide where and when to do it; a few years ago, this was exclusively the man's work. In a culture as gender conscious as the Quechua one, this amounts to a profound revolution.

Campeon said he felt ashamed when he saw women – sometimes with children on their backs – carrying out very heavy agricultural tasks. 'And yet', he added, 'we cannot and do not want to impose change from outside. Our most significant contribution is the impulse we provide by calling the communities to discuss issues and make their own plans. Our project does provide some help, but only when a community is resolved to act.[9] This is why we like to support the work of soil recuperation. For the Quechua Indians, nothing is more important than the land. It is not only a matter of production; it is a matter of personal and cultural identity.'

Over four years, approximately 50 hectares of unproductive *cangahua* have been recuperated in the communities of the Licto parish. This is an admirable achievement, which alleviates but does not solve the problem of land scarcity. People are still trying to get more land, for instance by buying back from the *haciendas* the fields on which their ancestors lived decades or even centuries ago.[10] CESA and others – including the Catholic church – have been giving them a helping hand.

First came a mule, led by a small child, then a few sheep, a black cow and a woman wearing a bright red shawl and a Borsalino hat. Behind her was another child directing a pig with a stick and man in a brown poncho with a hoe on his shoulder. Far behind was a small girl with rosy cheeks. She picked up a small dog and anxiously held it to her chest as our four-wheel drive car passed by, zig-zagging among potholes full of water. It was raining, but no one seemed to mind. The bland green of the pasture, the dark green of crops and the wet black of the soil glistened in an organic mosaic up to the far horizon.

We had been offered a ride by two doctors assisting health personnel in isolated mountain villages. They worked for a national non-governmental organisation and today were going to run a workshop on the prevention of cholera.[11] 'Did you see that family at the side of the road?' asked one. 'Early in the morning, this is one of the most common sights in the Andes – a family and all the animals in procession towards the fields.' High up, in the *paramo* above 4,000 metres, the clouds hung close to the ground, which was covered with lichens the colour of snow.[12] The mist briefly opened to give a glimpse of the majestic white cone of Chimborazo. The Quechua culture delights in understanding the world through complementary pairs of concepts such as father and mother, hot and cold, male and female. Even the word 'being' is double: what is one is incomplete. Chimborazo – a conical volcano usually crowned by clouds – is the 'great father' of all the mountains (and, at 6,310 metres, the tallest peak in Ecuador). The mother is Tunguragua – lower and gentler in shape, yet a powerful volcano which has erupted many times in the last 300 years.

Salinas parish straddled a great chunk of mountainside, encompassing wet sub-tropical forest in its lower reaches, some 800 metres above sea level, and the more barren *paramo* over 4,000 metres. Unlike other parishes, all its communities, locally called *recintos*, were involved in some sort of development initiative.[13] There were 17 small cheese factories, a wool-weaving industry with 80 employees, handicraft shops, a bakery, a hotel, a charcoal unit, a pork industry, mechanic and carpentry workshops, a mill, a women's enterprise producing sweaters, an artificial fishpond, a chocolate factory and much else besides. People had stopped leaving the area in search of work, and indeed outsiders had begun to settle there. In addition, the parish, and in particular the land around Salinas village, at an elevation of 3,500 metres, was known as one of the greenest and woodiest environments in the High Sierra. If you asked why the place is so special, everyone replied that people there are well organized, and that – of course – they have Father Antonio.

From Riobamba the trip to Salinas took us about ten hours. We had to get lifts with occasional travellers and wait patiently in between. No public transport served the parish and the road was a collection of potholes. As soon as we arrived we rushed to see Father Antonio, who was about to leave for Quito. We found him in his kitchen, greeting visitors, assigning duties to colleagues and frantically looking for a piece of machinery that he intended to take to Quito to be repaired. 'No, there was no initial coherent plan,' he said as soon as we had explained the purpose of our visit. 'Certainly, we built on the sense of the community among the people. It was an important strength – perhaps the only one we found here – although more a result of necessity than of conscious will. We in the mission tried to deepen it by adding a religious motivation – we are all sons and daughters of the same God – and by modernizing it to face the new realities.' When the mission arrived 23 years ago, poverty was striking. It was clear that people could not survive on what they produced from the land alone. Yet there was no salaried employment opportunity, and men were beginning to drift towards the cities. There was a clear need, said Father Antonio, to process the local crops, to start some industry and create jobs. The mission suggested to the people that they should unite in producer cooperatives.

Today, virtually all people in the parish of Salinas are organized in cooperatives, and all the cooperatives are associated in a union, the Union de Organizaciones Campesinas de Salinas (UNORSAL).[14] The cooperatives are rather unusual, since they do not divide profits among individual members but keep them as common property. Individuals get money for the products they bring to process – for example, milk, pork, wool – or a salary when they are employed. They also get some form of social security, for instance free medicines when they are sick. All profits, however, are reinvested for the common good.

'When I first arrived', explained Father Antonio, 'I was struck not only by the poverty, but also by the sad state of the environment, and in particular by the almost complete absence of trees. I always loved nature and started planting trees simply because I wanted to see more green in the area. Slowly, conversations arose on the ecological and economic benefits of trees. People felt that the environment was in need of care, but they could not afford to behave differently. They needed incentives, and the mission managed to procure some help from outside.' Incentives came in various forms, from long-term loans at favourable conditions to free technical advice, from linkage to markets to training fellowships.

Father Antonio looked at his watch, apologized and departed for Quito, instructing Bayron Casignia, a key technical adviser of UNORSAL, to show us round the parish. It was very cold and wet in Salinas and the only warm place in town was the eating room attached to the local bakery, appropriately called *Salon Caliente*, or Hot Saloon. We headed there with Bayron and sat down for tea, enjoying the dry heat and the pleasant smell of freshly baked bread. 'Sometimes, when you walk in the High Sierra, you still find a native tree', said Bayron, 'but usually nothing remains of the original forest. All you can see is grass, which offers the soil some protection, but the winter rains, the summer winds and the herders' fires inevitably lead to erosion of the land.[15] That's why we have landslides, sometimes of great proportions. Even the herders say that the pasture is drying out and that the seeds they spread for animal fodder do not do as well as before. There is a serious risk that the *paramo* will become a desert.' Bayron spoke with a soft voice, periodically stopping to sip some tea and greet those who came in to buy bread or simply to have a moment of warmth. 'But Salinas is much better than other areas in the Sierra,' he continued. 'Father Antonio did much to make people think about the environment. In the last two decades, we have planted some three million trees. The Grupo Juvenil alone planted 600 hectares, bought with the help of a foreign aid organization.[16] They carried on foot hundreds of thousands of seedlings to the area of reforestation, more than 10 kilometres from here.'

With the help of the Salesian Mission, a contract was signed between the Grupo Juvenil and EMDEFOR, a national company that provided pine seedlings and agreed to manage the trees for 60 per cent of the income expected from the timber. Little by little the idea of reforestation began to appeal to other communities which owned *paramo*. Today, more than 90 per cent of the communities of the parish have their own forested areas, all developed by *minga*. Most of the tree planting for intensive production involves pines, since local varieties take longer to grow and have less commercial value. Households, however, plant trees to prevent erosion, to improve the water retention of the soil and to act as windbreaks, and for these purposes local varieties are often chosen.

Reforestation has been fraught with difficulties. The Grupo Juvenil lost 300 hectares – nearly all planted – to some speculators. Local domestic animals found many seedlings too good to leave. Now the pine woods had to be managed, yet EMDEFOR was doing little to help. Every hectare of wood required about US$1,000 in tools and skilled labour and the parish had about 2,000 hectares in need of management. So far, the Inter-

American Foundation had provided financial support (a matching fund), but far less than was actually needed.

So how were the communities raising the finance required? 'We tried to sell firewood', replied Bayron, 'but a small truckload sells for 5–6,000 sucres (a few US$) and it costs 25,000 sucres just to cover the road. We tried to make charcoal, but pine produces too much smoke and not much heat, and the risk of fires is enormous when the wind blows hard in the dry season. We are in trouble, but we are not going to give up. We are now exploring whether we can get the management money from a small wood processing plant or from the resin we can collect from the pines.'

Victor Janchaliquin was more of a *Mestizo* than a pure Indian.[17] He was born in Simiatug, a remote community in the region of Chimborazo, and was the only one of seven brothers not to have migrated to a distant town. 'I like living here,' he said, scanning the horizon around us. We were standing at the top of a hill overlooking the village of Salinas. Behind the village, at the foot of a gorge, we could see a bubbling stream and a rocky area scattered with numerous pools. This was the salt mine, the *salina* that gave the village its name. A quarter of a century ago salt extraction was the main occupation of the village inhabitants.

In those days people were extremely poor, malnutrition was widespread and most children failed to survive beyond the age of five. Salt was the only resource people could exchange for food and other products, but the mine itself was property of the Cordobes family, who took 60 per cent of all the revenues.[18] Salt was greatly valued in the area, not least because communications with the coast, the only other source of salt, were very primitive.[19] Women would collect salty water from the mine and bring it to the village, where they would boil it to extract the salt. Men were in charge of collecting the wood to sustain the fires. It was common to see a man leading five or six mules down the mountain, all charged with firewood. As fires were burning constantly, the mules were constantly trekking up the mountains to fetch more wood. Eventually, the Sierra around Salinas was stripped of all trees.

This was the situation in the early 1970s, when the Salesian Mission settled in the parish.

The morning sky was clear blue, but we could see rain-clouds gathering in the distance. The landscape consisted of a mosaic of pasture, cropland and pine forest. Trees lined the fields and the road we took from the village up to the top of the hill. 'Most of all, I like planting trees,' announced Victor. 'Seven years ago I bought this piece of land in front of us and planted all the pines you see. Now I have enough firewood for cooking and for the fireplace, and I can even get some good pieces of timber. In about fifteen years, I will have a large harvest of timber to sell and will make lots of money from it. And, of course, there are the mushrooms.'

Victor was said to be one of the most capable mushroom collectors in Salinas. The mushrooms – *Boletus luteus* – were first noticed by Father Antonio, an Italian accustomed to eating wild mushrooms as a culinary delicacy. He had the mushrooms analysed, found them to be fit for consumption, and on the ground of the enormous quantities produced around the pines, suggested that they could be harvested and sold.

'At first', recalled Victor, 'we dried the mushrooms in the sun, but the wind used to blow many away. Sometimes it rained and the mushrooms rotted. In fact, the quality of the product was not constant nor very good. In 1990 however we decided to invest in the project, and acquired an industrial diesel dryer.'

So far, the production of mushrooms had been more important for its social benefits than for its economic profitability. Anyone is free to collect the mushrooms in the woods and sell them to the drying plant, and the poor were obviously the ones who took most advantage of this opportunity.[20] In 1993 the price paid for mushrooms at the drying plant was 90–100 sucres a pound, and a person could collect 100–150 kilos a day. It was a good source of income for individual collectors, but still a shaky business for the community group that managed it. In 1992, the parish produced 10,000 kilos of dry mushrooms, which was too much for the national market, but still too little for the international one. And the loan for the drying plant had yet to be paid. With the support of foreign volunteers, efforts were currently focused on improving the quality of the mushrooms and marketing them more effectively.

On our way back to Salinas, Victor pointed to a bunch of

mushrooms sprouting from the dark ground around the roots of a pine. They were small, solid and shiny. He picked the largest ones. 'Aren't they beautiful,' he said. Now and again he stooped to pick medicinal herbs: *matise* – for stomach disorders and skin diseases; *nisbe* – anti-inflammatory with some of the properties of penicillin; and *chicory* – good for the liver and the digestive system. He also pointed out a *floripondio*, a native tree covered with yellow-red bells which gave off a powerful, inebriating scent. The plant is known to have insecticidal properties, and the peasants extract from the bells a juice to fumigate potatoes. A decoction of the flowers is said to be a good analgesic and a cure for insomnia.

It was now midday and the first drops of what was soon to be torrential rain kicked up the dust on the road as we reached the edge of the village.

10

THE PHILIPPINES
The Hook and Line Fishers' Organization

'We'd sorted out the pirates and the coastguards; now we had to take on the trawlers'

'Fishing used to be so much easier!' exclaimed Beloy Alicaya, the chairman of SM79, a fishers' organization in the village of San Diego. 'Back in the 1970s and early '80s we used to catch many times more fish than we do now. Before the big trawlers and the purse-seiners came into our waters we could easily make 400 pesos a day. We were furious if we earnt less; now we'd be thrilled to get that much.' Beloy had been out fishing with his son for four hours in the morning; they had caught just 1 kilo of fish, worth approximately 20 pesos ($0.75). In a couple of hours they would be setting off again: February was generally a poor month for fishing and Beloy was pessimistic about the chances of a decent catch.

It was now mid-afternoon and a languid, heat-of-the-day feel had settled on the village. A muggy breeze rustled the nipa-palm walls of the hut where we sat and coconut fronds crackled above the thatched roofs of the fishers' homes. Near-by a group of men hammered and chattered as they put the finishing touches to a new *banca*, the traditional outrigger canoe used by the subsistence fishers of the Philippines. The acrid smell of distilled sugar jarred the senses, as did the sound of a man and woman squabbling behind us. 'Lovers' tiff,' grinned Beloy, a powerfully built man with a broad, handsome face.

Samahang Mangangawil 79 (SM79) – the Hook and Line Fishers' Organization – was initially established to counter the problem of piracy. Between 1969 and 1979 pirates from Manila Bay frequently journeyed south to rob the *bancas* on San Diego beach of their motors. 'On one occasion', recalled Beloy, 'we lost five motors; on another, four; once it was two ...' The fishers decided to organize vigils and every night for the past fourteen years a group of men has patrolled the sea front. There has been no more piracy. In 1979 SM79 was formally set up; with the help of university students who were undertaking community development studies, the fishers wrote a constitution and established an electoral system. At first members paid a due of 10 pesos a year; now it is 25 pesos a month and membership stands at around 120. Initially, SM79 was simply concerned with the immediate welfare of its members; for example, the membership fund was used to pay for searches when fishers disappeared at sea.

The local coastguards also took money from the fishers. In 1979 the fishers were told to pay 35 pesos registration fee for three years. 'That supposedly paid for the coastguards,' explained Beloy. 'We were dubious about that, but we still paid up.' In fact, the fee should have been 15 pesos, and when the fishers found out they protested. The official responsible for overcharging – he had siphoned the extra 20 pesos from each fisher into his own pocket – was transferred once the fishers discovered the ruse, and SM79's 120 members were paid back 20 pesos each. 'Well, that made 2,400 pesos', recalled Beloy, 'and we spent the money on a big celebration. After that we decided it was time to tackle the main problem – the declining fish catch. We'd sorted out the pirates and the coastguards; now we had to take on the trawlers.'

Under Philippine law the waters within 7 kilometres of the coast are reserved for the country's 700,000 municipal fishers – the men (and occasionally women) who fish from small wooden *bancas*; some use a hook and line, others use gill nets, small trawls, seines, fish corrals and push nets. Commercial fishing vessels over 3 tonnes are not allowed to enter within the 7 kilometre municipal limit. By the beginning of the 1980s the fishers of San Diego found themselves in competition with trawlers which ignored the law. 'Our first efforts didn't amount to all that much,' explained Beloy. SM79 took its grievances about the trawlers to the local mayors, to the coastguards, to the Philippine Constabulary and to the Minister of Natural Resources. As a result, the coastguard was ordered to apprehend trawlers fishing within municipal limits. 'We reported the trawlers which came inside the limit to the coastguard', explained Beloy, 'but they just paid a fine of 100 pesos and went straight back to fish the same water.' SM79 decided on a new tack: the members would sail out in their *bancas*, without coastguard officials, and catch the trawlers themselves. Since 1983 the fishers of San Diego have arrested getting on for 40 trawlers. In 1985 the fishers filed a complaint with the Philippines Navy after witnessing several trawlers actually being escorted by the coastguards. Once, SM79 even apprehended a trawler owned by a military man.

'On one occasion', recalled Beloy, 'we borrowed a shotgun off a retired colonel and bought some toy guns.' On 28 February 1991 300 fishers in 30 *bancas* gave chase to a trawler. The trawler refused to stop, so the fishers shot across its bows with the Colonel's shotgun, waved their pistols and made as if to dynamite their quarry (with bottles filled with sand to look like sticks of dynamite). The trawler stopped and its skipper signed a standard document, drawn up by SM79 and used in these situations; this attested to the fact that the skipper had voluntarily given up his catch and his registration forms. The fishers returned triumphantly to the shore and handed the registration forms to the coastguard. The confiscated catch was sold and the proceeds were used to buy rice, which was distributed to every household in San Diego.

'At one time, when the trawler problem was at its height, you could see twenty or more of them fishing inside our waters,' said Beloy. 'I think we've now won the battle against the small Filipino trawlers – but there's not much that we can do about the large Taiwanese vessels that come; you can't surround them with *bancas* and scale up the sides.'

At 5 o'clock in the afternoon – the sun already sinking fast over the South China Sea – we made our way down to the shore. The sandy beach was littered with colourfully painted *bancas* which had fine names like *Summer Kisses, Jesus Christ, Wilbert, Endless Love*... Beloy and his teenage son prepared their fishing lines, lit a paraffin lamp and pushed off into the dusk. Four hours later they returned home with the evening catch: 3 kilos of small fish.[1]

A generation ago fishing was a part-time occupation in most of the Philippines; it was something which men did to supplement their incomes as farmers or labourers. Talk to any of the older fishers in San Diego and they will tell you how they used to catch enough fish in one trip to feed their families for several days. In the 1970s and early '80s Beloy prospered: with the money he earnt from fishing he was able to build a house for his family. It has a concrete floor, a toilet, a kitchen, two bedrooms, electricity, hand-pumped water and a black-and-white television; the walls are more breeze block than bamboo and by San Diego's standards it is a substantial, typhoon-resistant dwelling. Those days of plenty have gone. As the population of landless rose, more and more people descended to the coast and took to fishing; denied the opportunity by the country's feudal system of land tenure to make a living as farmers, they turned understandably to the sea, whose resources, for a variety of reasons, were already in decline. Part-time fishers were forced to become full-time, and even so their living standards plummeted: no young fishers in San Diego today could dream of building a house like Beloy's. Indeed, a survey carried out in March 1991 put the net income of the motorized *bancas* on this stretch of coast at 1,830 pesos a month; that of non-motorized *bancas* at 665 pesos a month. The government's poverty threshold at that time was 4,162 pesos a month.

A complex mixture of factors has conspired to depress fish stocks. Commercial trawlers are obviously having a major impact on the coastal fisheries. Trawling – whether with bag-net or purse-seine – is a very efficient business, capturing large quantities of fish in a short period of time. It also tends to be a wasteful operation, as the trawlers often catch fish of no commercial value – trash species, as they are known. In shallow waters heavy trawling gear frequently breaks up coral reefs and damages the fragile sea bottom, and this has undoubtedly contributed to the present woes of the municipal fishers.

In the Philippines 2,000 species of fish, many of commercial importance, are associated with coral reefs, which provide a home, food and spawning grounds for a fabulous diversity of marine wildlife. Destroy the reefs and the sea is turned into an aqueous desert. In 1981 a survey of coral reefs in the Philippines found that only 5 per cent survived in a pristine or 'excellent' state; 70 per cent was described as 'poor', having lost half or more of its living coral cover. Coral reefs, it is said, can provide a sustainable fish harvest of 300 kilos per hectare a year; if this figure is correct, the destruction of reefs has deprived Filipino fishers of a potential catch of some 630,000 tonnes a year (or almost half the present annual catch). Trawling is only partly to blame for the loss of coral reefs; the municipal fishers themselves have done an enormous amount of damage by dynamite-fishing. This is a crude technique: sticks of dynamite are thrown into the sea and the explosion stuns or kills the fish, which float to the surface. The explosions also smash up the reefs on which the fishlife depends for its food and shelter.

'In 1981', recalled Beloy, 'SM79 decided to do something about the dynamite-fishing. We discovered that it was banned by law, so we went out and talked to the dynamite-fishers. At first we just explained that what they were doing was illegal – that it harmed the reefs and was bad for all of us. We confiscated their dynamite and warned them that if we caught them again we'd take them to the coastguard.' SM79 has managed to stop dynamite-fishing immediately off the shore of San Diego, but it continues in many other areas and remains a favoured practice among the fishers of Lumanyag, a village a few miles south of San Diego.

The use of cyanide has also contributed to reef damage: the poison is used by the suppliers of aquarium fish to stun their prey, and at one time the fishers of San Diego used a cyanide compound to kill fish. They would cut a block of sodium cyanide into small pieces, which they then stuffed inside fish bait. The bait was thrown into the sea where it was devoured by large fish, which floated to the surface. Once the public became aware of the health risk, many people stopped buying fish. SM79 managed to eliminate the practice in its waters and this has undoubtedly been a blessing for the coral, whose sensitive polyps were suffering from the poison.[2]

Coral reefs are one of nature's finest creations, formed by a symbiotic association between reef-building invertebrates and oxygen-producing algae: they are part animal, part plant. In order for them to thrive there must be sufficient sunlight to enable photosynthesis to take place; block out the sunlight and coral swiftly dies. Siltation smothers the coral, increases the turbidity of the water and inhibits photosynthesis. In the Philippines it is a major cause of coral destruction, and it is one of the consequences of deforestation, which, in many cases, happens scores and sometimes of hundreds of miles away from the affected reefs. There is little the fishers can do to counteract this. However, they are in a position to conserve the mangrove swamps which fringe the coast, and whose destruction also leads to an increase in marine siltation.

At the turn of the century there were probably half a million hectares of mangrove swamp around the Philippine coast; most of this was still intact in the 1960s, but it began to disappear at a rate of around 6,000 hectares a year in the 1970s and 20,000 hectares a year in the 1980s. Not much more than 100,000 hectares remains today.[3] The disappearance of mangroves has had a serious impact on fisheries. These bizarre, lustreless-leaved plants with their dense thickets of aerial roots play an important role in stabilizing coastal sediments. They are also highly productive: a study by the Asian Development Bank suggested that a hectare of mangrove swamp produces an annual harvestable yield of 100 kilos of finfish, 20 kilos of shrimp, 15 kilos of crabmeat, 200 kilos of mollusc and 40 kilos of sea cucumber. The same hectare also supplies an indirect harvest of up to 400 kilos of finfish and 75 kilos of shrimp which mature elsewhere – for example, on and around the coral reefs. Mangrove forests have been cleared for a variety of reasons; over half the Philippine swamps have been chopped down to make way for fishponds and the remainder have suffered from land reclamation, cutting for fuelwood and industrial pollution.

From the fishers' point of view, their disappearance is every bit as serious as the loss of coral reefs.

On our first morning Beloy went out to sea at 4 o'clock. He returned shortly after 8 o'clock with a small bucket of fish. After breakfast he was going to set off for a meeting in Nasugbu, a large port about an hour's drive by motor tricycle up the coast. He suggested we spend the day in and around the village. His wife Silving would talk to us about the women's group and take us to see the sugar distillery which was polluting the river behind the village. And we could talk to some of the fishers about the artificial reefs which they had constructed. Silving cooked us some rice and fish for breakfast; Ilyo Aala, the secretary of SM79, came to collect us soon after.

Ilyo was a delicate-featured man in his late twenties; he had a dark slash of moustache and a thin wisp of beard. On the way down to the beach we passed his new *banca*: it had taken just over two weeks to build and cost him around 5,000 pesos ($200). Once we reached the edge of the village we headed south across a patch of rubbish-tipped wasteground and climbed rapidly up the flanks of a scrub-choked hill. The scene which greeted us at the summit was breathtakingly beautiful. Immediately below lay the village of San Diego. On the seaward side was a dense cluster of small bamboo dwellings with grass-thatch roofs; further back, lining several wide streets, were 30 or so more substantial homes with brick walls and tin roofing. All lay under a swaying canopy of palms. The village was bounded on one side by a tidal creek, a long spit of soggy land and a golden swath of boat-strewn beach; on the other side its limits were defined by a small river, beyond which was a large sugar distillery floating in splendid if ugly isolation in a sea of sugar cane. Cultivated fields stretched far inland towards a jagged range of mountains, while the coast curved gently towards the north-west and Nasugbu.

However picturesque it looked from a distance, this was no tropical paradise. Most of the bamboo houses lacked electricity and only a fifth of the dwellings in San Diego had toilets, their occupants being forced to do their business either on the beaches (where they buried it) or on the wasteground beside the village. Conditions were exceedingly cramped despite the fact that there was plenty of land – used for neither agriculture nor housing – immediately outside the village. It was easy to see why the poor wanted land reforms: this unoccupied land belonged to people who refused to relinquish or rent it. Ilyo explained that SM79 had recently managed to procure a 3 acre plot of untitled land at the heart of the village; as a result 36 poor families had been able to build themselves small bamboo dwellings. This was a small triumph.

Ilyo felt that life was slowly improving for the fishers and their families, and he attributed this, in part, to the community's work with artificial reefs. 'We'd heard that other villages were using artificial reefs to attract fish', he explained, 'so we asked CERD if they would help us with a project here.' CERD – Community Education and Research for Development – is a Manila-based organization which has done much to help small fishing communities. 'CERD helped us to find out ways in which we could make artificial reefs and we submitted a proposal for funding, which they passed on to Oxfam.' The proposal was approved and in October 1991 SM79 and KAWAN, an organization of the poorest fishers who use non-motorized *bancas*, set about the task of building reefs using old tyres bought in Quezon City, a suburb of the capital. Each reef – or module – was made from 32 tyres lashed together and sunk in up to 30 metres of water; the fishers also constructed bamboo structures – *payao* – to attract migratory species of fish. Ilyo thought that the project had been successful. 'Before we built the reefs', he explained, 'there were many days when fishers would go out and catch nothing. But once the reefs were installed that seldom happened and the hook-and-line fishers increased their catch by a significant amount.' Unfortunately, the story has a sour ending. SM79 had recently done a survey of its artificial reefs: of the 24 original modules sunk at sea, it found only 8. The fishers assumed that the rest had been destroyed, some deliberately, by trawlers working illegally within the 7 kilometre limit.

Initially, artificial reefs do not increase fish stocks; they simply help to attract fish, thus making them easier for the hook-and-line fishers to catch. In the long term, however, artificial reefs accumulate coral polyps, shellfish and other invertebrate life and thus help to increase the biological wealth of the sea. Over time natural coral reefs are capable of recovering from ill-treatment, but this is a slow process and there is nothing the fishers can do to hasten it. Studies suggest that it takes around 38 years for half a dynamited reef to regenerate. Mangrove swamps, on the other hand, can be given a helping hand. In a village to the south of San Diego a group of fishers planted an experimental hectare of mangroves in 1992. Both CERD and Oxfam were keen to support the replanting of mangroves and in April 1993 Oxfam decided to spend a substantial sum of money – £39,011 – on an ambitious project which would, if successful, lead to the creation of 125 hectares of new mangrove swamp, double the area presently existing in Western Batangas, the local province.

Throughout the 1980s SM79 achieved a great deal with little help from the outside world. However, the recent involvement of CERD and Oxfam has clearly given a significant fillip to its activities and those of other fishing communities in the area. Before heading down the coast to San Diego, we visited Julio 'Juju' Tan, director of CERD, in his office in Quezon City. It was late in the afternoon, the light was fading, and soon after we arrived the daily brown-out – a euphemism for power cut – lowered visibility still further. CERD was set up in 1980 by a group of students and teachers from the University of the Philippines. 'We all had a background in community development', explained Juju, one of CERD's founders, 'and we decided it was time we practised what we preached.' CERD began by helping a farming community in San Carlos City, Pangasinan Province, to set up a primary health care programme. 'But our vision was to transform society', recalled Juju, 'and how could we do that by concentrating on health issues alone? We couldn't. Primary health care is a good "entry point" to helping a community, but that is not all that is needed.' CERD then decided to get involved with municipal fishers, who constituted one of the poorest and most neglected groups in the country. 'We did some thorough research,' said Juju. 'We looked at indigenous fishing technologies; we looked at the environmental problems which faced the fishers; and we looked at the whole issue of overfishing, especially by foreign vessels.'

Under Presidential Decree 704, the Marcos regime had given Japanese and Taiwanese trawlers the same access to Philippine waters as native boats; in return Philippine trawlers were allowed to fish in Japanese and Taiwanese waters. This was a grossly inequitable arrangement for several reasons. On the one hand, Philippine fishing vessels did not have the technical capacity to take advantage of the deal; in any case, Japanese and Taiwanese waters were already overfished. On the other, PD 704 also meant that Filipino fishers faced unfair competition within their own waters.

'It was inevitable that we'd start looking at government policy, at foreign investment and at overfishing,' explained Juju. CERD incurred the displeasure of the authorities for this and other reasons, not least its involvement with the fishers along the coast. In 1982 Juju and his co-workers were forced to retreat to the capital; around the same time one of the founders of the group, Manuel Mario Guzman, was arrested on trumped-up charges – he was accused of being a high-ranking rebel leader – and imprisoned for four years. 'Even though Marcos's people harassed us', continued Juju, 'we still managed to give the fishers some help.' By linking up with the churches, CERD was able to give leadership training to fishers' organizations; at the national level CERD helped various groups to work out a strategy to counter such problems as overfishing, dynamite-fishing and coastal pollution.

The Marcos government fell in 1986 and CERD began working once again with fishers' organizations in three municipalities in Western Batangas – Lian (which includes San Diego), Calatagan and Calaca. By early 1993 CERD had twelve staff in the area and it was working with around 2,000 fishing families. So far it has concentrated on those villages where it can make the greatest and most conspicuous progress. 'We can't be everywhere,' declared Juju. 'The testimonies of the fishers who are doing well will encourage others to organize.' CERD has run environmental awareness training programmes; helped to research and fund (through Oxfam) the building of artificial reefs; and provided all manner of technical advice on protecting coastal resources and managing fish stocks. 'We're not going into the villages and imposing our own ideas,' said Juju. 'We have a dialogue with the fishers. They tend to come to us with their own plans – such as building artificial reefs – and we help to refine them, to put them into practice.'

CERD has also helped the fishers to recognize the importance of existing law in asserting their rights to coastal resources. Although there is much wrong with the laws and decrees governing fishing practices, they are not entirely without virtue. They do establish a 7 kilometre limit within which commercial boats of 3 tonnes or more should not trespass, and they do prohibit dynamite-fishing, the use of poisons such as sodium cyanide and other destructive practices. Proprietorship also confers certain rights, and the fishers recognized this when they sank their artificial reefs. 'If you put a fish-aggregating structure in the sea', explained Juju, 'you have the right to protect it and determine who can use it.'

Paul Valentin, Oxfam's country representative, echoed these thoughts when we met him in his office a few minutes' drive away: 'Once people improve their fisheries, they become more vigilant. There has been a leap of consciousness in recent years and the fishers now see that the link between environmental health and economic sustainability is very clear.' Valentin had come to the Philippines some fourteen years earlier to work as a volunteer specializing in tropical agriculture. He spent nine years in Northern Luzon, the most populous island in the country, and married a Filipino. In 1988 he joined Oxfam and he is as articulate an observer of the development scene as one could wish to find.

Oxfam opened its Philippine office in 1987, a year after the overthrow of President Marcos. Valentin's predecessor had identified two groups of people who were notably neglected by the aid community. These were the country's indigenous peoples, who number around six million, and the fishing communities. The bulk of Oxfam's work today is geared towards helping these two groups. At the end of the 1980s Oxfam helped to establish an organization which brought together municipal fishers from across the country. 'That was a tricky game!' laughed Valentin. 'Every different political blood group was involved, but we did succeed in getting very diverse organizations to come together.' NACFAR, the National Coalition for Aquatic Reform, was formally set up in January 1990.

Oxfam decided at a early stage in NACFAR's life that it would not – indeed, could not, according to its own constitution – involve itself in lobbying for legislative changes. 'What we said we'd do', recalled Valentin, 'was work at the community level to pioneer initiatives which would favour sustainable resource management.' One of the pillars of NACFAR's programme is the Fisheries Code, which, if made law, will put coastal resources in the hands of the communities who use them. The Fisheries Code calls for the municipal exclusion zone to be increased from 7 to 12 kilometres and it proposes that coastal waters should be looked after by Resource Management Councils (RMCs). These councils would be made up of representatives of the villages (the *barangay* councils), the fishers' organizations (for example, SM79 and KAWAN in San Diego), the municipal government and the law enforcement authorities.[4] For Paul Valentin, RMCs are a critically important feature of the Code: 'At heart, it's an empowering mechanism which helps fishers to assert their rights over aquatic resources. At present, we are working towards the day when the fishing communities will be able to take control if "good legislation" comes into existence.' According to Valentin, SM79 was well on the way to protecting and managing its fishery resources long before anyone had thought about Resource Management Councils.

'Supporting small-scale initiatives in an area which has been earmarked for major agro-industrial developments seemed a bit of a gamble at first,' recalled Valentin. 'But the fishers in San Diego had already shown that they had the strength to achieve things on their own, and we saw this as a way to prove to the world – and to development agencies – that bottom-up, sustainable ventures are possible, that they can work.' Four years on and Valentin is very impressed by the achievements of SM79 and the other fishers' organizations which Oxfam has been working with. 'So far as the leaders are concerned', he said, shaking his head in admiration, 'it is 90 per cent pure sacrifice. They aren't paid for their work, and I know of one leader who had to sell his boat just to feed his family.' The fishers' groups are very 'transparent' with the communities, according to Juju Tan: 'They never hide anything,' he said. 'They're very democratic, very fair.'[5]

After dinner one evening we returned to the bamboo hut where we had first met Beloy. We were joined there by three women: Balbina 'Nellie' Destreza, Dominga 'Enggay' Alicaya and Beloy's wife Silving, with whom we were staying. The hut had been built by CERD and it doubled as a meeting place for the fishers and a temporary home for Lyn Lacsamana, CERD's women's organizer. The eldest of the three was the diminutive Nellie, who recounted in a quietly humorous manner the tribulations of the women's group, which had spluttered fitfully through the 1980s, occasionally sparking into life, but mostly lying dormant. The group was set up in 1979 and Nellie became its first elected leader in 1980. Initially, health – or ill-health, especially of the village children – was a major preoccupation. 'We went round from house to house asking mothers if they wanted a daycare centre,' recalled Nellie. 'Many of the children were sick and we decided we had

150

MAURITANIA

In the desert near Timbedra goat skins and inner tyres are used to carry water.
These women have had to walk over five miles to the nearest well.

A member of Timbedra Pastoral Association milking a cow at night.

The tree nursery at Um-Lehbal. Mohamed val Ould Essayed is on the left; Mohamed el Moktar is in the centre.

Under the second livestock project, pastoral associations have set up their own animal pharmacies. 'We've seen a great improvement in the health of our animals' said Mohamed Ould Beya, secretary-general of Timbedra-Est PA (on the left in this photo). The pharmacy is run by Mohamed Lemme Ould Khatty.

COSTA RICA

*While the industrial loggers use huge machines to extract timber, often causing
unnecessary damage, the ASACODE relies on Indian buffalo. This method causes
minimal disturbance to young trees, and the only fuel required is animal fodder.*

*Felix Vasquez can
identify over 60 species of
trees in their seedling
state, an astonishing
achievement beyond the
capabilities of most
botanists.*

Two members of ASACODE cutting up a Pilon tree with an Alaska mill. Industrial logging companies leave over half each felled tree to rot on the forest floor. ASACODE makes use of every cubic inch of wood.

Checking seedlings at ASACODE's nursery. From left to right: Felix Vasquez, José Luis Zuniga, Teodoro Lopez and Mel Baker.

Felix, Teodoro and friend dwarfed by a magnificent self-cotton tree. A logging company would pay around 3000 colones for such a tree; when processed by ASACODE it is worth 100,000 colones.

ECUADOR

The minga *is a central feature of Andean life. Here villagers from Laurel Gompueno work together to break up the hard soil – the first step in land recuperation.*

These two girls had collected 30 kilos of mushrooms by 11 o'clock in the morning. The girls clean and cut the mushrooms before weighing them and collecting their pay.

Two faces of Ecuador. The woman on the left is over 40, and is breastfeeding her sixth child. The woman on the right is working in an organic garden – there is an expanding demand for 'green' produce around Quito.

Victor Janchaliquin with wild mushrooms, which sprout from the base of the pines he's planted. The young trees provide firewood and a habitat for the mushrooms; once they mature, they will be felled for timber.

THE PHILIPPINES

San Diego village, with Nasugbu in the distance.

At sunset dozens of bancas put out to sea for the evening's fishing.

SM 79 recently procure a three-acre plot of untitled land at the hea of San Diego; as a result, 36 poor families have been able to build small dwellings like thi one. A pig pen can be seen on the left.

Silving Alicaya, one of the leading lights in the women's group and wife of Beloy, chairman of SM 79, the fishers' organization in San Diego.

and finally . . .

Among the bananas: Grazia Borrini Feyerabend, Charles Pye-Smith and Richard Sandbrook in Costa Rica.

to do something.' The women's group set about raising money and in 1980 it began a daycare centre in a building next to the church; a volunteer called Norma was taken on to run the centre. 'Small children were looked after during the day', explained Nellie, 'and if they were malnourished we'd feed them fish and soya milk.' For over a year the centre operated reasonably efficiently, but when the women's group asked for Norma to be paid a monthly salary, the mayor refused. The centre subsequently folded. The women raised some more money but one of the officials mishandled the fund. 'Then the group collapsed,' concluded Nellie with a resigned smile.

'Yes, it collapsed', agreed Silving, 'but some of us remained active, especially in the fight against the distillery pollution.' Earlier in the day Silving and a friend had taken us for a walk along the river which ran behind the village. A small ditch sliced through the fields from the distillery to the river: it was full of a substance the colour and texture of treacle. Four hundred yards further on, past a nipa-palm swamp and a scrubby patch of mangroves, we inspected the settling ponds; they were delivering a glutinous liquid into the river. 'In the old days', explained Enggay, 'before the distillery was built, people used to get plenty of fish from the river when storms prevented them from putting out to sea.' The distillery was built in 1975 and within a short space of time its effluent had rendered the river lifeless.

The women were convinced that many of the health problems in the village stemmed from drinking contaminated water. They began their protest against the pollution before the formation of the women's group and they continued, intermittently, to agitate against the distillery throughout the 1980s. In the early days the women held a protest rally in the nearby town of Lian, where they marched on the municipal offices and met the mayor, some *barangay* councillors and the distillery owners. The owners claimed that they were not polluting the river and they produced a glass of water as proof. 'Look', they said, 'this water is from the river and we'll drink it.' The women laughed at the memory and Silving took up the story. 'Yes, it must have been dyed with bromide or some food colourant. After they drank their water we produced some real water from the river – they didn't dare drink that, and the municipal officers said they couldn't even stand the smell!' Some time later a government doctor told the women that the distillery was not the cause of the pollution; rather, it was the villagers who were to blame. 'She told us we should ask for God's help,' said Enggay. 'We all cried and went home in despair.'

The women's group was inactive for many years, but it was re-established in 1987 with 120 members. Each paid a monthly due of 1.50 pesos and this was used to provide loans for sick women. The money did not last long and in a less than a year the group folded again. A non-governmental organization helped to rebuild the daycare centre, but it was destroyed by a typhoon. In 1988 the women raised more money and rebuilt it. It ran for a year, but closed down as many of the women could not afford the 50 centavos daily (0.5 peso) required for running costs. Yet another period of dormancy ensued, then in 1991 CERD came on the scene. With the encouragement of CERD and SM79, the women began to organize once again. In March 1992 they held a general assembly in San Diego, with 80 women founding the Samasaka-SD.

'Most of our problems', remarked Silving, 'stem from poverty – we decided that we had to set up some income-generating schemes.' The first priority was to earn enough money to buy food and send their children to school. Many of the children in the village were malnourished, and over 40 per cent received no education whatsoever; a mere 8 per cent went as far up the educational ladder as high school and only 2 per cent reached college. But finding enough time to make a living on the side was difficult for the women. 'We have to spend a lot of time helping our husbands,' explained Nellie. 'We prepare food, get the gasoline for the motors, mend the fishing gear, market the fish...' As Paul Valentin of Oxfam pointed out, it is the women who must keep families afloat in periods of economic distress: 'In extreme cases', he said, 'fishers' wives even turn to prostitution in order to feed their children.'

Silving, Enggay and Nellie seemed quietly optimistic about the future of Samasaka-SD. They had received considerable support from CERD and formed a very close relationship with Lyn Lacsamana; their husbands had also been more supportive than in the past. In the early months of 1993 they began their first income-generating scheme. With loans from a credit fund administered by CERD and provided by Oxfam, 25 women had been able to buy two piglets each and enough feed to fatten them. Their husbands had helped them to construct pigsties beside their homes. Beloy had made a solid one out of breeze blocks; others had constructed prettier affairs with bamboo poles. The women had decided to rear Large Whites; they would be ready for killing in four months, which compared favourably with the native russet-coloured hogs, which required at least six months to reach the same weight. When we were in San Diego the pigs were about a month away from their target weight. The women intended to take them into Lian and Nasugbu when the time came and replace them with a new batch of piglets. They did not expect the pig project to make them rich, but it would provide a boost to family incomes.

The women were going to continue their struggle against the distillery. 'We're also worried about the fact that the government has targeted Batangas for industrial growth,' said Silving. 'If they bring industry here, and roads and piers – well, it'll be the fishing people who suffer most.' It was hard to see what they could do to counter some of the major schemes, such as a new coal-fired power station at Calaca, which were being mooted by the government. After all, their protests over more than a decade had done nothing to improve the local distillery's pollution record.

One afternoon we went to see Roman Botones, the captain of San Diego *barangay* and a leading light in the Peoples' Committee Against Pollution, an organization set up to fight the distillery. 'We were very active in the early '80s,' he recalled. 'We photographed the dead fish; we took pictures of illegal waste disposal; we got the National Pollution Control Commission to call a hearing.' But the latter seemed to be in league with the distillery owners and the pollution remained as much a problem now as it was in 1979, the year when the People's Commission was set up. In fact, there were now four distilleries operating within the watershed, whereas there were only two then. 'In San Diego, we'll carry on with the struggle', said the captain, 'but in many other *barangays* people seem to have lost hope.' He attributed this to a mixture of weariness and fear: one night in 1984 two activists in the People's Commission – a couple who lived in Lian – were murdered in their home. It was assumed by many that they had been killed for their anti-pollution activities. 'After that', concluded the captain, 'we had trouble getting people to join us.'[6]

There was no proof that these murders were linked with

the pollution struggle, any more than there was proof that the high incidence of diarrhoea and skin diseases in San Diego was a consequence of the distillery's pollution. But in a country where the authorities frequently prefer foul means to fair, it was a reasonable supposition. Indeed, Beloy Alicaya had been persecuted by the military, evidently at the behest of the trawler and distillery owners. The military accused Beloy of being a rebel leader in the New Peoples' Army – a communist guerrilla group active in many parts of the country – and he was the subject of an 'Order of Battle' for much of 1991. 'This meant they could arrest me, or kill me if I resisted,' explained Beloy. The issue went to the Commission on Human Rights in Manila, which concluded that Beloy was not a subversive. Opposing those in power and those with wealth (the two tend to go together) requires considerable courage in the Philippines.

'One of the things we discovered then', said Beloy, 'was that many other small fishing communities were also being harrassed by the authorities for challenging trawlers.' This communality of experience has been one of the strengths of the municipal fishers' movement, and over the past few years the emergence of regional and national fishers' organizations has been of enormous help to smaller groups like SM79. While NACFAR has been able to lobby at the highest level for changes in the law, regional organizations have concentrated on issues too great for the village groups to handle, but possibly too parochial to command the full attention of NACFAR. In Western Batangas, for example, the regional organization of HABAGAT – it took its name from the south-west monsoon that lashes these shores – is an alliance of all the local groups like SM79. It has been especially active in pressing for stricter controls over foreign trawlers and in campaigning against industrial pollution and planned industrial developments which threaten coastal waters. HABAGAT is in a far better position than small organizations like SM79 to negotiate with the authorities at a municipal level, though of course it is only as strong as its constituent parts.

We met some of HABAGAT's campaigners on our last morning in Western Batangas. We had left San Diego the previous day and taken a motor tricycle down the coast to Ligtasan, a small settlement beside the tourist resort of Matabungkay. In the afternoon we swam across the local coral reef. Some of the reef was as nature intended: multicoloured fish fluttered around the coral heads like autumn leaves; sea cucumbers, brittle-stars and starfish glided across the sandy bottom. But there were large chunks which had been virtually destroyed by dynamite-fishing: here the sea bed was little more than a grey, lifeless ossuary.

Next morning we met several members of HABAGAT, including its president, Peter de la Salis, a fisher from Nasugbu. He was especially worried about foreign investment: 'The big problem is the Taiwanese trawlers – we've got to stop them fishing in our waters.' He felt that the fishers' organizations had achieved much in San Diego and many other villages: they had stopped piracy; they had protected natural reefs and created artificial ones; they had reduced dynamite-fishing and prevented illegal fishing by small trawlers; and they had done much to improve the living conditions within the villages. 'Now', said HABAGAT's president, 'it's time for the government to play *its* part in protecting the coastal resources.'

CONCLUSIONS

'Why should I care for the environment? I and my family go to bed hungry every night, that is what counts for us.'

'Why should I care for the environment? Any day I could be thrown off this piece of land. If I sacrifice my gain today, someone else will reap it tomorrow.'

'Why should I care for the environment? The others are exploiting resources as much as they can. Why should I behave differently?'

Questions such as these – questions of survival and rights – are at the heart of many local environmental problems. A misreading of these sentiments has led to a number of myths, for instance that communal resources are bound to end up in tragic mismanagement[1] or that only affluent people care for their local environment. We have found that this is not the case. Those who have very little other than their place of being need nature more than anyone else, and they know it. When they can benefit from local resources, when they feel reasonably sure of receiving a just compensation for their work, when they are not alone – people do care. In fact, we have found that many poor communities build their productive life and, at times, even their identity and pride, around caring for their local environment.

In the highlands of Ecuador, in the plains of Uganda, in the coastal villages of the Philippines, groups of residents are organizing themselves to make the most of their place of being, to exploit yet nurture their environment. Pastoral communities in Mauritania adapt old ways of living to new circumstances. Peasant families who recently migrated to the rainforest, in Costa Rica, learn completely new skills and activities. Ex-robbers in the marshes of Calcutta create new resources out of waste and degraded land. Until recently, many of these people were considered among the poorest of the poor. Today, they have found new sources of 'common wealth'; they are meeting their needs in harmony with their land and natural resources.

The communities we visited may at first appear to have little in common. They are surrounded by diverse natural environments, live under a variety of political regimes and belong to widely different cultures. They all, however, pool their strengths to manage the resources at their disposal and benefit in the process. They all succeed in *primary environmental care*. Learning from these communities was the aim of our travels. What we have learned is summarized in this last chapter.

The chapter is divided into three main parts: 'Anything new?', 'What makes a difference?' and 'What next?'. In the first part, we trace some historical and conceptual roots of community-based sustainable development. What we discuss is not new. Not at all. But realizing the potential of communities, today, is probably more urgent than ever. In the second part we draw a few general lessons from the experience of the communities described in the book. These lessons are brought to bear, in the third part of the chapter, for people, organizations and governments wishing to promote and multiply community-based initiatives. The three parts can be read independently.

ANYTHING NEW?

For about half a million years, our *Homo sapiens* species lived in small communities of hunter-gatherers.[2] Such groups, which numbered 20 to 30 people, combined swift mobility, good knowledge of resources and wildlife, minimal labour differentiation and ample leisure time.[3] They roamed the earth for hundreds of thousands of years, spreading from the savannah of Africa to the tundra of the North, from coastlands to mountains, from warm and fertile river valleys to cold and inhospitable forests. Two characteristics stand out as keys to their success. One was their capacity to adapt – biologically and culturally – to the opportunities and hardships of different environments. The other was their capacity to collaborate within the group – harvesting food, raising the children, passing on from generation to generation a body of knowledge about the land and its products.

Around 10,000 years ago, some of these communities of hunter-gatherers became so knowledgeable about plants and animals that they began to domesticate them, selecting and encouraging the most congenial varieties. Many communities maintained their original small group structure and moved from place to place as slash and burn agriculturists or nomadic herders. Some settled permanently around trading centres of particularly valuable commodities (like stone tools or pigments), or around areas where food species abounded. For a long time such settlements did not develop into large human agglomerations. As the historian H Pirenne wrote: 'A society in which the population lives by the soil which it exploits and whose produce it consumes on the spot cannot give rise to important agglomerations of human beings; each inhabitant being tied, by the necessities of life, to the soil which he cultivates'.[4] What certainly increased, however, was their collective understanding of the local environment, their body of 'local knowledge' accumulated by trial and errors in pursuit of survival.

Little by little, in many parts of the world, agricultural production rose, labour differentiation became important, communications improved, cities developed and the human population grew.[5] The process developed so slowly that when Columbus first reached the American continent, in 1492, large portions of the world were still dominated by a food collecting rather than a food producing economy,[6] and small human bands were a very common social phenomenon. In these small and self-sufficient communities it is rather obvious that collaboration within the group played an essential role for survival. The same was and is true, however, in all human societies – no matter how complex or sophisticated.[7] In fact, contrary to the stereotype of a purely competitive *Homo economicus*, history shows that association and kinship have always been essential components of economic life.[8] They contributed – in an infinite variety of forms – to the human talent for ingenious adaptation in different environmental niches.[9]

Today, small collaborative units appear dwarfed and overshadowed by large institutions – the state, the industrial giants, the banks, the corporations, the national and international systems of production and trade – and by the competitive attitude required by existing market systems. Credit and favourable terms of trade favour the 'fast and large' deals of corporations and rampant entrepreneurs rather than the slow and carefully evolving initiatives of small communities. Many national economies are dominated by big industry, large-scale agriculture and media cartels, often controlled by the same handful of people. But dissent exists. Several professionals and politicians – including some from 'giant institutions' – are questioning the sustainability and desirability of current economic systems. They wish to see more emphasis on equity and culture than on profit and consumption, more attention to the peculiar problems and opportunities of local environment, more people and communities involved in substantial roles in the initiatives that affect their lives. In a moment, we will see some of their arguments in a little more detail. First, however, we would like to stress that their ideas are not born today.[10]

Movements and ideas in recent history

In Europe and Russia, important precedents can be found among liberal, socialist and populist thinkers of the last century and, in our century, in the Peasant Parties of Eastern European states before the Depression era.[11] In the USA, the People's Party of the late nineteenth century[12] and the writings of Henry David Thoreau[13] are key cases in point, with direct links to the more recent idea of 'treason against natural societies' of Paul Goodman[14] and the appealing essays and poems of Wendell Berry.[15] In the East, many strands of people-oriented rhetoric are found in the programme of Sun Yat-Sen (the most influential Chinese political thinker at the beginning of our century) and in the writings of Mao Tze-Tung. Another obvious example is the philosophy of Mahatma Gandhi, with its emphasis on village-based production and the traditional values of frugality and collaboration.

In Latin America, the people's rhetoric was used to forward rather opposite political aims.[16] In Brazil, for instance, Catholic radical organizations like Acao Popular[17] were very active in the early 1960s. In the name of the people they conducted literacy campaigns and organized the peasants in rural syndicates against the indiscriminate power of large land-owners. Early after World War Two, in Argentina, president Juan Domingo Peron had used a similar language to pit recent urban immigrants against unionized labor. In the end, this favoured the interests of national capital. People-centred development was also advocated by many African leaders, who strove to maintain the traditional extended family and village councils as building blocks of post-colonial societies.[18] In the words of Peter Berger: '...various versions of the *negritude*... have a strong anti-modern and anti-Western animus and a desire to preserve some inner kernel of indigenous culture. [But] most of these movements and ideologies do not reject modernity out of hand. They still desire the "cargo" of good things that modernity promises, from better agricultural techniques to a longer life. The goal is to have these good things without the anomic features, the homelessness of Western societies.'[19]

In all continents we thus find examples of thinkers and movements with a stated trust in people's values and productive capacities, in community-based institutions and small-scale initiatives. Intriguingly, these values can be found to embrace considerably divergent political programmes, from liberal to socialist, from revolutionary to reactionary, from nationalist to communist. It is instructive to explore – albeit superficially – a few of these variations on the theme.

Among the first European political economists to articulate a position for small-scale productive units was the Swiss Simonde de Sismondi, in the early nineteenth century. Sismondi advocated a system of family farming, capable of distributing wealth throughout the population. The families would need access to capital, and security in land tenure. As a liberal, Sismondi believed in laissez-faire economic policies. For him, the potential polarization of wealth in society would be best kept in check by a large diffusion of private property (which could be achieved by dividing common lands into private holdings for landless labourers). Roughly at the same time, in England, an emphasis on small-scale cooperative organization among producers was put forth by several socialist thinkers who followed the economic theory of Ricardo.[20] Rather than supporting private property, they wanted to see land under state control and agricultural production in the hands of peasant cooperatives. Similarly, they suggested that small-scale artisans unite to overcome the control of the capitalist middlemen, who prevent labour from receiving its full and just returns.

The contradiction between private property and state property advocates was polemically resolved by the French P J Proudhon. In 1840, Proudhon published *What is Property?*, a treatise in which he states that property is theft wherever divorced from the actual use of the goods (the land, first of all). In other words, he argued that all revenues from rent, dividends, interest or profits not immediately related to the legitimate returns of labour are theft; the only legitimate use of land and natural resources is their direct use. For him, a just and equitable society could only consist of small produc- ers and artisans in control of their means of production, with competition among them regulated by professional associa- tions.

More than their English or French predecessors, the Russian populists[21] of the middle nineteenth century emphasized the human and spiritual advantages that artisans and peasants had over the new industrial proletarians. Not only political thinkers, but also artists, writers, theologians and philosophers asserted the wholeness and rustic grace of agricultural pro- duction by peasants and manufacture by artisans not alienated from the products of their labour. This utopian vision finds famous expressions in the writings of Pushkin and Tolstoy[22] and resonates in the People's choruses of Mussorgsky's *Boris Godunov*. The emphasis is on the deep-seated moral qualities of people, on the capacity to produce for one's own con- sumption and on the advantages of manual labour and the simple rural life. Common ownership of land and self-govern- ment by traditional institutions (like the *obshchina* and *mir*[23]) are important elements of such a populist vision.

The village as an economic unit in which peasants produce partly for self-consumption and partly – in cooperatives – for the market, was a key tenet of many Peasant Parties that developed in Eastern Europe between the First and the Sec- ond World War.[24] Industry was accepted so long as it remained relatively small scale, home or village based, and controlled by the workers themselves. These views – at times grouped under the label of neo-populism – differ from those of nineteenth century populism insofar as they approved of technological innovations and collective schemes (such as large cooperative associations of producers). In a world increasingly dominated by economic giants, it was becoming obvious that peasants and artisans needed collective strength to compete in producing, processing and buying. Following the populists, however, the neo-populists continued to oppose large-scale production – either capitalist or state owned – and the parasitic sectors that exploit the peasants and the factory workers. These ideas were accompanied by a profound distrust for the city and a renewed stress on the virtues of agrarian life.

The neo-populists managed to gain a substantial political backing, which peaked around the 1920s with hundreds of thousands of East European peasants organized in cooperatives. A Green International – to respond to the Socialist and Communist Internationals – was also founded. It was only after the Depression of 1929 that conservative and authoritarian forces managed to suppress the neo-populist sentiments, at times, as with the Romanian Iron Guard, incorporating some of their language and appeal. Unfortunately, the idealization of native peasants could easily turn into distrust and hate towards the middlemen, the urban dwellers and, little by little, foreigners in general and the Jews in particular. Yesterday as today, intolerance, fear and hatred for whoever does not fit the assumed ideal (ethnic background, racial characteristics, language, behaviour, etc) are an insidious danger for any movement that emphasizes 'fraternity' based on locality.

In the aftermath of the Second World War, both in communist states in the East and in the NATO countries of the West, industrialization and large-scale economic development were key tenets of virtually all governments. By the late 1960s, however, environmental concerns were becoming well established in the affluent and effluent West, and increasingly linked to issues of community and scale. In 1972, a powerful case in favour of self-sufficient communities was made in *The Ecologist* magazine, based on an analysis of environmental trends.[25] The thesis combined the ideas of people such as Schumacher (see below) and others who grew out of the radical movement of the 1960s in Western universities. By the 1980s, some of these ideas had become an important stream in European politics. At that time, a variety of Green parties emerged with platforms that can be associated – in various degrees – with populist roots intertwined with environmental concerns. Some members of such parties were inclined towards utopian-bucolic sentiments, and idealized the rural life. Others pointed at the exploitation of nature as merely another face of the exploitation of people. Some quite explicitly identified the large-scale industrial system as the main enemy, the heart of a system of 'exterminism' capable of undermining both nature and the peaceful coexistence of people.[26] Fierce controversies within the Green movement continue today over what socio-economic system can best assure environmentally sound policies. Unfortunately, this is not the place to do justice to this rich debate.

Social experiments in practice

From the beginning of our century a major collectivist movement of peasant workers developed in Palestine among the early Jewish colonizers. Several Israelis see in that movement the foundations on which their state was born. Literally, a *kibbutz* is 'a group', and the people who united in a *kibbutz* did so in the name of mutual assistance and to improve their productive capabilities. Collaboration was essential not least because the environment in which many of these groups worked was extremely difficult: rocky soils and a harsh climate in remote, disease-ridden areas. From early on, the farmers' organization centred around the collective ownership of goods and means of production and the equal duties and rights of all members in providing labour and receiving benefits, in particular the best possible education. The first *kibbutzim* comprised very few people, typically less than ten adults who worked together on a leased piece of land. Progressively, the groups became larger and more numerous, they acquired more and more tools and machines (as collective property) and developed small-scale industries. In the 1940s, nearly 50 per cent of the rural population in Israel was organized in *kibbutzim*. Particular values developed around this movement, in particular the abolition of patriarchal authority, the full emancipation of women, equity in education, voluntary adhesion of members, democratic decision-making, self-employment and close contacts with society at large.[27] Today, the *kibbutzim* remain a vital and evolving component of the modern state of Israel. While cooperation is still at the core of most economic initiatives, the social organization of the *kibbutz* is slowly evolving towards a more pronounced role for individual families.

Israel was not the only country to promote large-scale social experiments in community-based initiatives. Roughly in the same decades, countries like Mexico, Peru, South Korea, Tanzania and China were also putting into practice their national versions of community-oriented policies. In the 1930s, the Mexican president Lazaro Cardenas expropriated the land of large *haciendas* (farms) and divided it among the families of the resident peasant workers in the so-called *ejido* system. Basically, an *ejido* is a community that works a well-defined piece of land, lives off its products and can pass on the land rights to its descendants (through the family male line) but cannot sell it, cannot convert the land into money. In fact, president Cardenas declared the *ejido* land inalienable, fearing that the peasants could become the prey of speculators and end up selling their possessions. The starting of an *ejido* was voluntary and based upon a specific request by a group of at least twenty people. Some *ejidos* organized agricultural production in a collective sense, with tools owned by the community but revenues distributed according to individual inputs. Other *ejidos* organized both production and consumption around individual families. Still others were a mix of collective and individual enterprises. In 1950, about half the Mexican rural population was organized in *ejidos*. The Mexican government was supposed to provide several forms of support, in particular credit and connection to markets, but these did not always work out as expected. For decades the system has offered an example of a widespread land tenure arrangement that allows communities to play the main role in resource management. Results have been mixed. Several *ejidos* remained relatively poor and crowded communities, while others ran exemplary operations of combined sustainable resource management and productive businesses.[28]

In Peru, from 1963 to 1968, president Fernando Belaunde based his political programme on reviving and strengthening the traditional communal organization and mutual aid habits inherited from the Incas. The traditional element of his political platform was so strong that Belaunde himself used to dress as an Inca. He appealed to the initiative and self-help capacity of Indian communities in the Sierra, believing that the state should not compel them to act, but rather provide them with the technical and material support necessary to carry out the initiatives they themselves decided. The reorientation of his government programme was impressive: concern with the interior instead of the more developed urban population of Lima; decentralization and decision-making in the hands of the people rather than appointments and directives from the country's capital; investments in agriculture in poor mountain areas rather than in the irrigated coastal plains. University students were enlisted to help with teaching in remote villages during their summer vacations and public works, health care and credit schemes were widely promoted. Land redistribution was also initiated, although the issue was highly complicated by the very poor agricultural potential of much of the country's territory. In 1968, Belaunde and his party of Accion Popular were overthrown by a military coup.[29]

Meanwhile, in South Korea, the New Community Movement was enlisting rural villages and their councils as government partners in a variety of development initiatives. Villages were given the choice to select – in a given year – one intervention among a number that the government was willing to support. A village could choose a road project, a sanitation or water supply scheme, public baths, a school building, and so on. The villagers would provide the unskilled labour and some economic investments, the government would match that with skilled labour and resources needed to complete the initiative. The New Community Movement thrived and contributed to rapid improvements in rural welfare. There are few doubts, however, that the success of the programme was only partially due to the government policies in favour of rural communities and traditional institutions. At least as important were the strong community-orientation of Korean people and the wealth created by sustained industrial development in urban areas.

In Tanzania, President Nyerere focused the post-colonial development strategy around the *ujamaa* village,[30] a rural settlement where peasants were to produce food crops on individual land and cash crops on communal land, via an *ujamaa* farm association. From the late 1960s through the 1970s, millions of Tanzanians were administratively and at times physically relocated in these villages. (In some cases relocation was forced.) Nyerere wanted his programme to increase social equity and distribute resources throughout the country in a fair way. Unfortunately, he was facing enormous economic constraints, aggravated by the rising price of oil, the falling price of coffee and the heavy economic losses caused by the war with Uganda. This meant that there was very little the government could provide to support the *ujamaa's* agricultural development. And – because of equity considerations – that little was spread thin. Nyerere's programme succeeded in extending basic literacy, primary heath care and clean water to large sectors of the population. The communal production in *ujamaa* villages, however, proved a task much more complex and difficult than anticipated, and the government could provide only a minimum of technical and economic support. The villages remained, but communal agriculture never took off. Many villagers went straight back to subsistence agriculture in family plots.

As Nyerere's policies in Tanzania, the development plans of communist China emphasized equity (in particular the lowering of the urban–rural income differential), improving the living conditions of the rural peasants and developing small-scale industry in the countryside. Unlike Tanzania, however, China possessed a relatively strong industrial production capacity, well-educated technical cadres and a highly skilled peasantry. For decades, they were able to dedicate time and resources to enhancing productivity in the rural areas while maintaining low the wages of urban workers. This was accomplished by mechanizing agriculture as much as possible and progressively increasing the size and capital-intensiveness of rural industries. But the Chinese government also exercised a stringent authority over all aspects of the country's economy, from the very existence of competitive markets to the decisions made in the small communal farms. Given this, and despite all the rhetoric of the rural communes, one can hardly speak of 'people-controlled' development.

That China succeeded in creating spectacular improvements in nutrition, literacy and living conditions and a relatively equitable distribution of income is not in doubt. Yet, it did so at the price of the total control – often a coercive and violent control – of its people. As Kitching aptly pointed out: '...we have the paradox that it is only a massively centralized control of the macro-economic environment that makes the kind of "local self-sufficiency" viable. The small and beautiful, if it is not to be wiped out by competition, presupposes (ironically) the big and bureaucratic'.[31] In a similar vein, Fidel Castro's revolution in Cuba shows, from 1959 on, a continuous tension between the ever-present rhetoric of the supremacy of the will of the people and the need to control the politico–administrative system and improve its efficiency.

The environment–development dilemma

Development in the Third World has been the subject of much research and writing. While the mainstream of literature deals with conventional development theory and macro-economic interventions, the fringes are increasingly concerned with cracks in the system. Some authors swing between extremes of guilt and outrage at the status quo, not least concerning the disempowerment of people and communities in the name of development,[32] but relatively few concentrate on practical alternatives. A classic work that explicitly advocates small-scale, rural-oriented, people-centred development is E F Schumacher's *Small is Beautiful*, published in 1973.[33] The book offered a powerful manifesto in favor of artisanal, ecological and quality-oriented forms of production. Like Proudhon, Schumacher saw property as legitimate only at a scale that allows the owner to be directly involved with productive work. His book promoted an enormous interest in appropriate technology and quality of life versus quantity of production and consumption. Shortly thereafter, the economist Michael Lipton argued that the roots of poverty and drudgery in developing countries lay in the structural inequality between the urban and rural areas. For him, development programmes should emphasize small-scale agriculture and give it investment priority over any large-scale industrial scheme.[34] Meanwhile, the theorists and practitioners of liberation theology in Latin America rediscovered the common roots of 'community' and 'communion',[35] and Robert Chambers powerfully argued for reversing the policies that oppress the rural poor,[36] stimulating a world-wide interest in community-based assessment and planning.[37]

As the Green movement gained momentum in Europe in the 1970s and 1980s, so too did the environmental debate in connection with development. In fact, it soon became evident that the environment advocates were in a quandary as to what to recommend for developing countries. On the one hand, they believed that many environmental problems (eg poor sanitation, lack of safe water, land degradation because of overuse) were rooted in poverty and could be overcome by economic growth. On the other, such growth was bound to cause new environmental problems (pollution, depletion of marketable resources, loss of biological diversity and so on). These would be added to other undesirable consequences of growth such as enhanced disparity in income within and between countries, deteriorating socio-cultural customs and growing numbers of dispossessed and 'unemployed' people.[38] The dilemma prompted two basic kinds of answers.

On the one hand, are the answers provided by governments and the 'governmental establishment'. From the 1972

Stockholm Conference on the Human Environment to the 1987 report of the World Commission on Environment and Development such answers remained much the same. The call has been for 'more development', which has meant more industrialization, more modernized agriculture, more international trade, more high-tech research and more tasks, responsibilities and funds assigned to national governments and international institutions. Innumerable seminars, conferences and meetings have made hundreds of detailed recommendations to mitigate the undesirable environmental consequences of development, from assessing impacts to costing damages, from providing specific incentives and disincentives to expanding research. The great majority of recommendations, however, remained confined to the high sphere of ministries of finances and planning and to large-scale interventions. Very little attention has been paid to the peculiar characteristics of local environments, or the unique opportunities offered by local people and institutions.[39]

On the other hand are the answers of the 'non-governmental establishment'. These have been much more forthright in supporting small-scale initiatives and the diverse and complex potentialities of local communities. In this, non-governmental organizations have struck alliances with scholars and practitioners who long advocated a greater recognition of the knowledge and skills of local peasants.[40] In the urban field, they have associated with the health professionals and urban planners who successfully entrusted local dwellers – illegal residents included – with housing and environmental care initiatives.[41] They have joined progressive foundations in helping communities to run their own projects in a variety of countries.[42] Importantly, they have found in their midst an increasing number of professionals from the South who forcefully advocated that communities should be given a chance to care for their own environment. This is particularly true of India. To give one example among many, the Centre for Science and the Environment, in New Delhi, has long focused work on village-based initiatives. Blending traditional customs with an acute sense of the new problems facing the Indian poor, the Centre has worked out the requirements for an 'ecosystem-specific development'. Among those, is that villages should be legally recognized as administrative units and that village institutions should be put in charge of managing the common property resources in their surroundings.[43]

A new convergence

At least in the 'non-governmental establishment', the tension between environment and development advocates and practitioners is thus reducing as more and more of them discover common interests and perceptions. In Europe and to a lesser extent in North America, environment organizations (for example the World Wide Fund for Nature, WWF) and development organizations (for example Oxfam) not only have begun to talk a similar language, they often work together. In Australia, the Landcare programme provides an excellent example of the successful merging of the economic and environmental concerns of farmers throughout the country. In developing countries, environmental groups join development and human right organizations in common battles, for instance against large-scale initiatives that involve environmental disruption and the dislocation of people. Frequently, the convergence of concerns of environment and development advocates is centred around communities as caretakers of local environments. Indeed, our conclusions here can be seen as contributing to such an emerging convergence.

In the early 1990s, interest in a community-based approach to development and environmental care has bloomed. In 1990 and 1992, dedicated international workshops took place in Italy and on the island of Malta (a third and much larger one is due to take place in the UK in 1994). The workshop in Italy developed the basic tenets of a strategy named *primary environmental care*.[44] In Malta, the social dimensions of sustainable development were explored, and institutional arrangements to involve local groups in resource management recommended.[45] It is also significant that *Caring for the Earth* – the 1991 world strategy for conservation – devoted a full chapter to 'Enabling communities to care for their own environments'.[46] The strategy called for '... providing communities and individuals with secure access to resources and an equitable share in managing them ... supported by adequate financial and technical support ... and more effective local government'. Not least, in the run up to the June 1992 Earth Summit (the United Nations Conference on Environment and Development), prestigious international institutes published several statements of support for entrusting and supporting communities as agents of local development and environmental care.[47]

So where are we in 1994? The answer is, maybe, in a transition away from the conventional, centrally controlled, large-scale development towards a more community-based and decentralized alternative. *Agenda 21*, the principal planning outcome of the Earth Summit, reflects the status quo. On the one hand, it stays with top-down development. On the other, in its key third chapter that deals with poverty, it puts much emphasis on local solutions for both environment and development problems.[48] It remains to be seen how all this develops in terms of governmental priorities but, at the very least, some of the ideas that we owe to the past have been firmly revived in the present.

Four trends currently affecting the whole world are likely to influence what will happen and, if possible, complicate matters even further. First: the human population is growing – and the groups that are growing fastest, in a tragic attempt to improve their life, are the poor and dispossessed. Second: local environments and natural resources are being degraded and depleted – not least by the wealthy – while global ecological change is building up in a variety of ways. Third: the trend towards globalization continues apace. It affects trade, transport, mass communication and the all-pervading economic network which result in local issues being dominated by international factors. (African peasants are affected by the amount of cacao the European market is ready to import; European citizens have something to say about the Japanese wanting to kill more whales; the price of Middle Eastern oil influences the amount of South American land devoted to sugarcane; and so on.) Fourth: in income terms the rich are becoming richer and the poor poorer both within and among countries (a phenomenon alleviated but not compensated by a substantial rise in the quality of life as measured by life expectancy and literacy in most parts of the world[49]). The next decades will see whether these phenomena will hasten – or impede – the policies and supports necessary for community-based sustainable development to flourish. We suspect that, ironically, they might accelerate such policies, not least because 'international welfarism' is running out of steam.

In summary: is there anything new about community-based, environmentally sound development? No and yes. Little is new in the practice of meeting one's own needs by organizing and caring for the local environment, as exemplified by the communities described in this book: people have done it for thousands of years. Little is new also in discovering the wisdom and potential of small-scale, culture-rooted, community-based forms of development. Many books have been written on the matter, many rallies have been called in its support and some national policies have even prompted large-scale social experiments in different countries.[50] If anything, today we observe a new convergence of political positions around it. Liberals are attracted by the free enterprise opportunities when people are in control of local resources. Socialists find appealing the accent on solidarity and community values. Conservatives sympathize with the recognition of local wisdom and capabilities. Pragmatists and politicians are attracted by the simple fact that – particularly in very difficult environmental and social conditions – little else seems to be working, and that small-scale, community-based initiatives are usually both effective and efficient.

Yet, the stories collected in this book are the exception, not the rule. The practice of community-based development and the frameworks to support it are far from the mainstream of political practice. Major changes – in legislation, political structures, economic incentives, aid policies, development plans, research priorities, education systems, population policies and so on – are needed to give community-based development the attention and credit it deserves. Perhaps, above all, a change of attitude is required, so that the experts and the powerful come to respect the multiplicity of values and the variety of rights of different communities. We suggest and discuss some of those changes in our final two sections.

WHAT MAKES A DIFFERENCE?

The communities we visited are not a random sample. In fact, they were selected because they could be considered *exemplary cases of success* in what some of us call *primary environmental care* or PEC, for short. What do we mean by it? An example of PEC is given by any community or group of people that organizes and acts to meet its needs (eg income, health, housing) *while* taking care of its environment. Typically, it is a community where people recognize common interests and collaborate to meet them; a community that understands the peculiar problems and opportunities presented by local resources and finds ingenious ways of responding to them; a community, in other words, that prospers in a sustainable way.

Obviously, we did not choose all the examples we knew of and which responded to the above requirements. We selected our cases mostly to illustrate variety. We wanted this book to reflect the multiplicity of physical environments where PEC can work – from high mountains to rainforest, from coastal villages to the urban sprawl. We also wanted the book to reflect the different social institutions and aggregations that can be effective – from associations of heads of households to village committees, from traditional indigenous groups to young schoolmates. Finally, we wanted to show that PEC can work in heritage environments (where unique resources need to be protected and maintained), in common environments (where non-unique resources need to be used in a sustainable way) and in degraded environments (where the most urgent action is the restoration of an ecological equilibrium, or the appropriate treatment or use of waste).

In recent years, several people had met to list and discuss conditions for success in PEC initiatives. To be honest, when we embarked on this project we expected to find more confirmation than disproof of their conclusions.[51] This expectation may have influenced us, but it also made us aware of the need to understand a whole range of issues. How did people become conscious of common problems and opportunities? How did they organize? What was 'special' about their community? How did they reconcile environmental values and their own interests – often of a monetary nature? Did they need to acquire some specific piece of information, technology or knowhow? Was there a local institution in charge of managing resources? How did they obtain enough capital to work with? Was there any help from governmental staff, such as extension officers or health care workers? Was there any help from local leaders, non-governmental organizations, aid agencies, friends from other communities? How did their initiatives take off and evolve along the way?

In our visits to the communities whose stories we told, we asked such questions and discussed the answers with many people. Often, however, we also learned by looking around, or chatting casually. At times, people told us much more than we knew how to ask. In a few cases, we left with doubts and unanswered questions in our minds. What has thus 'made a difference' in the communities we visited? As G B Shaw said, 'the only golden rule is that there are no golden rules'. We found *no single condition that plays an important role everywhere*. Every case is a case in itself, with a community seeing as a challenge and an occasion to organize what another community considers an insurmountable obstacle. But common features exist.

To begin with, in most cases *the government allows the locals to have access to resources and play a substantial role in their management*. This is very clear in Zimbabwe, where the Campfire initiative stems from the legislative act of 1975, which assigns to eligible districts the authority and responsibility to manage wildlife resources. The whole process of Campfire, in fact, is centred around a progressive devolution of power from national to district bodies, from districts to wards, from wards to villages. As decision-making gets closer and closer to them, people become more aware of the pros and cons of potential choices, they know more, they benefit more and they care more. In Mauritania, the main reason that moved pastoral associations to become active is the withdrawal – for all practical purposes – of the state control over local economies. In this case, 'the government allows' means that government has to let go of regulations that – respected or ignored, viable or absurd – stand in the way of local institutions and locally crafted arrangements. Perhaps unexpectedly, given much of its record, the World Bank played a major role in this case in prompting the government to give people a substantial resource management authority. The critical importance of exposing and stopping the pretence of state management of resources is also patent in Nepal's story. After the problems of the recent past, the government has recognized the community-based Conservation and Development Committees as the best caretakers of their forest resources and assigned to them a formal role in forest management.

In Costa Rica and the Philippines, our stories have told of struggles against governmental laws (or interpretations thereof) that are biased against small-scale enterprises. In both cases, people's access to resources is 'assured' by law, but laws are not automatically enforced or easy to comply with. In Costa Rica, it takes time, courage, capital, local support and a great dose of enterprise to bypass the tree-cutting regulations that favour the large companies. Only the latter have the resources to be represented by the state-required engineer, to travel far and wide in pursuit of permits, and to oil all reluctant wheels. In the Philippines, it takes bravery to face the law-breaking trawlers knowing that some authorities are allied to them and that they would probably protect them in court. In fact, the government has gone as far as signing international treaties that benefit large companies only. In countries such as these, we can only imagine how fairer and more sympathetic authorities might encourage and promote community-based initiatives.

Other elements fostering success are *traditional associations and customs that can play a role in local resource management*. Four of our stories are examples of initiatives carried out by resource-user groups that have strong traditional roots. The resources are herds (and thus pasture) in Mauritania, fisheries (and thus coral reefs) in the Philippines, crops (and thus land and water) in Ecuador and water and wood (and thus forests) in Nepal. Groups of pastoralist (clans, extended families) are a feature of Mauritania's dry land as much as the camels, the mint tea and the sand dunes. Today, the government is building upon them by assigning clear administrative and management authorities to pastoralist associations. The fishers of the village of San Diego organized themselves as a group only about fifteen years ago, but the tradition they follow is much older. In fact, the Philippines has long harboured resource-user associations. The *zanjeras* – for instance – are rural groups created to manage scarce water resources. They have been assuring adequate delivery of irrigation to villages for more than two centuries.[52] In Nepal, local forests had been traditionally managed by village committees. It was only in the late 1950s that the government declared the forests state property, to be directly and exclusively managed by state agencies. The policy, compounded by phenomena like internal migration and population growth, initiated a period of indiscriminate exploitation or 'open access' to the forests themselves.[53] This is only now slowly reversing, with the village committees resuming their prior role.

The Indian communities of the Andean region have centuries-old experience in collaborating to raise their crops in one of the most difficult environments on earth. Having to cope with steep grounds, difficult soils, unpredictable rains and a very harsh climate, they accumulated a tremendous wealth of biological diversity – thousands of plant varieties adapted to peculiar conditions – and a detailed knowledge of where and how to grow them. This could only develop through a wide exchange of seeds and information and through the communal work of the *minga*. (Family members alone could never build all the terraces, irrigation channels and so on needed in the Andes.) In the north of Peru, old customs such as regional fairs are currently being revived. After the main annual harvest, people from different communities congregate and camp for a few days in an open area, exhibiting, selling, buying and exchanging their crops and seeds. During these annual fairs, some non-governmental organizations and researchers from the University of Lima have promoted local competitions and offered prizes for the best products and the most detailed knowledge of properties and conditions for optimal growth. In this way, building upon old traditions, the conservation and development of local biodiversity is given one more chance to survive.[54]

Traditional associations have many advantages over other resource management options. Most obvious are their compatibility with local culture and the respect and trust they are likely to enjoy among local people. Some laws and regulations may be already adapted to their presence and they may have a tradition of dialogue with government officials and representatives of other communities. Moreover – given their experience with local issues – traditional associations can be highly effective and efficient in their tasks. But they have disadvantages too. For example, they may be perpetuating some features not conducive to people's well-being or environmental protection. In Mauritania and in some Nepalese villages, traditional groups may not accept women or lower-cast people as prominent members. In Ecuador, they may deny medical treatment to a severely wounded victim until the community assembly has decided who is at fault in the accident. (We actually witnessed such an event during our visit.)

Yet, traditional associations can change, adjust to new roles and interact with a variety of new partners. This was apparent in Ecuador, where the Indian communities are transforming fast under the pressure of male migration and the need to face market forces. Women become more prominent in the monthly assemblies, book-keeping is introduced and part of the resources, instead of being spent on food and drinks, is reinvested in community ventures. In the parish of Salinas, virtually every community has established its own cooperative, something unheard of until twenty years ago. In the Philippines, a multilevel network of associations is in place, with village groups united in regional bodies, in turn members of a national organization. This is exactly what is needed to face the powerful interests that could never be defeated by a group of fishers from a remote village.

Another lesson surfaces from our case studies. Communities confronted by a variety of problems gain the confidence to take action when *some leaders pull together the local forces and show that success – even a limited success – can be rapidly and visibly achieved.* The best examples of this we encountered in Uganda and the Philippines. It is hard to describe the pride and inner strength of the people of Kapuwai, a community that solved – by its own will and money – some of its worst health problems. As the old wise men said to the youth of the student association: 'You tell us that something can be done. Show to us that what you say is true, and we will give you our support!' That is exactly what happened. Now, having won its battle against the major child diseases, the community is ready to tackle land degradation, the encroachment of swamps and the disappearance of the few patches of forests still left in the area. We can imagine the same feelings of pride in the hearts of the fishers of SM79, returning home after having stopped a pirate trawler, confiscated its catch and made the owner sign a statement of guilt. The money of the confiscated fish was transformed into rice for the whole community, and every grain of rice must have tasted like victory, must have spurred the desire to go ahead with the fight.

Something similar happened in Poland. Darek Szwed and his friends of the Green Federation needed concrete evidence that recycling can pay before approaching the city government. They enlisted the support of the residents of a Krakow suburb, collected waste paper, sold it to a paper mill and made a profit. Then, and only then, they went to the authorities and to the schools, and explained the recycling proposal. From Costa Rica comes the stirring example of the ASACODE sawmill. People who were once sceptical are now seeing with their own eyes that Gregorio and his family are getting more money for their trees, that they choose the ones to fell and that their piece of forest is left in good conditions when extraction is done by buffalo and not by the tractors of the logging companies. As we were leaving Talamanca, new members were joining in the ASACODE scheme.

Pooling resources and demonstrating that 'it can be done' is only the beginning. As clearly shown in the Los Angeles case, the strength of a movement lies in the *continuity of the process*, in *building upon solidarity and the efficiency of working together*. Carlos Molina could have fought alone for decades without achieving much. With time, with others, he was able to influence the highest air quality authorities in Los Angeles. In the soggy marshland of Calcutta's periphery, the first six families that made their livelihood from fishing scratched a modest existence for decades. In the late '50s, they even ended up being exploited by speculators who gained control over the marshland resources. All changed when 53 members pooled together their savings and managed to lease back the land. From this moment on, they really begun to prosper. The same happened in Uganda, where only the solidarity of a large group of people could provide enough savings and enough labour for the health care activities. And, important for the environment, efficiency of working together may also mean using resources more sensibly. The small-scale producers of ASACODE recover all the timber of a felled tree, and not just the straight and large pieces. The school children of Krakow get badly needed income from paper, which would otherwise be only a burden for the community, in ecological and economic terms. It was impressive for us that the environmental benefits of activities such as these were not only appreciated because of material consequences, but often celebrated in themselves.

The experience of Campfire, in Zimbabwe, is another case that illustrates the important of continuity of purpose. The Campfire Association, which at the beginning gathered only representatives of district councils, has now opened its membership to ward councils. It was only with the passing of time and the gathering of concrete experience that the process evolved towards more and more control by local communities. Another initiative which is destined to expand with time is the eco-tourism business in Costa Rica. For such a business to be viable a broad association of communities is needed, to allow tourists to explore a variety of environments in the area, but also, and more importantly, to consolidate a biological corridor where plants and animals can continue to live and exchange genetic material. The Ugandan case also illustrates that people get easily involved when *the most highly felt problems are tackled first*. Building upon the success in health, the

Kapuwai community is now diversifying and expanding activities in environmental care. Similarly, the Licto communities, in the Andes, have chosen to work first of all for their most precious possession: land. And the women's groups in the Philippines are renewing their commitment to generate some income, without which all other initiatives seem to fail.

It is interesting to compare the approaches of the Labor/Community Strategy Center in Los Angeles, and of PACODET in Uganda. For the former, the analysis of the situation, the goals ahead and the strategy to reach them must be clear and set in the minds of the organizers. When the residents of Wilmington are woken up by an explosion at the refinery in their backyard, the organizers are there and able to provide immediate help. They have given much time to articulate a position and an ideological explanation of the problems of poor communities in Los Angeles. Now they are confident they can guide people to understand the entangled issues of pollution, labour demands and the 'right to know' applied to local health hazards. They intend to change society, and they think they know how to do it. By contrast, one cannot say that the Ugandan PACODET committee – Stanley, Filder, Amos, James, Lawrence, VV, Ann – have everything nice and clear in their minds, not even the exact objectives they would like to reach by the end of next year. They are searching, discussing, finding out about their resources and problems, taking a step at a time while maintaining only the broadest long-term goals. The very fact of seeing their land from a hilltop – which they hardly ever did before – is opening up for them a new perspective on what is happening and what they can do.

The intriguing point is that both approaches seem to be working. At least in part, this may be due to the widely different environments (from the most modern and industrial to the most traditional and rural) and the different roles of the groups. (The Labor/Community Strategy Center is composed of full-time organizers, the PACODET committee is made up of farmers, teachers and agricultural extension workers.) The matter, in any case, brings forth the issue of leadership. Is enlightened leadership necessary to pull together a community-based initiative? Should leadership be 'internal'? Can it be accomplished by external individuals, possibly professional organizers? The only lesson we can extract from our cases is that some leadership is needed but – indeed – there is not much else that can or should be specified beyond that. If anything, we have found that *effective leadership stimulates people to act for what they need and want*, as Guillelmo Teran told us in Licto. Sometimes the leadership is driven by ideology, but sometimes definitely not. Mel Baker recalled for us that the Fundacion ANAI, in Talamanca, started by helping communities set up their own nurseries. It was an act of leadership, but of a kind that provides opportunities – to diversify production, to discuss issues, to gather local energies together – and there was no problem for ANAI when the communities that built and used the nurseries decided they no longer needed them, having profited and matured in the process.

Father Antonio, in the parish of Salinas, is perhaps the leader par excellence among the people we met. He provided his flock with an uninterrupted flow of ideas and support – from the most spiritual, such as religious teachings, to the most mundane, such as grants and favourable-term loans. He is the spine of the place and also its most serious weakness, since so much that has been accomplished is due to his work. Yet, one must consider the ground that the people of Salinas have covered in barely twenty years. Father Antonio has promoted a unique situation – without someone like him, another Salinas could not exist – but he and his parish have shown that things can change. They are not offering a model that can be easily replicated, but a model from which others can learn. Less impressively but no less importantly, local leaders such as Min Bahadur Gurung, in Nepal, and Elliot Chauke, in Zimbabwe, were key for the success of various initiatives in their villages. They were willing to spend time in voluntary duties, capable of coming up with ingenious proposals, respected enough to be allowed to resolve conflicts, articulate enough to represent the community's position in front of authorities and the authorities' position in front of their community's fellows.

In fact, the issue of leadership easily takes us to the larger context of 'partnerships'. Our cases show that communities successfully engaged in primary environmental care tend to *work in effective partnership with external individuals and institutions*. Often, these external agents fulfil a limited and well-defined need. In Calcutta, the encouragement to restructure the ponds and plant trees provided by the dedicated ecologist Mukut Roy Choudhury and the legal and political support of Dr Dhrubajyoti Ghosh were essential for the fishermen's cooperative to prosper. In the Philippines, non-governmental organizations like CERD and aid agencies like Oxfam closely follow the initiatives of village fishermen and support them in crucial ways, for example by training local managers and obtaining capital for the first artificial reefs. Successful external support is generally coupled with an attitude of service and respect for local values rather than commanding expertise and objectivity. Very often, it makes use of techniques designed to facilitate, encourage and enable local people to find their own solutions and incorporate advice as they decide, as in the participatory assessment exercises we witnessed in Uganda.

In Zimbabwe, the partners in the process represent different expertise and interests in the management of natural resources. Zimtrust – a development organization – supports Campfire with training, workshops, research and funding of selected activities. The multispecies programme of WWF provides advice to establish the safe culling quota of wildlife and to outline the particular requirements of different species. The social scientists from CASS, at the University of Zimbabwe, counsel practitioners and the government on the policies that can sustain the initiative – for instance policies regarding communal property resources. Together, they work with government representatives and local authorities in a competent, interdisciplinary and flexible partnership. Only such a powerful and sophisticated arrangement could provide effective help to the one and a half million people engaged in the sustainable management of wildlife in the country. A similar interesting arrangement is found in the Annapurna Conservation Area Project of Nepal. ACAP's employees act as *facilitators and match-makers*: they help local communities identify their needs and opportunities, plan projects and find sources of revenues, information or whatever else is missing. In this way, ACAP supports a broad range of initiatives: from the reforestation of degraded areas to the construction of small hydro-electric plants, from the installation of toilets to the maintenance of trails.

For the Kapuwai community, in Uganda, two individuals have acted as key partners and match-makers. One is John Okodoi, a highly educated and respected government official who retired early from active duty due to a disabling stroke. From 1979 until his death, in 1993, he acted as patron of the PACODET association, providing them with advice, unfailing trust and important connections with national authorities and foreign organizations. The other is Dr Tom Barton, one of those 'citizens of the world' who seem to be born to help others and, in the process, find great rewards for themselves. Tom has been mostly a friend for the Kapuwai community, but a friend with pockets full of information, suggestions, tools and sources of capital for small projects. With the same warm and personal orientation, but with more of a long-term institutional basis, the Fundacion ANAI of Costa Rica has offered, for over twenty years, ideas, technical and managerial support, a variety of training courses and community credit schemes. There is little doubt that their support has been crucial for the people of ASACODE to assert themselves in front of large companies and corrupt government officials.

Finally, a feature that we did not expect to find with such a consistency. Most communities of our successful cases *are linked with (external) markets and private businesses*. This is obvious for the communities we visited in Nepal and Zimbabwe, for which tourism is a main source of revenues. Their conservation initiatives receive a substantial income from foreign visitors and depend on various private ventures and companies. The safari operators, for instance, are essential for Campfire. They have made holiday packages an art, proposing all sorts of strong emotional experiences, from surviving a close encounter with a buffalo to using a flush toilet in the jungle and without them no rich hedonist would dream of leaving his or her money in a poor and remote community. In fact, Zimbabwe shows that a regulated market – even in the case of controversial products such as ivory and wildlife trophies – can provide essential support for conservation initiatives that also benefit poor communities.

A connection with markets outside the local area is basic not only for tourism enterprises, however, but for all sorts of commercial ventures. First of all, since many environmental care initiatives require cash investments, most people see cash returns as essential. Then, a connection with markets is necessary to procure inputs (for example technology for the micro-hydro-power plants in Nepal and mosquito net material for the women's workshop in Uganda). It is also essential to provide outlets for sustainable local production, in both familiar markets – for products like timber, fish, carpets and cheese – and 'green' markets – for products like organic mushrooms and recycled paper. Even the subsistence economy of the Ugandan villages we visited is beginning to branch out, with people selling rice and importing handicraft tools. The existence of markets for such goods is essential for them to start new initiatives. Finally, as the activists of the Labor/Community Strategy Center in Los Angeles told us, a market in safely produced, ecology minded industrial products is the key for any environmentally sound and equitable future.[55] The 'entrepreneur' is alive and well in the great majority of our cases.

Let us summarize the main features we observed to 'make a difference' in the communities we visited. The most basic condition is that local people have access to resources and can play a substantial role in their management. Sometimes this is in direct continuity with tradition, with existing groups remaining in charge and old customs revitalized to face new requirements. At other times, groups are formed ad hoc and, little by little, find their optimal structure and functions. A favourable milieu includes markets and business ventures that can link with environmentally sound productive activities. The markets may deal with typical 'green' commodities (like organic mushrooms, recycled paper, walks in conservation areas and non-polluting, non-hazardous products) but also with all-colour commodities, like fish, rice, timber, meat and the opportunity to exercise a gun on wildlife.

Besides markets, we found community-based initiatives to profit from partnerships with a variety of external individuals and institutions, which supply – as needs arise – information, legal and technical advice, financial assistance, credit, training, technology, facilitation, managerial assistance and so on. A crucial role is the one of match-makers – people or institutions who identify and contact all partners potentially interested in a given initiative; they make a world of difference for many local communities. Partnership and leadership are linked issues. Whether the people who initially promote activities are born locally or come from outside has little to do with the ultimate results. It is rather more important that leaders stimulate the will and sense the capability of a community, for instance by calling people to discuss a highly felt problem and finding out together that success can be achieved. As usual, deeds are clearer than a thousand words. In the long run, solidarity around common goals and the productivity gain of working together tend to foster the continuity of the process.

There is a common feature among our cases that we have not yet mentioned. It is a sense of togetherness and pride, a desire to work and take responsibility for one's own future, a 'spirit of the community' linked more with culture and history than economics and development programmes. It includes a pride in building and maintaining a beautiful place. It is the light in the eyes of people when they speak of their dreams, the bent back of someone who has done volunteer work, the attentive faces and the broad smiles at a community meeting. This spirit can emerge as a reaction against injustices and a common enemy. It can also be born out of a sense of wonder, and celebration for what has been and can still be achieved.

WHAT NEXT?

This book is about communities that succeed in primary environmental care. We told their stories and explored the characteristics and conditions that 'made a difference' for the people involved. It was not our aim to provide an exhaustive case for community-based management of natural resources.[56] Nor was it to suggest that all environmental and social problems can be solved locally. In fact, there are irreplaceable roles to be played by national and international authorities. Even a hypothetical society in which all local communities are fully involved in primary environmental care would need coordinating and supporting bodies at various levels, especially – but not only – in those activities for which the economy of scale is most important (eg formal education, curative health care, disaster relief). Still, we believe that *community-based initiatives* such as the ones described in this book demonstrate benefits to the participants and to society at large, and offer hope for a more equitable and sustainable future. These initiatives *deserve to be extensively replicated and spread*. It is with this objective in mind that we asked ourselves 'what next?'.

The first and rather obvious answer is that we hope this book inspires yet more to act in their own neighbourhood. Whether we live in a rural or urban area, we are likely to understand the peculiarities, problems and unique advantages of our immediate environment. We may know of an unclean garbage collection site, of a river where fish are becoming less abundant, of a dangerous crossroads or of a wood degraded by fire and lack of care. We may also know of an untapped water source, of a local business association willing to contribute to social activities, of an area where the micro-climate favours the cultivation of a valuable market product, or of a traditional way of sharing tasks and profits in managing the local forest. By talking and getting together with other residents, we can act upon that knowledge. In the spirit of primary environmental care we would give priority to initiatives that benefit the environment while bringing other returns – for example economic, aesthetic, health related – to the community as a whole.

There is something 'natural' about caring for one's own environment, especially in those communities where families have lived in the same place for a long time. In many cultures even the simplest gesture – like stopping on the way home and casually removing stones and dirt from a drainage channel by the side of the road – reveals a sense of stewardship. Nothing to brag about. Nothing even to notice. But if everyone, on the way home, behaved in such a way, there would be no flooded road in the winter, no repairs to be carried out and much smaller management costs. It is by re-establishing a sense of local pride, a sense of belonging to a place and community, that primary environmental care will naturally replicate. But this cannot be provided from outside. It can only grow from within, taking nourishment from culture and history. It can only be created by us in our own neighbourhood.

The role of outsiders – national governments, local agencies, non-governmental organizations, business, credit institutions, aid agencies and so on – is to provide *favourable conditions and appropriate forms of support* for local initiatives. We hope that this book is read also by people who, because of their profession, activities or concerns, can influence those conditions and offer that support. We need to stress, however, that the size of the task is enormous. There exist innumerable environments in which community-based initiatives could make a world of a difference for both the people involved and the environmental conditions. If feasible replication is at stake, outside agents need to figure out what little support can obtain large results. In other words, we should ask ourselves 'what next, in a cost-effective way?'. The stories collected in this book provide us with several indications. We summarized them under four main headings.

1. Decentralize control over natural resources

For people to become active in environmental care a basic condition is that they have the authority and responsibility to do so. Much presumed 'lack of care' arises because people do not feel in charge or, indeed, do not have the power to act. If a national or local government wants to involve people in the sound management of local resources, it can, first of all, review the legal basis for such an involvement. Private property of land is a well-known way of assuring local control over resources. (It does not, however, necessarily guard against abuse and waste.) Communal property of land and/or resources represents a significant alternative.[57]

This is not the place to discuss the variety of legal arrangements for communal access to resources. What we wish to emphasize, however, is that private ownership is not a necessary condition for success and governments do not need to relinquish all their rights. On the contrary, a variety of co-management arrangements – such as long-term leases, limited resource-extraction permits, limited rights of use or of change of destination – are suited to combine formal ownership by the government with *people's security of access through time.* One example beyond those in the book serves to illustrate the point. In India, following the National Forest Policy of 1988, the forest departments of several states assigned to local communities the usufruct rights over their neighbouring forests. The rights included the extraction and use of all non-wood products and of a percentage share of the wood products – subject to successful forest protection and other conditions approved by the state. The local management plans were developed jointly by community organizations and state foresters, with the support of non-governmental organizations whenever necessary. The result? A clear reversal of forest degeneration and dramatic increases in productivity, all at minimal cost.[58]

This example – as well as several others collected in the book – suggests that governments have much to gain by decentralizing control and responsibility for local resources. The national regulatory framework can be left flexible enough to accommodate local peculiarities, but it is desirable that local regulations end up being specific and stringent.[59] Who is benefiting from local resources? Who is in charge, and responsible for their management? Who is directly accountable for the results? To whom? With what possible consequences? When questions such as these can be answered in a straightforward way, it is unlikely that the local environment is abandoned and degraded. As in many of our stories, local control over and responsibility for resources is the other face of local environmental care.[60]

2. Strengthen local institutions for resource management

Many readers will be familiar with wards, parishes, communes, panchayats, counties, districts and so on as their smallest units of local government. In an ideal world, government and communities merge at some point, and there is perfect coincidence of interests and intent. Sadly, this is extremely rare. In fact, it is rare even to find an explicit dialogue between many 'authorities' and 'communities', for instance to agree on common objectives and negotiate respective responsibilities. Many institutional arrangements for the management of resources, for instance, do not correspond to units of production and benefit. This makes little sense, since for a group of people to spend time and effort in environmental care they must perceive a clear link between the quality of management (including their work input) and the magnitude of benefits in return.[61] As pointed out by Marshall Murphree[62] – effective care of resources may require that even single individuals providing differential inputs receive differential benefits.

An essential element of sound resource management is a local body that discusses, organizes, plans, takes action, responds on a human scale and, not least, provides for an equitable matching between inputs and benefits. Many such local bodies have existed as administrative units for centuries – examples are the community assemblies in Ecuador or the parishes in the UK. Others have only recently been recognized by state acts – such as the peasant associations in Mauritania or the development committees in Nepal. Some groups are mostly interested in the use of a particular resource, an example being the Mudialy cooperative, in Calcutta. Others, such as PACODET in Uganda, aim at a general improvement of living conditions. As in our Los Angeles story, the 'local body' may not be directly in charge of resource management but have taken upon itself to convey the interests and concerns of people to appropriate authorities. In all cases, the important point is that local institutions exist, assume responsibility over local resources and are recognized by and accountable to both local people and national authorities.[63] Amazingly, this essential aspect of organization – the effective link between national authorities and people – is so often ignored by the central governments and the development process.

Moreover, what in development jargon is referred to as 'capacity building' rarely includes substantial attention and investments at the local level. The cases illustrated in this book demonstrate that this is a mistake. Governments and development agencies can expect great returns if they strengthen local institutions for resource management and provide them with incentives to act. At least in part, our cases are successful because local institutions have been recognized and nurtured. For instance, for years Zimtrust has been offering training, workshops and networking for the ward and community councils involved in Campfire. Similarly, leadership training by CERD played a key role in the development of effective local organizations in the Philippines. And Fundacion Anai promoted local institutions in Costa Rica in many indirect ways. In their rotating fund programme, for instance, they asked communities to take collective responsibility for the individual repayment of loans, and only someone presented by a local 'credit committee' was given access to loans. In this way, communities that wished their members to apply had to get organized.

3. Match-make for partnership and support

Even when people and local institutions have a reasonable amount of control over local resources and possess the relevant skills, a community needs a catalytic impulse to get organized and act: the social equivalent of the grain of sand that prompts an oyster to create a pearl. That grain of sand can be provided by leaders/organizers/facilitators who help the community pull its energies together, scout for external support and match various social actors for common goals. These leaders/facilitators can belong to the community or come from outside – moved by professional, political, religious motivations, or even by a not easily specified sense of solidarity and friendship.

In practice, what does the process entail? It can all begin by gathering community members around a project everyone easily approves and supports (such as a nursery, in Costa Rica; recycling paper, in Poland; or setting up a health care scheme, in Uganda). It may also begin by rallying people to solve a strongly felt problem (such as the depletion of fisheries in the Philippines, or the deterioration of trails in Nepal). Or it may begin by a systematic, interactive exploration of local needs and resources (as in participatory appraisal exercises such as the one we witnessed in Uganda). Specific action can then be agreed upon in community meetings and planning workshops. Action can also arise spontaneously because some individuals are highly motivated. The essential point is that one or more persons make it their business to catalyse the community's energy and ingenuity, and to look intelligently beyond its immediate boundary for the inputs and support that are not available locally. Such 'match-making' usually links the community with governmental services and non-governmental support, be it from private individuals, business groups, international organizations, aid agencies, or any other body capable and willing to help.

Facilitators and match-makers can be trained, and many development organizations are beginning to do just that. Even some aid agencies are currently examining how they can best 'institutionalize' their support for PEC initiatives. Changes to a variety of elements in the work of organizations – from the attitude of professionals to disbursement procedures; from conditionality issues, to programme formulation activities will have to be made.[64] A few governments are actively involved, for instance the government of Nepal, which is providing support to the *lamis*. Unfortunately this is rather uncommon.[65] More often than not, the grain of sand does not come from coherent governmental programmes but from the serendipitous initiative of community members, the personnel of non-governmental organizations or friends and concerned professionals from a variety of sectors.

A variety of forms of support can help a community engage in primary environmental care. Small grants, for instance, can make a world of a difference. They have been used to enable community members to visit others and observe what they do, to prime local 'rotating funds' or to import critical technology and tools. Similarly, credit schemes and matching funds can be used to increase a community's capital base and build upon existing knowledge and capabilities. Training in business management and technical skills allows people to begin new activities as do key material inputs such as seeds and tools. Often, legal assistance is required for communities to find out about and act upon their rights. On-going provision of simple and effective technical advice and technological innovations helps, as does support for communication and networking. Although the time frame of the experiences we examined varies from one year to several decades, it is the common perception of all the people we met that community initiatives fully develop over a long period, and thus require continuity of support (although not necessarily the same kind of support at various stages).

Last but not least, the success of the initiatives we encountered appears in no small measure tied to the approach and style of people involved – as both local players and external supporters. Human qualities like enthusiasm, perseverance, courage, patience, willingness to work hard, honesty, openness to new ideas and the capacity to communicate, although difficult to include in a 'what next?' recipe, may be essential ingredients for replicating and spreading primary environmental care. At the root of everything well done, we always seemed to find generous people.

4. Make markets work for people

In many areas of the world, the *dominance* of market forces is a relatively recent phenomenon. Although exchange of products has been important in all human societies for thousands of years, it is only in the recent past that the fine tuning of subsistence in traditional communities has been shattered by the increasing local demand for cash. With that demand, surplus-generation and profits have become crucial in the decision-making of households and producers, with momentous consequences for local environments and communal life.[66] This phenomenon cannot be ignored. Moreover, it cannot be ignored that, as mentioned in the previous section, many community-based initiatives that appear sustainable and socially beneficial are related to business ventures and markets – including sophisticated and controversial international markets. And that many sound environmental-care practices require cash investments – which people are willing to make only when cash returns can be confidently expected. As a consequence, for governments and institutions interested in multiplying primary environmental care initiatives there is a clear indication that

189

they should promote access to markets – and even create new markets wherever the local economic environment is sluggish and uncooperative. But, *what kind of markets?*

Even in very remote places – as every traveller knows – there is little problem in finding soft drinks or avenues for exporting highly profitable raw materials. The markets we are talking about, however, are different. They are *regulated markets*, in which sustainable production is encouraged and an equitable flow of benefits is assured. In such markets, profits would reward those who produce with consideration for the environment and the health of workers, whose products contribute to meeting the needs of local people, and whose work creates more work in local communities. In this sense, there is a great challenge ahead for policy-makers to develop and enforce appropriate regulations. To start, it is important to remove disincentives, such as low taxation for production processes that dump on society the cost of environmental damage and reduce local opportunities. Instead, products designed to respond to ecological *and* social criteria can be given incentives, with advantages for both producer and consumer communities and for the sustainable development of countries, much less the globe.[67] The same challenge applies to private and community-based business, which will hopefully respond with ingenious and socially responsible enterprise.

Among the ecological and social criteria that could identify positive initiatives are: the sustainability of production processes; the promotion of biological diversity and the protection of unique habitats and environmental functions; the strict compliance with public health regulations; the creation of jobs and the enhancement of local skills; the creation of widely spread rather than individual benefits; the reinvestment of profits in the producer community; and the promotion of community well-being and cultural identity. Beyond such general considerations, the meaning of 'regulated market' must be left unspecified – it is too dependent on the national economic situation and social background to be described in detail outside a specific context. Such markets, however, can be expected to reconcile the liberalization of trade[68] with full protection and support to valuable ecological and socio-cultural environments.

It would be naive to disregard the fact that a process by which communities acquire control over local resources, organize themselves in management institutions, strengthen their capabilities, enter into a variety of partnerships and gain full access to regulated markets, has fundamental political implications. Yet, this book is not a political treatise. We gladly leave to others the task of articulating a coherent political message based on primary environmental care – if any can be. We only wanted to tell the stories – fascinating for us – of communities who have taken the future into their own hands. We offered our reflections on how their example can be replicated and expanded upon. They offered us many reasons to hope.

NOTES AND REFERENCES

CALCUTTA

1. The society has approximately 100 full members, 176 nominal members and 150 casual labourers.
2. The following publications give an excellent overview of the East Calcutta Marshes, the Mudialy fishery and the whole issue of low-cost, self-help sanitation:

   Ghosh, D and Sen, S (1987) 'Ecological History of Calcutta's Wetland Conversion', *Environmental Conservation*, Vol 14 No 3.

   Ghosh, D (1990) 'A Low-cost Sanitation Technology Alternative for Municipal Wastewater Disposal Derived from the Calcutta Sewage-Fed Aquaculture Experience', in Edwards, P and Pullin, R S V (eds) Wastewater-fed Aquaculture, Asian Institute of Technology, Bangkok.

   — (1991) 'Self-help Sanitation – Towards a Third World Option,' *Global 500 Newsletter*, UNEP.

   — (1992) *Urban Sanitation Ecosystem in the Wetlands to the East of Calcutta*, Ashoka Foundation, Calcutta.

   Mukul, (1992) 'To Save the Wetlands: Struggle by a Fishermen's Cooperative in Calcutta', in *Frontline*, 20 Nov.

   World Wide Fund for Nature (WWF) – India (1991) *The Wetlands of Calcutta – Sustainable Development or Real Estate Takeover?*, WWF, Calcutta.

3. The National Environmental Engineering Research Institute (NEERI) published its *Water Quality Studies of the Jeel in Calcutta Port Area* in 1990. The studies included an analysis of water quality in the area leased by the Mudialy Fishermen's Cooperative Society. Biological oxygen demand (BOD) was measured at 77.58 mg/l in the incoming water and 15.00 in the outgoing water. 99.9 per cent of faecal coliform bacteria coming into the system was removed during passage through the ponds. Mercury levels in the incoming water were measured at 4.52 g/l; NEERI was unable to detect any mercury in the outgoing water.
4. In 1945, the wetlands covered approximately 20,000 acres; of this, 11,570 acres were devoted to sewage-fed fisheries, the rest

lying fallow. Sewage-fed fisheries now cover just under 7,500 acres.

NEPAL

1. For a good critical assessment of ACAP, see *A Profile and Interim Assessment of the Annapurna Conservation Area Project, Nepal*, by Michael P Wells, prepared for the Liz Claiborne Art Ortenberg Community Based Conservation Workshop, December 1992. ACAP has produced a variety of progress reports, published by the King Mahendra Trust for Nature Conservation (PO Box 3712, Jawalakhel, Kathmandu).
2. According to one unpublished study, social problems related to tourism include 'drug use and idle youth who seem unenthusiastic about taking up rural lifestyles'. Trekkers periodically offend local sensibilities by dressing immodestly and failing to respect religious customs and monuments.
3. Village Development Committees replaced *panchayats* in 1990 when the monarchical system gave way to the democratic. Within each VDC there are nine wards and members of the VDC are elected by the constituents.
4. Mustang was opened up to foreigners in March 1992 with the Ministry of Tourism delegating responsibility for the management of the Upper Mustang Conservation and Development Programme (UMCDP) to ACAP. The number of tourists allowed into the region is controlled, each paying $700 for a ten-day trek ($70 for each additional day). Sixty per cent of this revenue will go to the UMCDP. The money will be used to help local people manage the environment in a sustainable way. A range of projects – covering everything from health to education, the restoration of Buddist *gompas* to the provision of solar energy – is being considered by the villagers. Critics of the UMCDP point out that ACAP has little authority to control the numbers of tourists and the sorts of businesses which will emerge to serve the new tourist industry.
5. ACAP's Minimum Impact Code, which tells visitors how to 'step gently' in this fragile region, is published in a leaflet about ACAP which is given to every trekker when he or she applies for a permit to visit the region. ACAP also has permanent displays explaining its work and entreating trekkers to help in the conservation effort at Pokhara and Ghandruk.
6. Conservation and Development Committees were originally known as Forest Management Committee. Each CDC has fifteen members, including nine people representing the nine wards of the VDC, the VDC chairman and three people (two women and

one low-caste representative) chosen by ACAP. CDCs meet on the first day of the Nepali month (the Nepali new year begins on 13 April and the Nepali calendar is 57 years ahead of the Gregorian). CDCs are supported by sub-CDCs and each employs two or three *sangracchan beralos,* or conservation guards.

7. At the time of our visit, ACAP was shortly going to appoint another woman to the committee.

8. In March 1993, 29 children attended the daycare centre. The parents paid 25 rupees a month for each child and supplied some rice; the four children of low-caste parents were exempt from charges and the teachers were trying to encourage other low-caste families to send their children too. The Mothers' Group had raised 8,000 rupees to set up the centre, and ACAP paid the teachers and helpers as well as the rent.

9. The agro-forestry programme was now in its third year. Under the guidance of Filip Debruyne, a Dutch agriculturalist, a variety of demonstration plots had been established. These were used to show farmers that it was possible to grow good crops without using artificial fertilizers and pesticides; there was a heavy emphasis on mulching, inter-cropping and the integration of trees within the agricultural system. ACAP had also established a network of 'conservation farmers', enthusiastic individuals who were prepared to impart to others the knowledge gained from training courses. This they did in return for training by ACAP and free seeds.

ZIMBABWE

1. General descriptions of the historical development, aims and strategy of Campfire can be found in the following:

Centre for Applied Social Sciences of the University of Zimbabwe (CASS), World Wide Fund for Nature (WWF) Multispecies Animal Production Systems Project and Zimbabwe Trust (Zimtrust) (1989), *Wildlife Utilization in Zimbabwe Communal Lands,* CASS/WWF/Zimtrust Coordinating Committee, Harare.

Child, B and Peterson, J H (1991), *Campfire in Rural Development: The Beitenbridge Experience,* Joint Working Paper Series, CASS, Harare.

Dept of National Parks and Wildlife Management (revised version 1986), *Communal Areas of Management Programme for Indigenous Resources,* Zimbabwe.

Environmental Consultants Ltd (1990), *People, Wildlife and Natural Resources: The Campfire Approach to rural Development in Zimbabwe,* Zimtrust/Dept of National Parks and Wildlife Management/Campfire Association, Harare.

— (1992), *Wildlife: Relic of the Past or Resource of the Future?*, Zimtrust, Harare.

2. See Thomas, S (1991), *The Legacy of Dualism and Decision Making: The Prospects for Local Institutional Development in Campfire*, CASS, Harare, p 7.
3. The value of the Zimbabwe dollar has decreased in recent years. One US$ was valued at about Z$2.7 in 1990, Z$5 by October 1992.
4. Historical and current land use in Zimbabwe is discussed in Murphree, M W and Cumming, D H M (1991), *Savannah Land Use: Policy and Practice in Zimbabwe*, CASS/WWF Paper no 1. The impact of government policies is illustrated in Jansen, D, Bond, I and Child, B (1992), *Cattle, Wildlife, Both or Neither*, WWF Multispecies Project, Harare.
5. It is essential to understand how the various interests at stake in wildlife management can be satisfied in an *equitable* way. For an in-depth discussion of this issue see the following:

    Murombedzi, J (1991), *Decentralizing Common Property Resources Management: The Case of Nyaminyami District Council of Zimbabwe's Wildlife Management Programme*, IIED, London.
    Murphree, M W (1991), *Communities as Institutions for Resource Management*, CASS, Harare.
    Thomas, S J (1992), 'Equity in Campfire: wildlife as a communal property resource in Zimbabwe', Zimtrust manuscript, Harare.

6. The term 'alienated' means land under private ownership, as opposed to communal land held under a communal tenurial arrangement.
7. The Department remains the responsible authority over all wildlife even today; as such, it can step in in cases of abuse and even has the power to withdraw 'appropriate authority' status.
8. This is an important step towards communal management of natural resources and a most promising approach to conserving the environment while meeting the needs of local communities. For discussion of the subject in general, see the following:

    Berkes, F (ed) (1988), *Common Property Resources*, Belhaven Press, London.
    Bromley, D W and Cernea, M M (1989), *The Management of Common Property Natural Resources*, Discussion Paper no 57, World Bank, Washington, DC.
    McCay, B J and Acheson, J M (eds) (1987), *The Question of the Commons*, University of Arizona Press, Tucson.
    Murphree, M W (1991), 'Communities as Institutions for Resource Management', *CASS Occasional Papers*, Harare.

Ostrom, E (1990), *Governing the Commons: The Evolution of Institutions for Collective Action,* Cambridge University Press, New York.

9. The concept of 'producer community' is often used when discussing communal resource management systems. In the case of wildlife, the concept is complicated by the fact that the resource at stake is migratory, and may be found in different areas according to seasons, weather, population pressure etc. Since the Campfire regulations establish that safari revenues must accrue to the district/ward in which an animal is killed, inequities may occur when most of the costs and damages from an animal have been inflicted on a district/ward different from the one in which the animal is killed. Some, in fact, would maintain that a 'producer community' is essentially the community that bears the costs (including the opportunity costs) related to the survival or maintenance of a particular resource.

10. Prof Murphree suggests that the ideal size of a producer community is 100 to 200 households, eg large enough for a wildlife programme, and small enough for all households to be involved and accountable to one another. See Murphree, M W (1989), *Research on the Institutional Context of Wild Life Utilization in Communal Areas of Eastern and Southern Africa,* CASS, Harare.

11. For instance see:

    Barbier, E, Burgess, J, Swanson, T and Pearce, D (1991), *Elephants, Economics and Ivory,* Earthscan, London.
    Keuter, U P and Simmons, R (1992), 'The economics and politics of African elephant conservation', paper presented at the conference of the International Association for the Study of Common Property, Washington, DC, 17–20 Sep.

12. Robert Monroe points out that, while critics have every right to hold this opinion, the SACIM (South Africa Centre for Ivory Marketing) Treaty, signed by Zimbabwe, Botswana, Namibia, Malawi and Zambia in 1991, binds the signatories to allowing *all* revenues from ivory to go direct to SACIM (bypassing national treasuries), to be used exclusively for elephant conservation.

UGANDA

1. An excellent, if brief, history of PACODET's activities is given in *Pallisa Community Development Health Care Centre – A Community Participation Model Project* by John Okodoi, 1992. John Okodoi, PACODET's patron, was an eminent and much travelled individual. From 1979–85 he was the Permanent Secretary in the Ministry of Cooperatives and Marketing, and he was a keen supporter of PACODET's activities. News of his sudden death reached us shortly before we went to press.

2. Some members of the community wished to make larger contributions than 100 shillings. However, it was decided that everyone should give the same sum, and that this should be affordable to all.
3. The volunteers represented specific communities that were very keen for the volunteers to be trained.
4. According to *Provisional Results of the 1991 Population and Housing Census* (Ministry of Planning and Economic Development, Kampala, June 1991) population growth in the Pallisa district during the 1980s was 2.9 per cent per year.
5. The capital for the rotating fund – about 200,000 shillings – was raised from members' dues and from the profits made from selling bricks by the community. The credit idea is well understood and for many years families have borrowed from churches, school funds and so forth.
6. It seems that rice paddy provides a more favourable breeding habitat than natural marshland for malaria-transmitting mosquitos. See Steyn, J J (1946), 'The effect on the anopheline fauna of cultivation of swamps in Kigezi district, Uganda', *East African Medical Journal*, vol 23, pp 163–9.
7. In the autumn of 1993, USAID agreed to fund the setting up of a sewing/carpentry workshop. In Kapuwai people often complained that they were cold at night during the winter months as they had no blankets; they were also much bothered by mosquitos. With the founding of the workshop, they will now be able to make mosquito nets and quilts.

MAURITANIA

1. In July 1993 US$1 = 120 ougiya.
2. For an excellent summary of the achievements of Mauritania's Second Livestock Project, see *Resource Management and Pastoral Institution Building in the West African Sahara* by Shanmugaratnam, N et al, World Bank Discussion Paper 175. This paper also looks at projects assisted by the Bank in Niger, Mali and Senegal. A useful resumé of experiences in these countries is provided by Djeidi Sylla in a recent paper for a research workshop 'New Directions in African Range Management Policy', organized at Woburn, UK, 31 May to 4 June 1993 by IIED, ODI and the Commonwealth Secretariat. The budget for the Second Livestock Project (1987–92) in Mauritania was $18.9 million, $2.4 million of which was allocated to pastoral organization and training. The World Bank instigated the project, but loans were also received from OPEC and the African Development Fund.
3. The Republique Islamique du Mauritanie became an indepen-

dent state in 1960. During the colonial period the French ruled this part of its West African Empire from St Louis, which is now in Senegal. The capital city, Nouakchott, was founded at the time of Independence.

4. General assemblies are held every two years. According to the World Bank Discussion Paper 157 (see note 2), 'The 20 days for establishing one PA left only a few hours for meetings and discussions in each village – too short a time for any real participation of the pastoralists to take place.'

5. The sands of the Sahara are tremendously fertile; lack of rain, rather than low fertility, is the limiting factor. Areas which have become 'desertified' since the droughts are not lost forever: regular rain would bring them back to life.

6. In addition, many of the best grazing lands have been converted to croplands over the past few decades, which has further reduced the amount of land available to pastoralists.

7. This sounds contradictory, and the pastoralists seemed somewhat uncertain about the value of hay-making. If in the future they built up a sedentary milk herd, then the hay will undoubtedly be of local use. But really to make the enterprise profitable, the PA must transport the hay to the region around the capital where there is a serious demand for it.

8. There is much debate among pastoral experts about the desirability – and feasibility – of conserving dryland pastures. Many believe conservation programmes in these regions to be a waste of time and money (although foreign aid agencies may be prepared to foot the bill) as dryland pastures will almost invariably regenerate when they receive sufficient rain. During our travels in Mauritania we heard much about the need to conserve pastures, but it is unclear whether the idea came originally from the pastoralists themselves or whether they were simply 'toeing the line' to impress the World Bank, the main paymaster of the Second Livestock Project.

9. In each case, the PA will contribute 10 per cent of costs for well-building and well-renovation. If its members provide manual labour and help supply materials such as stone and sand the PA will earn back its 10 per cent contribution.

KRAKOW

1. Over 1,100 buildings in Old Krakow have been listed as historic monuments. UNESCO has recognized Krakow's architectural importance by declaring the city a World Heritage Site.

2. The original twelve apostles are housed in a shed behind the church; the ones on show in front of the baroque facade are modern copies. For details of the city's restoration work, see

Cracow: history, art, renovation, published by the Citizen's Committee for the Restoration of Cracow's Historical Monuments (undated).
3. Figures supplied by the Polish Ecological Club.
4. Steel production has fallen from a high of 6.5 million tonnes a year to around 3 million tonnes a year.
5. *The Times*, 15 April 1988.
6. The Green Federation has no written constitution, no formal membership, no power structure of any sort. There are approximately twenty groups spread across the country; all are run along anarchist lines. As it is not officially recognized by the state, the Green Federation cannot apply for grants from other organizations; the Foundation for the Support of Ecological Initiatives fulfils this function on its behalf.
7. Cited by Grzegorz Peszko and Wojciech Stodulski in *Green Brigades*, issue no 7, spring 1992.
8. For a good discussion of the problems of recycling, see *Costing the Earth* by Frances Cairncross (Economist Books, London 1991), pp 201–21.

LOS ANGELES

1. In the words of a local real estate agent 'Good air quality is one of the primary determinants of property value in the area'.
2. Emitters include road vehicles (cars, trucks) and other mobiles (aeroplanes, ships, trains, construction equipment), industrial plants and manufacturers, commercial services (for example dry cleaners, car body shops, painters) and consumer products (hair sprays, windscreen washer fluids, household pesticides, radiator and brake fluids, household cleaners, body lotions, air fresheners and disinfectants). Transport is primarily responsible for the emission of carbon monoxide and nitrogen oxide, while the industries and manufacturers are the primary emitters of toxic particulate matter.
3. Photochemical smog was revealed for the first time in Los Angeles in 1944 by people investigating damage to vegetation, eye irritations and reduced visibility. It forms when nitrogen oxides react with volatile organic compounds in the presence of sunlight. Contrary to common belief, low-altitude ozone is not restricted to urban areas. The pollutant can rapidly move to rural areas and there is evidence of extensive damage to European forests as well as a potential 5–10 per cent loss in crop yields both in Europe and the USA.
4. As reported by the AQMD, LA is regularly first among US urban areas for the number of days with ozone measurements exceed-

ing the federal standards. The world's highest ozone concentration value was measured in LA in 1955. (See also note 7.)

5. See Mann, E (1990) in *The Nation*, 17 September, p268.
6. Information from a briefing paper issued in 1990 by the AQMD. In the paper it is stated that the ozone in LA's air has been reduced by about 50 per cent since the 1950s, despite the increases in population, jobs and traffic. If no control had been put in place, the levels would have soared to four or five times what they actually are. A comprehensive plan to achieve state and federal standards of air quality is currently being implemented, and includes provisions for the use of cleaner fuels, the rapid introduction of cleaner vehicles, energy conservation, reduced emissions from all sources of pollution and reduced vehicle miles travelled and trips taken.
7. In the late 1980s, however, several corporations have initiated ambitious programmes of pollution abatement coupled with extensive publicity.
8. An example of such choice would be the conversion of a military industry into an industry producing mass transportation vehicles. This would need substantial government support, and the new industry would produce less toxic waste and pollution, and offer safer but fewer jobs. The key questions in this example, are: what happens to the workers laid off? and, since public money is involved, should the new jobs remain with the previous workers or go to the unemployed in the community – for example the black women who never managed to get proper training and a proper employment? The answers are not at all straightforward.
9. WATCHDOG members estimate these to be physical responses to acute hydrogen sulphide exposure.
10. Individuals in the USA are rarely requested to show identity or residence papers. Many recent or illegal immigrants, although important parts of the labour force, do not possess legal documents.

COSTA RICA

1. Squatting is one way of getting rights to land in Costa Rica. Prior to the 1980s Costa Rican law required individuals to clear forest in order to acquire the right of possession. Taxes on land with natural forest were also higher than on 'improved' land. Today squatting is totally prohibited, in theory, in Indian reservations. See Utting, P (1991), *The Social Origin and Impact of Deforestation in Central America*, UNRISD Discussion Paper 24, UNRISD, Geneva.

2. There were 200 colones to a pound sterling in May 1993.
3. Many companies hire workers for less than three months in order to avoid providing the benefits generally accorded by Costa Rican law. This creates a population of transient young men who go in and out of employment: a recipe for alcohol abuse, violent crime and forest encroachment.
4. Tax breaks and other incentives have led to the area under commercial banana plantations in Costa Rica rising from 20,535 hectares in 1985 to 32,000 by 1992. The banana industry imports almost a third of all pesticides used in Costa Rica, with an average 250–300 cases of severe pesticide poisoning involving agricultural workers being reported each year. The use of pesticides has undoubtedly had a deleterious impact on river life and may be affecting the country's fringing coral reefs. It seems certain that spray-drift affects the wildlife in forests beside banana plantations. There is an urgent need for research on the impact of pesticides on Costa Rica's wildlife. See Lewis, S A (1992), 'Banana Bonanza', *The Ecologist*, Vol 22.
5. ANAI has also offered a small-scale credit programme to villagers and helps communities to set up a rotating fund managed by elected committees. Committee members undergo an ANAI-sponsored training course in financial management. Individuals can apply to the committee for a grant, which must be paid back within a stipulated amount of time. If the community maintains its capital intact for at least 3 years, the fund is assigned to it permanently.

ECUADOR

1. The parish of Licto comprises 26 separate communities and is situated in the canton of Riobamba, province of Chimborazo. The land surface is 6,446 hectares, with the population thinly dispersed (an average of 100 families per community and 5 persons per family).
2. The term *Indios* is the generic name for indigenous people in Ecuador.
3. Subsistence agriculture is the main productive activity in Licto, and local income is generally supplemented by male migration. (In a few communities, more than 50 per cent of income comes from the remittances of migrants.) The main crops are maize, wheat, potatoes and barley. Only a few of Licto's 26 communities are served by irrigation and many do not have tap water, although nearly all have electricity. Infant mortality is much higher than in the rest of the country, and common diseases are TB, diarrhoea, parasite infections, skin diseases and alcoholism.

In the last couple of years, fourteen local peasants died of cholera.

4. This ecological distinction is very acute in Licto, and has remarkable socio-economic consequences. In the lower communities, the land is flatter and more productive, there is some irrigation, nearby *haciendas* offer employment opportunities and few people need to migrate. Communities at mid-elevation are in a critical condition: land is poorly fertilized and extremely hard to work and a large proportion of the population is migrant. In the communities settled at higher elevation, well irrigated land is quite productive, but where water is scarce and erosion has set in migration is high. It is in the communities at mid-elevation that people are most active in recuperating the soil.

5. The process is called *minifundization*, from the Spanish word *minifundio*, which literally means 'small agricultural plot'. In article 66 of the *Agrarian Law of Ecuador*, minifundio is defined as a land holding whose extension does not allow productive employment of all members of the peasant family and does not generate income compatible with the satisfaction of their basic needs or the generation of product for the market. In Licto, the average number of children per woman was, until quite recently, well above four. In the last few years, however, the birth rate has fallen by about 20 per cent throughout the Andean regions. Contributing factors include male migration and employment differentiation of women. In a specific Andean area where women have access to salaried work in haciendas for the production of flowers the birth rate has plummeted.

6. To understand the importance of the *minga* tradition it is useful to set it within a larger cultural context. Most indigenous inhabitants of the American continent resisted foreign invasions with wars, whilst the Indios were more easily dominated, but actually never destroyed. A typical characteristic of their culture is that every community, clan or household is a nucleus of its own – they do not combine to build great powers, but unite only for specific purposes. Some scholars see an important defensive strategy in this 'logic of fractionalism' which enhances the local capacity to resist foreign influences. The dominant attitude is retreating and inward-looking, with a strong attachment to households, clans and communities, to their systems of interchanges, reciprocities and solidarity and to their precise organization of space, time and work (of which the *minga* is the most characteristic expression).

7. In the last decades, a differentiation arose within Indian communities. For the sectors that participate in the processes of modernization a slow, hidden, but continuous tendency to favour the private over the communal interests can be detected. For some of these people, participation in a local *minga* becomes less and

less attractive. On the other hand, many indigenous organizations are progressively taking up the role of 'development' promoters, finding new ways of reconciling cultural ties and economic improvements. Even in the modernized sectors, however, ties have so far remained universally strong with Quechua customs like religious rituals and festive occasions.

8. In the parish of Licto, 70 per cent of all women (and 50 per cent of the population) are illiterate.

9. The assistance provided is in the form of technical advice, training, demonstration plots, tree nurseries, agricultural tools, seedlings and seeds, preventative health care, medical care and veterinary services. All of the various forms of assistance are integrated as much as possible. In general, CESA promotes agro-economical methods, including the use of manure rather than chemical fertilizers, a variety of soil conservation practices (terraces, drainage ditches, raised beds), selection of seeds, conservation of local varieties and small-scale reforestation near the homes. Increasingly, one of the reasons why peasants do not apply appropriate soil conservation practices is because their plots are so small and fragmented that there is barely enough land to plant, and no space can be spared for ancillary purposes. The incorporation of trees in the fields is easier, since the benefits are more easily perceived.

10. An interesting fact in the Andes is that people remember exactly where their ancestors have lived and what kind of rights they had over what land. Usually, there is no conflict among communities about what land they have rights to claim and/or buy.

11. There was a cholera epidemic in Ecuador in 1992 as well as in many other South American countries.

12. The *paramo* is an ecological system of tropical latitude and high altitude (approximately over 3,800 metres) characterized by dry and wet seasons and generally covered by low vegetation (bushes and *paia*, an abundant local grass with sharp edges). More tender grass is seeded for pasture during the summer months.

13. Canton of Guaranda, province of Bolivar. The parish extends on 491 square kilometres, with an approximate population of 6,000 people distributed in 21 *recintos* (communities) and the main village of Salinas, which alone counts 500 residents.

14. For more information on the organization of people in the parish of Salinas see Andrade, M (1991) *Tres Ejemplos de Empresas Campesinas: Salinas, Pastocalle, San Antonio* Desarrollo Partecipativo en los Andes and FAO, Quito, or write to UNORSAL, Salinas (Guaranda), Ecuador. Other publications on the various activities in Salinas can be obtained from the publishing house Abya Yala, Casilla 17–12–719, Quito, Ecuador.

15. Cattle do not like to eat old and dry *paia*, the typical grass of the *paramo*, and some herders burn it so that the animals can eat the

freshly sprouted grass. This practice is known as *quema del paramo*.

16. The Grupo Juvenil is one of the member organizations of UNOR-SAL. Despite the name, which means Youth Group, its members are people of all ages. It is one of the oldest and most active cooperatives in Salinas – although not the most economically successful or independent.

17. *Mestizos* are the descendants of both European colonizers and *Indios*. The distinction between *Mestizos* and 'pure' *Indio*, however, is more of a socio-cultural than a genetic nature.

18. Legally, they should have got only the 15 per cent, but people say that in practice they got most of the revenues.

19. The salt from the Salinas mine is excellent because it contains iodine and many essential minerals.

20. Potentially, an income of up to $15–20 per person per day. About fifty people regularly bring mushrooms to the drying plant, and four people work in the plant itself and in the commercialization of the product. The main limitation on local income is posed by the finite capacity of the drying plant, which at times cannot process the whole amount of supplied mushrooms, and by the scarcity of reliable, long-term buyers. There are plans to buy another drying plant in the near future.

21. The minimum monthly salary in Ecuador is 65,000 sucres – about US$35.

THE PHILIPPINES

1. There is a voluminous literature dealing with the plight of the municipal or small-scale fishers of the Philippines. Issues of *LUNDAYAN*, a quarterly publication of the Tambuyog Development Center, provide an excellent introduction to the subject. Contact: The Communications Desk, Tambuyog Development Center, Room 108-A, PSSC Building, Commonwealth Avenue, Diliman, Quezon City.

2. Again, accurate figures are hard to come by. However, one study suggests that there are 3,000 aquarium fish collectors operating in the Philippines, and that each one sprays 50 coral heads a day for an average 225 days a year. This means over 30 million coral heads are sprayed with cyanide each year. Other activities which damage reefs include *muro-ami* fishing, when divers smash the coral with rocks suspended on ropes, and *kayakas* fishing, which is similar to *muro-ami* and is practised in shallower waters. These methods are said to damage 36,000 hectares of coral a year in the Philippines.

3. Estimates for the rate at which mangrove swamps have disap-

peared vary. For those who wish to explore the matter further, see Bina, R (1988), *Updating Mangrove Forest Statistics in the Philippines*, NATMANCOM Workshop on Mangrove Research, Environment, Policy and Information, 28-30 Nov, Sulo Hotel, Quezon City.

4. A word about the administration of the Philippines. The country is divided into 72 provinces, each of which is sub-divided into municipalities, which are made up of *barangays*, or village communities. San Diego *barangay* lies within the Lian municipality in the province of Batangas. The elected leader of the *barangay* is the *barangay* captain. The word *barangay* comes from the large and ancient outriggers which carried up to 90 passengers and were used by the Malays when they migrated to the Philippines.

5. Over the past few years Oxfam has funded CERD's fisheries programme in Western Batangas to the tune of around £57,500. Trochair, Oxfam's Irish counterpart, has also contributed to the programme. Oxfam's support has enabled CERD to conduct training courses on ecology, leadership, women's issues and so forth, and it has financed specific ventures such as the building of artificial reefs and the setting up of a credit fund for small 'livelihood' projects.

6. Under Presidential Decree 704, the discharge of factory refuse or any substance deleterious to fishlife is prohibited. The anti-pollution campaigners thus have the law on their side. However, this is a tricky issue, not least because the economy of Nasugbu and Lian is based on sugar. If the distilleries and factories were to close down, large numbers of workers would lose their jobs. Moreover, many of San Diego's fishers earn money working in the cane fields at harvest time.

CONCLUSIONS

1. See: Hardin, G (1968), 'The tragedy of the commons', *Science*, 162, pp1243–; Hardin, G (1976), 'Carrying capacity as an ethical concept', in Lucas, G R and Ogletree, T W (eds), *Lifeboat Ethics*, Harper and Row, New York; and Feeny, D, Berkes, F, McCay, B J and Acheson, J M (1990), 'The tragedy of the commons: twenty-two years later', *Human Ecology*, 18 (1), pp 1–19.

2. Also scavengers of carcasses killed by large animals, and fishers. Communal hunting is likely to have been a key reason for humans to socialize in small bands.

3. See: Washburn, S L (1961), *Social Life of Early Man*, Aldine, Chicago; Simmons, I G (1989), *Changing the Face of the Earth*,

Basil Blackwell, Oxford; Oliver, R (1991), *The African Experience*, Pimlico, London.

4. Page 215 in Pirenne, H (1936), *A History of Europe*, University Books, New York.

5. This is not the place to enter into the most interesting debate on whether the increase in agricultural production stimulated population growth or vice versa. For a brief summary of such a debate see Harrison, P (1992), *The Third Revolution*, Penguin, Harmondsworth.

6. Simmons (1989) op cit, p 47. These areas included the whole of Australia and North America and a good part of South America, while in the rest of South America and in the African continent south of the Sahel a food-collecting economy existed alongside agriculture.

7. For a detailed account of collaborative institutions in various times and places see Kropotkin, P (first edition 1902), *Mutual Aid*. Kropotkin wrote in reaction to the common misunderstanding of Darwin's concept of 'struggle for survival', pointing that such a struggle is commonly directed outside rather than inside a species. He stated: 'Sociability and need of mutual aid and support are such inherent parts of human nature that at no time of history can we discover men living in small isolated families, fighting each other for the means of subsistence' (p 153 of the 1955 reprint of *Mutual Aid* by Extending Horizon Books, Boston, Ma). Kropotkin stressed that many rural small-scale institutions were violently broken up by the state (eg in France and England from the fifteenth to the nineteenth centuries) by innumerable acts and decrees and, most importantly, by the violent seizure of communal lands and its conversion to private property (enclosures etc). Collaboration, however, should not be emphasized to the point of neglecting other powerful social phenomena, such as competition. In the words of M Mead: 'No society is exclusively competitive or exclusively cooperative. Both competitive and cooperative habits must coexist. Nor [does] competition necessarily mean conflict, and cooperation solidarity [...] The Maori strove to outdo one another in bird snaring and were honored publicly for their success, but the cooperative distribution of the catch was not affected; the rivalry served only to create higher productivity' (p 460 in Mead, M (1961) (ed), *Cooperation and Competition among Primitive People*, Beacon, Boston).

8. See Polanyi, K and Arensberg, C M (1957) (eds), *Trade and Markets in the Early Empires: Economies in History and Theory*, The Free Press, Illinois. As stated by Fusfed in the book (pp 342–55): '...the motivations of economic life in modern society were definitely not the rule in primitive societies [...] the production of goods and services was embedded in political, religious, social

and kinship institutions'. Closer to our times – for instance for the guilds of Florence in the fourteenth century – the purpose of association was not first and foremost to make money. It was rather '...to preserve a certain orderly way of life – a way that envisaged a decent income for the master craftsmen but which was also [...] designed to ward off struggle between the members [...] Competition was strictly limited and profits were held at pre-scribed levels. Advertising was forbidden, and even technical progress in advance of one's fellow guildmen was considered disloyal'. (p 35 in: Heilbronner, R L (1968), *The Making of Economic Society*, Prentice-Hall, New Jersey).

9. Illuminating examples can be found in Reader, J (1990), *Man on Earth*, Penguin Social Sciences, Harmondsworth.

10. In the following we will limit ourselves to movements and ideas from the last couple of centuries. Prior examples of great interest exist, but we chose not to explore them in any detail.

11. See Kitching, G (1990), *Development and Underdevelopment in Historical Perspective: Populism, Nationalism and Industrialization*, Routledge, London. Much of the following discussion on neo-populism and populist perspectives in Tanzania and China takes this book as main reference.

12. The party – born in the US political scene in 1891– was support-ed mostly by commercial farmers, petty capitalists and entrepre-neurs living in the small towns of the US heartland. It asserted that the common person should have greater access to positions of profit and political power. In moral terms, it stressed simplici-ty, civic dedication, democracy and egalitarianism (see Hof-stadter, R (1969), 'North America' in Ionescu, G and Gellner, E (1969), *Populism: its Meanings and National Characteristics*, Weidenfeld and Nicolson, London). The etymological origin of the word 'populism' goes back to this People's Party. The con-vergence of intents between this party and the Russian corre-spondent *narodnicesvo* (which also means movement of peo-ple) ended up making the term international. It is significant, however, that while the US People's Party was made *by* farmers, the Russian one was *about* farmers, but substantially created and supported by urban intellectuals.

13. In his essay on civil disobedience (1863) Thoreau writes that: 'The character inherent in the American people has done all that has been accomplished [in the USA]; and it would have done something more if the government had not sometimes got in its way.' The quote is from Horowitz, I L (1964) (ed), *The Anar-chists*, Dell Laurel, New York p 313.

14. Goodman, P (1946), *Drawing the Line*, Random House, New York.

15. See, for instance: Berry, W (1990), *What are People For?*, North Point, San Francisco; and Berry, W (nd), *Collected Poems: 1957–1982*, North Point, San Francisco.
16. See Hennessy, A (1969), 'Latin America', pp 28–61, in Ionescu and Gellner (1969) op cit, (note 12).
17. The organization flourished between 1962 and 1964, and was then forced underground.
18. See, for instance: Kenyatta, Y (first printing 1932), *Facing Mt Kenya*; and Nyerere, J (1967), *Freedom and Unity*, Oxford University Press, Oxford.
19. Berger, P (1976), *Pyramids of Sacrifice: Political Ethics and Social Change*, Anchor Books, New York, pp 194–5.
20. The best-known Ricardian socialists are Thomas Hodgkin, John Gray, William Thompson and John Francis Bray.
21. See Walicki, A (1969), *The Slavophile Controversy over Capitalism: Studies in the Social Philosophy of the Russian Populists*, Clarendon, Oxford.
22. See: Pushkin, A, *Boris Godunov*, first set to music by Mussorgsky in 1869; and Tolstoy, L (first edition 1886), *What Then Must We Do?*.
23. The *mir* was a council of peasant elders responsible to the landowner for the work of the peasants of the village commune (*obshchina*). Before the abolition of serfdom, in 1861, the mir had the power of allocating land to peasants for their subsistence use. After the abolition of serfdom, many Russian populists hoped that the *mir* and *obshchina* could remain as institutions of communal control over the land, fending off capitalist greed and the exploitation of peasants' labour. There was a debate, however, over whether these institutions needed to be modernized by state intervention (eg by creating producer cooperatives) or left to their own. About this, and about divergence of opinions among Marxist theorists and revolutionaries, see the illuminating discussion by Kitching (1990) op cit (note 11).
24. See Ionescu, G (1969), 'Eastern Europe', in Ionescu and Gellner (1969) op cit, (note 12), pp97–121.
25. 'Blueprint for survival', *The Ecologist*, vol 2, pp 1–43, 1972.
26. See New Left Review (1982) (ed), *Exterminism and the Cold War*, Verso, London, and, in particular, the article by Rudolf Barho.
27. See: Darin-Drabkin, H (1970), *Le Kibbutz Société Differente*, Seuil, Paris; and Massari, R (1967), 'Pianificazione rurale e collettivismo agrario in Israele', *Giurisprudenza Agraria Italiana*, 9, pp 3–61, Sep.
28. The literature on *ejidos* is immense and will not be listed here. For a discussion of 'success' cases in natural resource management see, however: Anderson, E N (1992), 'Can *ejidos* work? Forest management in a Maja community', paper presented at

that all who prayed,
   with strength, or feebly,
   or not knowing that they prayed, all
moved earth and heaven to our aid.

   You all are miracles:
thanks be to God
and you.

> Don Chatfield
> Evanston, Illinois, 1980

the Conference of the International Association for the Study of Common Property, Washington DC; and Richards, E M (1992), 'The forest *ejidos* of South-East Mexico: a case study of partici-patory natural forest management', *ODI Rural Development Forestry Network*, paper 13c.

29. The ideas of Belaunde are expressed in his books *Pueblo por Pueblo* and *La Conquista del Peru por los Peruanos*, published in Lima in 1959. See also Kuczynski, P P (1977), *Peruvian Democracy under Economic Stress*, Princeton University Press, Princeton, NJ. When Belaunde came back to power several years after the coup that ousted him, his political platform had radically changed.

30. See Nyerere, J (1964), '*Ujamaa*: the social basis of African socialism', in Friedland, W H and Rosberg, C G, *African Socialism*, Stanford University Press, Stanford, CA.

31. Kitching (1990) op cit (note 11). To this point see also Khor, L (1973), *Development Without Aid*, Schocken, New York.

32. Typical examples are: Fanon, F (1963), *The Wretched of the Earth*, Grove Press, New York; Rodney, W (1972), *How Europe Underdeveloped Africa*, Bogle L'Ouverture, London; Amin, S (1976), *Unequal Development*, Monthly Review Press, New York; Davis, S H (1977), *Victims of the Miracle*, Cambridge University Press, Cambridge; Lappé, F and Collins (1977), *Food First*, Ballantine, New York; Murdoch, W W (1980), *The Poverty of Nations*, Johns Hopkins University Press, Baltimore; Jackson, T (1982), *Against the Grain*, Oxfam, Oxford; Bodley, J B (1982), *Victims of Progress*, Benjamin and Cummings, Menlo Park, Ca; George, S (1988), *A Faith Worse than Death*, Penguin, Har-mondsworth; Frank, L, *The Development Game*, Granta, London. Ivan Illich and his followers also articulated a scathing – albeit conspicuously non-constructive – criticism of the whole devel-opment enterprise as destructive of convivial lifestyles: see Sachs, W (1992), *The Development Dictionary*, Zed Books, Lon-don.

33. Schumacher, E F (1973), *Small is Beautiful. Economics as if Peo-ple Mattered*, Harper and Row, New York.

34. Lipton, M (1977), *Why Poor People Stay Poor: a Study of Urban Bias in World Development*, Temple Smith, London.

35. See, for instance, Boff, L (1979), *Jesus Christ Liberator*, Orbis Books, New York.

36. Chambers, R (1983), *Rural Development: Putting the Last First*, Longman, London.

37. See the recent assessment provided by the same Robert Cham-bers (1992): *Rural Appraisal: Rapid, Relaxed and Participatory*, Institute of Development Studies, University of Sussex, Brighton.

38. See, for instance: Adelmann, I and Morris, C T (1973), *Economic Growth and Social Equity in Developing Countries*, Stanford Uni-

versity Press, Stanford, CA; Murdoch, W W (1980), *The Poverty of Nations*, Johns Hopkins University Press, Baltimore and London; and Todaro, M P (1985), *Economic Development in the Third World*, Longman, New York and London.

39. Going through UNEP's (1981) *In Defence of the Earth: the Basic Texts on Environment: Founex, Stockholm, Cocoyoc*, UNEP, Nairobi, and WCED (1987), *Our Common Future*, Oxford University Press, Oxford, one is surprised to find only low-esteem references to real people. They are the hungry and wretched to be saved; the ones who multiply beyond the capacity of the environment to sustain their consumption or the ones to be cared for and environmentally educated by their government. The word 'community action' probably occurs once or twice in these voluminous studies and definitely in minor contexts.

40. Significant but certainly non-exhaustive references are: Chambers, R (1981), 'Rapid rural appraisal: rationale and repertoire', *Public Administration and Development*, 1, pp 95–106; Richards, P (1985), *Indigenous Agricultural Revolutions*, Unwin Hyman, London; and Altieri, M A (1987), *Agroecology: the Scientific Basis of Alternative Agriculture*, Westview Press, Boulder, Colorado.

41. See Hardoy, J E and Satterthwaite, D (1989), *Squatter Citizen*, Earthscan, London.

42. See for instance, many project reports of the Ford Foundation, the Inter-American Foundation etc.

43. Agarwal, A and Narain, S (1989), *Towards Green Villages*, Centre for Science and the Environment, New Delhi.

44. The workshop defined primary environmental care (PEC) as 'a process by which local communities – with varying degrees of external support – organize themselves and strengthen, enrich and apply their means and capacities (know-how, technologies and practices) for the care of their environment while simultaneously satisfying their needs'. In synthesis, PEC was meant to integrate three objectives: meeting needs, protecting the environment and empowering communities. The workshop took place in Siena, in January 1990, and produced a Report for the OECD/DAC Working Party on Development Assistance and the Environment (*Supporting Primary Environmental Care*, DGCS, Rome, 1990) and a book of proceedings (Borrini, G (1991) (ed), *Lessons Learned in Community-based Environmental Management*, ICHM, Istituto Superiore di Sanità, Rome).

45. The Malta workshop took place in La Valletta, in April 1992 and produced a report published by UNRISD (1992), *Development, Environment and People*, Geneva.

46. IUCN, UNEP, WWF (1991), *Caring for the Earth: a Strategy for Sustainable Living*, IUCN, Gland (Switzerland), and Earthscan, London.

47. Holmberg, J (1992) (ed), *Policies for a Small Planet*, IIED/Earth-scan, London; Davidson, J and Myers, D with Chakraborty, M (1992), *No Time to Waste: Poverty and the Global Environment*, Oxfam, Oxford; Ghai, D and Vivian, J (1992) (eds), *Grassroots Environmental Action: People's Participation in Sustainable Development*, Routledge, London.

48. The chapter makes forceful reference to '...increased local control of resources, local institutions strengthening and capacity-build-ing [...] greater involvement of non-governmental organizations and local level of governments as delivery mechanisms [...] focus on the empowerment of local and community groups [...] and community organizations...support [for] a community-driven approach to sustainability'.

49. UNDP (1992) *Human Development Report*, Oxford University Press, Oxford.

50. This is not the place to discuss the results of such experiments and policies, each of which would require an in-depth historical analysis. If only one lesson can be drawn from them, however, is that community-based sustainable development is concerned with much more than locality and the small scale. Indeed the whole society, and the government in particular, needs to pro-vide a supporting framework for a variety of aspects and condi-tions.

51. In particular in the Siena meeting in 1990 (see note 44) a num-ber of 'conditions for success in primary environmental care' were identified. These include: capacity to organize, participate and influence development priorities; integration of local knowledge and awareness of the environment; access to natural resources and financial resources; access to environmentally sound and socially responsive technologies and practices (eg participatory assessment and planning); access to information and public accountability; support by governmental (eg exten-sion agents) and external institutions (eg training, research insti-tutions); and appropriate time frame and adaptive planning in the management of aid projects and programmes.

52. Siy, R J Jr (1982), *Community Resource Management: Lessons from the Zanjeras*, University of the Philippines Press, Quezon City.

53. Karmacharya, S C (1992), 'Equality or equity? Perspectives of Nepalese community forestry', paper for the Conference of the International Association for the Study of Common Property, Washington DC.

54. See Tapia, M and Rosas, A (1992), 'Seed fairs in the Andes. A traditional strategy for *in situ* conservation of phytogenetic resources', paper presented at the seminar Local Knowledge and Agricultural Research, Brondesbury Park (Zimbabwe).

55. See, to this point, the recent report by the Labor/Community Strategy Center (1993), *Reconstructing Los Angeles from the Bottom Up*, Los Angeles.

56. To this point, see: McCay, B J and Acheson, J M (1987) (eds), *The Question of the Commons*, University of Arizona Press, Tucson; Berkes, F (1988) (ed), *Common Property Resources*, Belhaven Press, London; Ostrom, E (1990), *Governing the Commons: the Evolution of Institutions for Collective Action*, Cambridge University Press, New York; Jodha, N S (1990), *Rural Common Property Resources: Contributions and Crisis*, ICIMOD, Kathmandu; Stevenson, G G (1991), *Common Property Economics: a General Theory and Land Use Application*, Cambridge University Press, New York.

57. For an illuminating discussion of alternative property systems see Bromley, D W and Cernea, M M (1989), *The Management of Common Property Natural Resources*, Discussion Paper no. 57, The World Bank, Washington DC. It is interesting to notice that while private property tends to work very well for high productivity resources, for resources of low productivity – like a summer pasture in the Swiss Alps – communal property is the regime of choice (see p 49 of Bromley and Cernea (1989) op cit).

58. See: Dhar, S K, Gupta, J R, and Sarin, M (nd), 'Participatory forest management in the Shivalik hills: experiences of the Haryana forest department', working paper no 5, Ford Foundation, New Delhi; and Poffenberger, M (1990) (ed), *Forest Management Partnerships: Regenerating India's Forests*, Ford Foundation, New Delhi.

59. See a number of specific examples in: Conroy, C and Litvinoff, M (1988), *The Greening of Aid: Sustainable Livelihoods in Practice*, Earthscan, London; Drijver, C (1990), 'People's participation in environmental projects in developing countries', *IIED Dryland Networks Programme Papers*, no 17; Development Alternatives (1991), *Community-based Management of Natural Resources*, DA, New Delhi.

60. The view is forcefully put forward by F Amalrik and T Banuri (1992) in 'Population, environment and responsibility', manuscript, IUCN Pakistan, Islamabad.

61. See numerous examples in: Gow, D D and VanSant, J (1981), 'Beyond the rhetoric of rural development participation: how can it be done?', *IRD Working Paper* no 9, Development Alternatives, Washington DC; Borrini, G (1991) (ed), *Lessons Learned in Community-based Environmental Management*, ICHM, Rome; Scoones, I and Matose, F (1992), *Woodland Management in Zimbabwe: Tenure and Institutions for Sustainable Natural Resource Use*, Zimbabwe National Forest Policy Review.

62. Murphree, M W (1991), *Communities as Institutions for Resource Management*, Center for Applied Social Sciences, University of Zimbabwe, Harare.
63. See, to this point: Ghai, D (1988), 'Participatory development: some perspectives from grass-roots experiences', *UNRISD Discussion Paper 5*; Renard, Y (1991), 'Institutional challenges for community-based management in the Caribbean', *Nature and Resources*, 27, 4, pp 4–9; Uphoff, N (1991), 'Local institutions and participation for sustainable development', *IIED Gatekeepers Series*, no 31, London.
64. See: DGCS (1991), *Primary Environmental Care: Proposte Operative per la Cooperazione Italiana*, DGCS, Rome.
65. Other interesting examples of governmental agencies in the process of changing their roles and attitudes are reported in Poffenberger, M (nd), 'Joint forest management in West Bengal: the process of agency change', *Sustainable Forest Management Working Paper*, no 9, Ford Foundation, New Delhi; Peluso, N and Poffenberger, M (1989), 'Social forestry in Java: reorienting management systems', *Human Organization*, 48, 4, pp 333–44; Gronow, J and Shrestha, N K (1990), 'From policing to participation: reorientation of forest department field staff in Nepal', Nepalese Ministry of Agriculture and Winrock International, Kathmandu. See also Korten, D C (1980), 'Community organization and rural development: a learning process approach', *Public Administration Review*, pp 480–511, Sep–Oct.
66. As pointed out by Kitching, it is also the case that today's artisans and petty producers – in particular in developing countries – are no longer struggling against industrial competition, but rather depending on it for their activities to prosper. For instance, many are involved in the repair and maintenance of cars, bicycles and machines, in catering to factory workers and in recycling discarded products (Kitching (1990), op cit (note 11), p 100).
67. A thorough discussion of economic incentives and disincentives to promote conservation of biological resources at community and national level – as well as numerous detailed examples – can be found in McNeily, J A (1988) *Economic and Biological Diversity: Developing and Using Economic Incentives to Conserve Biological Resources*, IUCN, Gland.
68. See the illuminating discussion by Robert Repetto (1993) in 'Trade and environment policies: achieving complementarity and avoiding conflicts', *WRI Issues and Ideas*, July.